IRELAND'S Ocean

IRELAND'S
Ocean
A NATURAL HISTORY

MICHAEL VINEY & ETHNA VINEY

The Collins Press

Published in 2008 by

The Collins Press

West Link Park

Doughcloyne

Wilton

Cork

British Library Cataloguing in Publication data

Viney, Michael, 1933-

Ireland's ocean : a natural history

1. Marine ecology - Ireland

I. Title II. Viney, Ethna

577.7'09415

ISBN-13: 9781905172665

Design and typesetting by Nevil Swinchatt

Typeset in Myriad Pro 10 on 15 pt

Printed in Ireland by ColourBooks Ltd

Photograph on p.i: flukes of humpback whale (*P. Whooley*)

FSC

Mixed Sources
Product group from well-managed
forests and other controlled sources

CONTENTS

Preface

This book was born above the Bay of Biscay, with the shimmer of a sunlit Atlantic gilding the window beside us. We were flying home from a rare holiday and talking about food and the Spanish feeling for the sea. That took us to the curious divorce from ocean life that Ireland had endured for so long, then to our mutual need for being near to the sea – yet still how little, like most people, we knew of what went on below the waves. Here was Ireland spending millions on marine research and making maps of its share of the continental shelf – a vast area of sea floor – and still there was no Irish book of general interest that might open windows to the ocean's life and promise. This is what we set out to put together, helped by the vibrancy and enthusiasm of today's marine science.

It is not the happiest of times at which to plumb the ocean, even at a studious remove through scientific papers, websites and reports. Half a century ago the ocean still seemed endlessly, robustly prolific, majestically indifferent to us as largely land-bound mammals. Both are still true, in the stern Gaian sense. But the reckless and wasteful plunder of overfishing, insidious pollution, and the imminent stresses from increased CO_2 all threaten now to tip ocean ecosystems out of balance with scarcely guessable trends and consequences. At the same time, science has been reinforcing a new sense of responsibility towards the natural world, a new and vital necessity for it, indeed. As the ocean is explored and parsed to ever-greater depths, both for knowledge and new human resources, the mantras of 'sustainability' and 'ecosystem approach' begin to speak for a wiser discipline and understanding.

This introduction to Ireland's ocean – broadly, the northeast Atlantic – can do only partial justice to its complexity of life. We have tried to show how the knowledge about it is organised, and to choose species as examples of particular morphologies (body forms and structures) and lifestyles. There are plenty more fish in the sea, certainly, than appear in these pages.

We are particularly indebted to Ireland's research scientists, some of whom we are lucky to count as friends. While taking full responsibility for errors, omissions and failures of understanding, we would like to acknowledge the work of Simon Berrow, Rick Boelens, Robert Brown, Oliver Ó Cadhla, Mark Costello, Don Cotton, Robert Devoy, Boris Dorschel, Tom Doyle, Edward Fahy, James Fairley, Kevin Flannery, Anthony Grehan, Michael Guiry, Dan Minchin, John Molloy, Charles Nelson, Bernard Picton, Cilian Roden, Andy Wheeler, Ken Whelan and Noel Wilkins. Other researchers are acknowledged in the text. For patient assistance beyond the call of duty, we also thank John Joyce of the Marine Institute and Enda Gallagher of the Geological Survey of Ireland (GSI). For marine photography we are especially indebted to the Marine Institute, the Geological Survey, Simon Berrow, Don Cotton, Michael Guiry, Stefan Kraan, Nigel Motyer, Andrew Wheeler, Padraig Whooley and a host of others who generously helped us with illustrations. In fond appreciation we have spiced the odd chapter with gems from Séamas Mac an Iomaire, whose century-old chronicle from the coast of Connemara is such an authentic delight.

Michael Viney, Ethna Viney
Thallabawn, County Mayo, 2008

Abbreviations

BIM	Bord Iascaigh Mhara
CMRC	Centre for Marine Research at NUI Cork
CPR	Continuous Plankton Recorder
GSI	Geological Survey of Ireland
ICCAT	International Commission for the Conservation of Atlantic Tuna
ICES	International Council for the Exploration of the Sea
IMAGIN	Irish Sea Marine Aggregates Initiative
INSS	Irish National Seabed Survey
IPCC	Intergovernmental Panel on Climate Change
IWDG	Irish Whale and Dolphin Group
MCCIP	Marine Climate Change Impacts Partnership
MOC	Meridional Overturning Circulation
MRI	Martin Ryan Institute
MPA	Marine Protected Area
NAO	North Atlantic Oscillation
NEAFC	North East Atlantic Fisheries Commission
NOAA	National Oceanic and Atmospheric Administration
NPWS	National Parks and Wildlife Service
RDS	Royal Dublin Society
SAC	Special Area of Conservation
TAC	Total Allowable Catch

CHAPTER 1

Into the Depths

The pulse of the ocean drums most keenly among Ireland's southwesterly islands: among the Blaskets, say, or the Skelligs, whose western cliffs receive the endless procession of Atlantic swells. Here, on one height or another, one feels the wind at full fetch and looks out across the glitter and drifting cloud-shadows to the farthest horizon on Earth. The ocean seems truly enormous and revelatory; its seismic vibrations seem to tremble in the rock beneath one's feet.

At these jagged sandstone cliffs and pinnacles, the massive sundering of crustal plates that set Newfoundland edging away from Ireland is all too readily rehearsed; the boiling and leaping of foam evokes the violence of that distant, smoky cleft in the ocean floor where the New World began to take

St Brendan.

its leave from the Old some 175 million years ago. The science of the birth of the Atlantic is scarcely less fabulous than the *eachtraí* and *immrama* of early Irish sailors, the adventures in 'rowing about' to magical lands and their beckoning sirens preserved in Irish history and folklore.

The first people to settle on the island of Ireland came by sea, whether they sailed up from Spain or North Africa, crossed over from Europe directly, or came across the Irish Sea from Britain. They were fisher-gatherers rather than hunter-gatherers, catching salmon, bass, flatfish and eels from the estuaries and eating shellfish from the shore. For many centuries afterwards, movement from one part of the island to another was more easily accomplished by boat around the coast than by the forested or marshy interior. And having discovered Ireland to be an island,

what more natural than to suppose others, even more promising? Today's new charts of seamounts and coral reefs inherit the quest for Hy Brasil – the mythical, shape-shifting Isle of the Blessed, so boldly inscribed west of Ireland on certain medieval maps.

The lure of unknown islands also ran through *Navigatio Brendani* – the famous voyage of St Brendan the Navigator (a tale that might more properly have been assembled by the monks of the Great Skellig with their sublime prospect of the sea, but which was probably written [and lyrically embroidered] in a monastery in France). When Tim Severin set out in his cowhide currach in 1976 it was from a creek on the Blaskets' own peninsula and, in replicating that staggering adventure for television, *The Brendan Voyage* spun enduring images of an intimate and awesome bargain with the ocean. In the creaks and groans of leather and timber, the bubbling rush of water a mere hand's reach away, the compulsive early journeyings and pilgrimages seem all the more improbably heroic.

Whether the *Navigatio* was a real account of a voyage undertaken by Brendan the Navigator or an amalgam of sailors' tales, the places described in it fit very well with the islands between Ireland and Iceland. It describes an island full of sheep and lambs, which could be in the Outer Hebrides, and a mountainous island with fire billowing from a peak that fits well with Mount Hekla's restless eruptions in Iceland. Irish monks were to settle there. Indeed, religion and pilgrimage, along with trade, propelled the busy maritime traffic, notably with Spain and France as well as in the Irish Sea. Later, the ocean would be a means of escape to better things, whether for rebelling earls and their defeated soldiers, or for refugees from poverty and hunger.

For Ireland's coastal communities, progress in exploiting the sea was to become closely subject to colonial economics. In medieval times, the east coast ports joined in the pursuit of vast shoals of herring and exported them, salted, to Britain, and after colonial conquest the fortunes of Irish fisheries continued to ebb and flow according to Britain's needs (in the nineteenth century, as much for the supply of potential naval seamen as for fish). Away from the Irish Sea, local hookers, *gleoiteogs* and *púcáns* were often no match for the robust fishing fleets from Spain, France and Holland that arrived inshore, with or without permission, from the seventeenth century onwards.

Dunmore East Harbour in the mid-twentieth century.

To Newfoundland

When, early in that century, the rich cod fishery of the Great Banks was discovered, Waterford business-men set up operations in Newfoundland, and arranged ships that brought thousands of fishermen there from the southeast of Ireland. They travelled to Newfoundland on April's easterly winds and returned before the ice set in, their catches dried for the Irish and British market. These Waterford fishermen joined the rush to claim drying sites on the spruce-clad Newfoundland shore, and left a caretaker there to guard them during the winter months. Many finally settled there and, through visiting back and forth with the home country, it became the basis of an Irish settlement. But as Mark Kurlansky notes in *Cod: Biography of the Fish that Changed the World* [1998]: 'Except Ireland, which was too impoverished to develop a distant water fleet, the ports that remained important to the Newfoundland fishery . . . were those in the European regions closest to Newfoundland.'

Salted herrings, along with mackerel, continued to fill the barrels on Irish quays, but in widely fluctuating quantities. The apparently fickle behaviour of herring stocks in frequently changing their shoaling grounds is notorious in fishing history. We know now that the behaviour of the North Atlantic Oscillation (see p.23) has helped to swing Northern Europe's weather between cool, dry years and warm, wet ones with matching trends in sea surface temperatures. These in turn have affected the food chain of marine life, from plankton upwards, in very complex ways, including the abundance and behaviour of stocks of cold-water species such as herring, mackerel and cod.

No doubt Ireland's fishermen had their own theories to explain the non-arrival of the shoals, a particular blow when fishing boats were small and local fleets were sometimes numbered in hundreds, many of them merely currachs. During a herring fishery in the early 1800s, there were sometimes 600 boats in the rudimentary harbour of Roundstone in Connemara. The region boomed during the Napoleonic wars, when the demand for salted fish, along with young cattle, flax and *póitín*, made it, in Kevin Whelan's phrase, 'the best poor man's country', and the later desertion of the fish was just one of the miseries that arrived at the wars' end.

The Famine question

In *The Great Hunger*, her classic chronicle of the Famine, Cecil Woodham-Smith addressed the question posed by so many observers of Irish history: how could it be that the thousands of people living along the coast did not catch and eat fish? She quoted James Hack Tuke, a Quaker philanthropist, who 'standing on the cliffs of Achill, looked down through the clear Atlantic water and saw "shoals of herring and mackerel in immense quantities", while farther out, in the deeper waters, were cod, ling, sole, turbot and haddock. Nevertheless, around him stood starving creatures that made no use of this inexhaustible supply of food.' The most immediate cause was simply that 'when the potato failed, fishermen all over Ireland pawned or sold their gear to buy meal'. But this rash action reflected, as she saw it, rational attitudes born of the natural handicaps of long stretches of the Atlantic coasts: lack of timber for deep-sea boats; perilous shores without piers or harbours and wild, unpredictable weather. But even in established ports and harbours, the history of Ireland's fisheries has often alternated between prosperity and despair.

At the end of the 1920s, as the new Irish state was struggling for stability, the herring and mackerel fisheries collapsed with the loss of European markets for cured herring and the United States market for cured mackerel. This left the Irish drift netting fleets with the wrong boats and gear for catching demersal (bottom-living, or 'white') fish, and with a home market already well supplied from Britain. A state-sponsored fishermen's co-operative, offering trawlers and demersal gear on hire-purchase, made slow headway.

The long decline in fishing activity from pre-Famine Ireland was not arrested until after the Second World War. Even in 1958, as offshore banks were avidly trawled by boats from Britain and the Continent, the Irish fishing industry was still administered under the Department of Lands. In a development programme its minister announced that year, the stress was on 'exploratory and experimental fishing'. Odd as this emphasis may seem at such a late stage of the island's development, it was to help reassert the role of marine science in Ireland's relations with the ocean.

Many ingenious devices

Individual fascination with sea life is as old as Aristotle: 'In marine creatures one may observe many ingenious devices adapted to the circumstances of their lives.' But wider interest had to wait on social movement beyond the merely utilitarian attitudes to nature. Even then, the activities of individual naturalists became entwined with upper-crust aesthetics in the patronage of fine book illustrations and the middle-class passion for collecting fossils, seashells and seaweeds. 'My Patellas [limpet shells] are nearly extirpated,' complained James Clealand of Bangor, County Down, in 1823; 'they became so much the fashion that the Visitors who frequented Bangor, as Sea Bathers, during the last two summers, employed the children to collect them and there is not one to be seen now.'

Maude Delap reared jellyfish in the Valentia rectory.
(Courtesy of Mick Delap)

The nineteenth-century nature field clubs of Belfast and Dublin were more disciplined in their dealings with rock pools. They inherited an interest in marine life that had been under way since the eighteenth century, mostly in the hands of Protestant clergymen inquiring into the wonders of creation, and of gentleman-naturalists with an omnivorous interest in the ordering of nature. John Templeton, for example, whose family had been among Antrim's earliest settlers, collected seashells for decades for the catalogue of Irish molluscs he completed in 1816: the dredging he began in 1790 could be seen as the start of marine biology in Ireland.

Templeton was primarily a botanist, like most naturalists of his time. At the other end of the island, on a small estate overlooking Bantry Bay in west Cork, lived another botanist, Ellen Hutchins, a magistrate's daughter and the first of the great women collectors. Her pioneering fascination with cryptogamic plants – the ferns, mosses and liverworts that reproduce by spores, not seeds – had her wading into rock pools for seaweeds to draw and identify. A similar rapt spirit was to drive Maude Delap, rearing jellyfish in her bubbling aquariums in the Protestant rectory on Valentia Island, County Kerry, in the early 1900s.

The plankton net

As with any other branch of Irish natural history, most of the nineteenth-century names and events associated with marine biology derive from a colonial ascendancy. John Vaughan Thompson, a British army surgeon posted to Cork in 1816, was a specialist in planktonic larvae who got the acorn barnacle moved into its proper 'regiment' – the crustacea, not the molluscs. But science history remembers him also for a simple but significant technological advance. He discovered the potential of a muslin hoop-net towed from the stern of a ship 'occasionally drawing it up, and turning it inside out into a glass vessel of sea water, to ascertain what captures have been made.'

The plankton net was to become an everyday tool on the momentous around-the-world voyage of HMS *Challenger,* taking three years to sample the seabed, chemistry and organisms of the ocean. When it sailed from Portsmouth in December 1872, the director of its civilian scientists was Wyville Thomson, a remarkably energetic Scot who had spent seventeen years as Professor of Natural History and Geology in Cork; Professor of Natural Science in Belfast, and of Botany in Dublin. He had already pioneered the dredging of the Atlantic seabed to the west of Ireland and Scotland (despairing, as he wrote in *The Depths of the Sea* [1874] of the 'old prejudices' that prevented fishermen from bringing ashore any unfamiliar creatures that were hauled up in their nets: 'Fishermen are often so absolutely ignorant of the nature of these extraneous animals, that it is conceivable to them that they may be devils of some kind . . .').

From HMS Porcupine *came more proof that 'life extends to the greatest depths'.*
(NOAA Photo Library)

Bottom of the locker

In 1869 Thomson was aboard a converted British Admiralty gunboat, HMS *Porcupine*, on a voyage off the southwest of Ireland to the edge of what is now called the Porcupine Abyssal Plain. At that date there was still uncertainty as to how much life, if any, could exist at abyssal depths. Early in the century, the ocean explorer Sir John Ross had retrieved bottom-dwelling organisms, including starfish and worms, from a depth of 1.8 km in Canada's Baffin Bay. But in 1843 the respected Edward Forbes framed his Azoic Theory that the ocean below 300 fathoms was not only dark and cold, but lifeless. Aboard the *Porcupine*, Thomson and his team sent down a dredge to 2,435 fathoms (4.5 km), with tangled, hempen deck swabs attached to it. Finally retrieved and swung on to the deck at one o'clock in the morning, its load of chalky mud held quite enough species of molluscs, echinoderms, worms and other seabed organisms to justify Thomson's conviction that 'life extends to the greatest depths and is represented by all the marine invertebrate groups.'

The first careful surveys of the Atlantic were those setting out from the American coast with the aim of finding a telegraph cable route to Europe. In 1856 the US steamer *Arctic*, equipped with new 'sounding machines', made the first voyage from Newfoundland to Valentia Island, taking twenty-four deep-sea soundings on the way. The *Porcupine* itself was subsequently sent out from Ireland to examine a 'curious dip from 550 to 1,750 fathoms . . . about 170 miles to the west of Valentia', a foray towards the shelf-edge that discovered the 'Porcupine' Bank.

The mid-nineteenth-century transatlantic soundings, by both American and British hydrographers, found precipitous deeps. But the colossal relief of the Mid-Atlantic Ridge, with its deep central canyon, was recorded only as a central rise on the seabed that became 'the Telegraph Plateau'. It was not until the 1950s that echo-sounding profiles disclosed the 'notch' at the top and running along the length of the ridge, which became so hugely significant in the recognition of plate tectonics.

Agenda for oceanography

The soundings on the *Challenger* voyage, however, made with a simple 100-pound weight on a rope during five crossings of the Atlantic, did nourish one of the first maps to show the great zip-fastener course of the mid-ocean ridge into the southern latitudes. A painstaking programme of research also

HMS Challenger: a pioneering voyage at the start of oceanography. (NOAA Photo Library)

H.M.S. CHALLENGER UNDER SAIL, 1874.

pioneered the agenda for the science of oceanography. At each of its 362 'stations' around the globe, it sampled not merely the seabed, but the flora, fauna, water chemistry and temperature at different depths from the surface to the bottom. The dredging and netting yielded 13,000 specimens of plants and animals, many of them new to science.

They bore out the vast diversity of marine life already anticipated in Thomson's *The Depths of the Sea*. The new mass audience for natural history made best-sellers of such titles, so that many other scientists found it worthwhile to share their enthusiasms at a popular level. A Limerick Quaker, W. H. Harvey, Professor of Botany in the Royal Dublin Society

(RDS) and in Dublin University, produced some weighty marine floras, including a *Phycologia Britannica*, but also *The Sea-side Book*, a popular introductory guide.

Official academic interest in Ireland's ocean microfauna waited until the 1880s, when research from the *Challenger* expedition was heading towards its final 29,500 pages (the volumes are still treasured by the Irish Marine Institute in its base at the head of Galway Bay). With grants from the Royal Irish Academy, paddle-powered steamers such as the *Lord Bandon* and the sea-going tug *Flying*

Falcon were commissioned to take more marine biologists and naturalists on trawling and dredging cruises. Expeditions to the deeps off the southwest coast in the 1880s were planned and organised by the energetic Alfred Haddon, Professor of Zoology in the Royal College of Science for Ireland, and drew enthusiasts from a wide mix of sciences: geology, botany, ornithology – even entomology.

Among them, in 1888, was Robert Lloyd Praeger, whose curiosity included all these sciences and more. In his classic memoir *The Way That I Went* (1937), he described a *Flying Falcon* expedition from Cobh to trawl the deepest water yet. The tug used 1,270 fathoms (some 2.5 km) of the newly introduced steel wire rope, and came up with 'a splendid catch of marvellous creatures. There were great sea slugs, red, purple and green; beautiful corals, numerous sea urchins with long, slender spines; a great variety of starfishes of many shapes and of all colours, including one like a raw beefsteak, which belonged to a new genus; strange fishes and many other forms of life.' Like many naturalists then and since, Praeger was especially intrigued by the haul's display of brilliant colours – 'for what is the use of colour in absolute darkness?'

The 1888 expedition was led by the adventurous rector of Carrigaline, County Cork, the Rev William Spotswood Green, who, after some serious mountain climbing in New Zealand and Canada, became fascinated by fish and left the church in 1890 to become one of three Inspectors of Irish Fisheries. In 1890–91, for the Royal Dublin Society, he led survey cruises of fishing potential around the entire coast of Ireland and later helped the RDS to establish Ireland's first marine laboratory aboard the *Saturn*, a brigantine berthed near the mackerel-fishing harbour of Cleggan, County Galway.

Praeger, meanwhile, became absorbed by the post-Darwin focus on island biogeography, and from 1909–11 organised the remarkable Clare Island Survey, in which more than 100 scientists made an inventory of every species they could find, from the top of the mountain to the depths of the intertidal zone and even, with dredges and nets, to the seabed. The intertidal inventory filled about a quarter of the survey's publications. Eighty years later, in 1991, the Royal Irish Academy launched a complete re-survey, providing an ecological baseline for the changes expected from climate change. Its intertidal studies concentrated on the island's most exposed rocky shores, as a habitat at Europe's extremity.

Into the Trough

The years up to First World War brought intense and enthusiastic attention to the fish in Ireland's ocean, making the Rockall Trough, in particular, the cradle of deep-sea biology. The first permanent fishery research body was set up in Dublin in 1900 by the Department of Agriculture and Technical Instruction, and Green, now Chief Inspector, was put in charge of it. The steam cruiser *Helga* was diverted from fishery protection to research into the life-cycle of commercial species. Much of its time was given to trawling and tow-netting cruises planned by the newly established International Council for the Exploration of the Sea – now the powerful ICES – which was co-ordinating the study of fish eggs, plankton and hydrography.

The drive of marine investigation from Ireland of the 1890s and early 1900s, with the Rockall Trough and Plateau as the main area of study, was not to be equalled for another half-century. Among the fish recorded and described in successive reports were species that 'have, and perhaps deserve,

Watched by Valentia Islanders, the first transatlantic cable was brought ashore in 1866.
(Courtesy of The Cable Museum, Valentia Island Heritage Centre)

but little esteem among fishmongers'. They included *Chimaera monstrosa*, with its bulging eyes and rat-like tail, already known as rabbit fish to the trawlermen of Grimsby and today considered (suitably filleted away from the consumer) a promising new food species. Many other specimens from below the 50-fathom line were either new to science or not readily recognisable. The Department made no apology for devoting such resources to delving into the shadows of what had been, very largely, *aquae incognitae*. Ernest Holt, who succeeded William Green as Chief Inspector, set out the principles in the annual report for 1906:

> We have to deal with a vast number of organisms, the presence of which on or near our coast was unsuspected or at least unrecorded, while many of them are new to human observation. Before proceeding to an orderly survey of the distributional relationships of these forms as elements of the whole fauna, and to speculations as to their influence upon the present or probable future objects of commercial fisheries, it is essential to obtain a knowledge of them individually. Their treatment, therefore, on a strictly zoological basis, is to be regarded not as a diversion of the energies of fishery officials into the realms of what is called pure science, but as a preliminary to the necessary collection of all the factors which may affect the commercial fish supply.

This broad, holistic spirit of inquiry prefigures the thinking of today's ecosystem approach to fisheries management, turning away from a narrow obsession with profitable food species to deal with the ocean as a whole (see Chapter 7).

While the Irish Free State had a Minister of Fisheries for a time, research was a low priority and largely confined to freshwater trout and salmon. A negligible sea fishing fleet waited until the economic revival of the 1960s for any development, and the low regard for Ireland's marine potential was reflected in the negotiations for membership of the European Economic Community: the Republic traded much of its fishing rights for agricultural advantage. For information about new or unfamiliar species, the Fisheries Department and scientists were greatly dependent on trawlermen and interested individuals in the fishing ports. A special example of the latter was Michael Long, an amateur naturalist of Dingle who owned a pub on the quay, and who died in 1980. Because of his interest, fishermen brought him any strange fish that were caught in their nets. Up to 1978, according to Arthur Went, an assiduous government fish scientist, Michael Long 'was responsible for bringing to notice 82 per cent of all individuals of interesting, scarce or rare fishes handled in the Department of Fisheries and 76 per cent of all species.'

Elsewhere in the North Atlantic, one of the most significant avenues of research was into the basic food supply of fish: the growth of plant plankton (phytoplankton) and the animal plankton (zooplankton) that feeds upon it. The importance of all plankton to the food web made it the focus of exceptional scientific effort, and the Continuous Plankton Recorder (CPR), set up by Britain's Sir Alister Hardy in 1931, is unique in marine biology. On certain standard sea routes, many of them passing to the north and south of Ireland, it has maintained a virtually unbroken monthly coverage since 1948, sampling plankton automatically from a standard depth of 7 m. Its network of volunteer ships

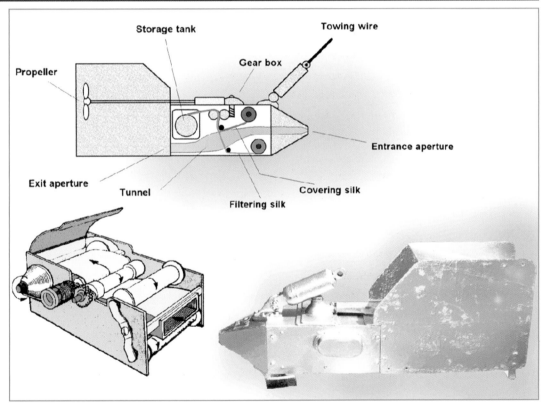

The workings of the Continuous Plankton Recorder. (© SAHFOS)

from nine countries (England, Scotland, Norway, Denmark, Sweden, the Netherlands, Iceland, Canada and the US) has towed recorders for more than 4 million miles, collecting some 200,000 samples of plankton from all over the North Atlantic. Today, phytoplankton research is a priority of Ireland's Marine Institute, particularly concerning the harm that toxic blooms can cause to the island's fast-developing aquaculture industry.

Raymond Keary
took geology into
the ocean.
(Geological Survey of Ireland)

The transatlantic telegraph cable laid with final success in 1866 was followed by a telephone cable almost a century later, in 1956, from Newfoundland to Scotland, and by the first fibre optic cables, including one from Ireland to New Jersey, in the 1980s. Attracted by their magnetic fields, sharks began to chew on them, and bottom trawling added more damage. Today they are buried for most of their length and the exposed stretches over rock are inspected and retrieved for repairs by robot submarines.

Mapping the blue

Up to the 1960s, the geological maps of Ireland ended at the tideline: every-thing beyond was blankly blue. The mapping of the vast economic zone of seabed, begun in 2000, came as a final satisfaction for one outstanding Irish geologist. Raymond Keary had spent much of his professional life, first in NUI Galway, and then the Geological Survey of Ireland, agitating for just such a venture. In his early years, seeking to map the seabed of Galway Bay, he famously improvised a heavy marine sledge containing a microphone: dragged behind the 12-m ketch that was the college's research vessel, it recorded different sounds from scraping over sand, gravel or rock. His 'rooting around on the seashore' of Connemara became an obsession that later, as head of the GSI's marine division, he brought to surveys of the glacial sand and gravel resources of the Irish Sea. He also plotted deposits, in several Irish bays around the coast, of heavy mineral sands, some promising prosaic iron and titanium, but others sparkling, discreetly, with garnets and even gold.

By the 1980s, Ireland's offshore hydrocarbon basins were already attracting costly oil/gas exploration. The first promise to Ireland, under the United Nations Convention on the Law of mineral rights extending towards the Atlantic's Abyssal Plain, filled Keary and his GSI colleagues with eager speculation. In the journal, *Marine Mining*, they even discussed the chances of finding cobalt-rich manganese nodules, the mysterious lumps of interleaved metal ores known to litter deep seabeds ever since the dredgings of HMS *Challenger*. 'In our present state of ignorance,' their paper lamented, 'all that can be said is that it is possible that there are large deposits of manganese encrustations, placer deposits associated with seamounts, and conventional ore deposits close to the seabed in basement rocks, and that manganese nodules may be discovered.'

Keary saw that the only way to secure funds for seabed geological research was to promise knowledge of commercial importance. A first step in 1996, which brought the Geological Survey and Marine Institute into partnership, was the GLORIA survey, the use of sidescan sonar to map the deep sedimentary basins from the Porcupine Seabight to the Rockall Trough – prime hydrocarbon territory of the future. Peadar McArdle, Director of the Geological Survey, was now fully convinced that, as Keary had argued for years, the entire seabed area should be surveyed, and a formal proposal was submitted to government. Then, three years before his death in 2003, Keary saw the launch of the full seven-year national survey, replete with multibeam sonar and a government budget of some IR£21 million (€26.7 million). Its maps and databanks would serve, he promised, 'engineering, fishing and mineral exploration interests, as well as . . . scientific workers interested in all aspects of seabed biology, chemistry and physics.' In 2002 he was made an honorary Doctor of Science in NUI Galway, and thanked for 'educating a nation into the importance of its hidden territory.' A group of carbonate mounds to the northeast of the Fangorn Bank have been named *Cnocáin Uí Chiardha* in recognition of his involvement in the setting up of the Irish National Seabed Survey (INSS).

This 'handsome' coral, dredged up by Wyville Thomson in 1869 and named Lophohelia *by him, was an early sample from the Atlantic's cold-water coral reefs, under close exploration today as islands of deep-sea diversity. (From* The Depths of the Sea, *courtesy of Library of Congress, Washington)*

Exploration of the tumbled, silted slopes below the edge of the continental shelf, initially by commercial oil/gas prospectors in the 1990s, brought one of the most dramatic discoveries in the history of Irish – indeed, European – marine science: clusters of hundreds of mounds topped with cold-water corals, as rich in species as any tropical reefs. In Wyville Thomson's cruises on HMS *Porcupine* in the summer of 1869, his dredgings of the seabed down to 600 fathoms between Shetland and Stornoway, at Scotland's northwest corner, produced clumps of 'the handsome branching *Lophohelia prolifera*', which, as he wrote in *The Depths of the Sea*, 'forms stony copses covering the bottom for many miles, the clefts of its branches affording fully appreciated shelter to multitudes [of other species].' *Lophelia pertusa*, as it is known today, is the coral that built the deep and ancient reefs on the slopes of the Irish shelf: new objects of wonder for an age that now has to fret for their survival.

The new M6 weather buoy, keeping watch at the Rockall Trough.
(Marine Institute)

CHAPTER 2

The Restless Ocean

Along the top of the most exposed cliffs of the Aran Islands and set back several metres from the edge, ridges of jumbled blocks of limestone rise like primitive ramparts piled against the wind. But the wind itself constructed them. Its rushing energy raised huge swells in the ocean surface and drove them for hundreds of kilometres across the long fetch of the Atlantic until, rearing up the cliffs, they lifted the uppermost layers of rock and heaved them back across the land. On the middle island, Inis Meáin, the ridge climbs almost to Synge's Chair, more than 50 m above sea level. Even at this height, most of the blocks would take many men to move.

Such titanic effects are rare in human experience and limited to the kind of sea that swamps the summits of lighthouses. In *The Perfect Storm* (1997), Sebastian Junger unfolded a mesmerising chronicle of Grand Banks swordfish longliners caught and drowned in such a modern tempest. The cruise liner, *Queen Elizabeth II,* once met a 29-m high rogue wave during a hurricane in the North Atlantic. And in just three weeks of 2001, the radar satellites of the European Space Agency collected ten rogue waves of more than 25 m, piled up in oceans around the world. But the high storm beaches of Ireland's outer isles, however 'over the top' in their implicit drama, remain the work of basic ocean physics, written in a giant hand.

Borrowing from the wind

The power of waves is that of energy borrowed from the wind and, given enough of it, waves will grow and grow as they journey across the ocean. 'Fetch' is the distance that wind blows over water without changing its direction, so in theory a mere ripple in the Caribbean can reach the Irish coast as a great breaker hustled ashore in Kerry in a southwesterly gale. Most of our big swells, however, are born in storms to the east of Newfoundland: more can be traced to tropical storms that spin up the coast of Florida. As their local violence eases, the crests of waves are smoothed and become more widely spaced. Rolling on for thousands of kilometres and passing above the Mid-Atlantic Ridge, they meet the newest of Ireland's yellow weather buoys, the M6, moored above the Rockall Trough, far to the west of Aran. Tethered to a 3-tonne block in 3,000 m of water, it takes note of the swells' height and period (the time, in seconds, for the passage of successive wave crests), the salinity and temperature of the water, the wind speed and direction, the atmospheric pressure and weather systems that prevail. Its figures, transmitted every hour, take the pulse of the one of highest sustained wave-power levels in the world. As the swells roll on across the shallowing shelf, they feel the first drag of the seabed and begin to crowd in on each other. Steepened also, perhaps, by local winds or collision with tidal currents, they may reach heights of 4–5 m before breaking, with some grandeur, on the shore. These modest, everyday heights may be eclipsed in conditions of extensive low pressure at sea. In late November 2007, for example, the Marine Institute warned of exceptional 14-m high waves, rolling in to the western shores.

Aill na Searrach, a great wave shelving at the Cliffs of Moher, is the newly discovered challenge of Irish surfing. The surfer here is John McCarthy. (Ronan Gallagher)

The travel of a wave is an illusion: its water is going nowhere. Out at sea, its particles are spun like a wheel but left back more or less where they were: what travels on is the energy, the momentum, expressed in the shape of the wave. As it approaches the shore, the wheel of energy drags on the bottom and becomes an ellipse. The wave slows. The following crests pile in behind it, it rears in height and begins to curl, before finally collapsing in foam. The turbulence helps to spend its energy: even the sound it makes is energy returning to the air.

Not everyone finds big waves frightening. The serious surfer is quick to learn the three main kinds: spilling, surging and plunging. Each depends on the contours of the beach and the steepness of the wave before it enters shallow water. A gently sloping beach will produce the spilling breaker, its crest beginning to melt into foam a good distance from the shore. The surging breaker doesn't break at all, but rushes up a steep beach to hurl itself, perhaps, at a sea wall with an impact of several tonnes per square foot.

The thrilling prize the surfer seeks is the great plunging breaker, driving up a moderately steep beach until, as it begins to spill, its crest curls over in a glassy tube of water. In recent years, long-distance swells from Atlantic storms have made western shores an exciting destination for surfers, and the challenge of one wave, in particular, is famous across the surfing world. It borrows an ancient name, *Aill na Searrach* (Cliff of the Foals), from a distinctive cluster of rocks beneath the towering Cliffs of Moher in County Clare. Here, in certain predictable conditions, the wave rears up majestically as the swells begin to shoal. Once discovered, its awesome 10-m face was ridden for the first time on 15 October 2005, when surfers were towed out from Doolin by jet-ski to be launched upon its fast-moving crest.

Power in the tides

The power of gravity creates massive oscillations of the ocean that alternately hide and uncover the shore. Earth's gravity holds the sea in place, and the pull from the moon heaps it into a bulge on the planet's nearest side. As Earth spins, and the moon follows its orbit around it, the bulge remains at the point directly under the moon and travels as high tide around the coasts. The sun's gravitational pull holds the planets in their orbits and also affects Earth's ocean, causing tides only about half as high as those gathered up by the moon. But during the full moon and new moon, the sun, moon and Earth are aligned in a straight line. The tides then rise higher and fall lower than usual and are called 'spring' tides. At other phases of the moon, it and the sun are at right angles to each other in respect to Earth, and the resulting 'neap' tides do not rise or fall as much as usual.

So much explains one high tide a day, but there are two. They arise from two travelling bulges in the oceans, one on the side nearest the moon and another on the opposite side of the planet. How can this be? As Earth and its moon follow their whirling partnership around the sun, and are held together by gravity, they are also spaced apart by centrifugal force. This force is strongest on Earth's surface at the point farthest from the moon's gravitational pull. Here, the water is flung out into a second bulge of high tide, but a smaller one than that produced directly beneath the moon.

(Geological Survey of Ireland)

In the open Atlantic the surge of the tidal flood is small, but it builds as it flows across the continental shelf and is channelled into estuaries and the Irish Sea. Halfway up the Shannon Estuary, for example, the average tide is 4.5 m, but at the head of the estuary it is almost 1 m higher. At Carnsore Point, at Ireland's open southeastern corner, the mean spring tide has a range of a mere 1.75 m, but sweeping through St George's Channel into the confines of the Irish Sea, its rise on the great cockle strands of Lancashire can reach a formidable 8 m. High tide enters the Irish Sea from both ends and meets, quite peacefully, just southwest of the Isle of Man; its currents turn and retreat almost simultaneously.

In the uncertain future of climate change, the possible extremes of tidal reach worry many Irish coastal communities. Storm surges are already familiar: when atmospheric pressure of deep Atlantic depressions is low and allows sea level to rise, then long, violent winds press the waves of high tide into narrowing bays and estuaries. Increases of up to 1 m above predicted high water level have already been recorded on Irish coasts, and Cork and Dublin have both suffered physical damage (see map p.187).

As local familiarities of weather start to play disconcerting tricks and their wider connections become apparent, the ocean's cardinal role in Earth's climate – both in causes and effects – calls out for a better understanding. The ocean deals every day with the planet's heat, the engine of atmospheric flows. It stores vast amounts of it and gives it up slowly, in balanced and stabilising ways. Evaporation sends water from tropical seas into the atmosphere to fall again in high latitudes as rain or snow, releasing heat in the process. Evaporation and precipitation affect the saltiness of water and thus the patterns of density which shape the circulation of the seas. Winds both promote evaporation and produce the strong currents that take warm water to the cold polar regions. The ocean is restless but not aimless, its liquid machinery running to a rhythm that engages seamlessly with climate.

Rivers in the sea

To the well-tried image of currents as rivers in the sea one could add others from the urban world: tube trains at different levels, flyovers and railway junctions. Even free-flowing motorways and inching-along tailbacks have their metaphorical uses. But this is to picture currents in motion, fast or slow. What starts and sustains them? In the ocean's upper layers, the energy of obsessive winds will drag water into motion, even to considerable depths: it initially affects the top 200 m but reaches down over time, its impact gradually waning, to perhaps 1,000 m. A mass of water is slow to move but, once flowing, has stubborn inertia. Below the currents set in train by the energy of winds are slower, 'geostrophic' currents generated and maintained by the wrestling of great physical pressures: the mounting weight of water as depth increases and the balance of this with something called the Coriolis force. This mighty planetary muscle was named after a nineteenth-century French physicist who noted that the Earth's rotation acts on any object in motion, even winds and water currents. It pushes them to the right in the northern hemisphere and to the left in the south; deflecting them in proportion to their speed and where they are on Earth (the maximum push is at the Poles). Temperature and salinity, too, have a role, since cold and salty water is denser, or heavier, than warm, fresher water and will sink beneath it: physics, as we shall see, is key to ocean circulation.

Inshore in Ireland's ocean, the currents set up by the higher ranges of tides and their flow or

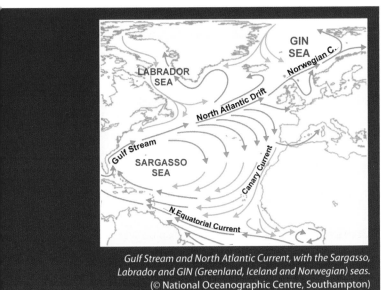

Gulf Stream and North Atlantic Current, with the Sargasso, Labrador and GIN (Greenland, Iceland and Norwegian) seas. (© National Oceanographic Centre, Southampton)

channelling over different seabed contours have a daily impact on sea life, keeping the water column mixed, changing its temperature, churning up nutrients and shifting sediments around. Although wind-driven currents are important around the coasts, especially at the northwest and southwest corners, the predominant circulation in Ireland's ocean is south to north, following the edge of the continental shelf and driven more by currents arising from differences in salinity and temperature. In the broader, equally restless ocean, similar distinctions hold true.

The powerful currents of the wider North Atlantic follow an enormous clockwise circular gyre, driven by the prevalence of particular winds. Like the currents, these need explaining. The sun heats the planet unevenly and, as hot air rises, cooler air is sucked in to take its place: this is wind. In the North Atlantic, hot air rises at the Equator and flows towards the North Pole. As air is drawn in, it spreads both southwards towards the Equator and northwards towards the Pole. The Coriolis force acts on both, swinging them to the right: the southward flow as the trade winds (blowing east to west), and the northward flow spun into the Atlantic westerlies, joined by the rightward (west to east) flow of risen air.

It is the trade winds and westerlies together that set up the big gyre of surface waters. Water is pushed to the west by the trade winds off West Africa, becoming the North Equatorial Current. Off South America this splits into two branches, one heading north past the West Indies to Florida, the other into the Caribbean, where it is joined by the Guyana Current from the south. Water piles up and swirls around the Caribbean before rejoining and boosting the northward flow of the Florida Current. This colossal river of warm water is now perhaps 800 m in depth and flowing at some 30 million cubic metres of water per second. It follows the continental shelf as the Gulf Stream until, just north of Cape Hatteras in North Carolina, it swings away into the Atlantic, urged eastwards both by winds and the Coriolis force. As it slows, it loses the sharp definition imparted by the shelf and throws off great swirling meanders. Some break off to become rings 200 km across and reaching the full depth of the ocean.

The flyovers and tailbacks of the North Atlantic Current. (Illustrated by Jack Cook, Woods Hole Oceanographic Institution)

A wedge of cold current from Labrador helps to lever the Gulf Stream away from the North American shelf above Cape Hatteras and, in mid-Atlantic, on a level with Portugal, it splits into several currents. Some swing south in a recirculation around the becalmed ellipse of the Sargasso Sea, a lens of clear warm water 1,000 m deep. But at the Grand Banks off Newfoundland the largest flow presses on towards Europe as the North Atlantic Current (also called the North Atlantic Drift).

This, too, spins off smaller currents as it surges on northeastward towards Europe. Some flow south to become the Canary Current, ultimately completing the huge Atlantic gyre in the westward sweep of the North Equatorial Current. Others swing away north towards Greenland to become part of a sub-polar gyre, curling back westward to join the Labrador Current, flowing south along the coast of Canada. Out on the Grand Banks, this current's cold winds mingle with the warm, moist winds of the Gulf Stream to produce some of the densest, most enduring fogs of the world.

Origins of warmth

At the final reach of the North Atlantic Current, flowing past the northwest of Ireland and Scotland and on into the Norwegian Sea, the original sea temperatures of the Gulf Stream have fallen substantially. They have, however, helped to warm the westerly winds reaching northwest Europe. As these approach Ireland in winter, they may pick up more warmth from the Rockall Trough, where waters overturn annually to a depth of hundreds of metres. A warm, salty Slope Current flows northwards from the Bay of Biscay region, through the Rockall Trough, and on through the Faroe–Shetland Channel into the Norwegian Sea. This helps to isolate the shelf waters from those of the deep ocean and to feed them with winter nutrients. A stronger, shallower, more salty filament of the Slope Current, 50 km wide, is called the Shelf Edge Current. This provides a hospitable route for migrating fish and also carries a planktonic community that originates in the Mediterranean Sea. Surfacing at the south and west coasts of Ireland, it is credited with delivering many of Ireland's Lusitanian species.

The ocean is not only a maze of swift-moving currents, but of different kinds of water, held in masses, layers and lenses and sometimes separated as if by glass walls and floors. Temperature and salinity (which refers to all the salts dissolved in sea water: see Ocean Chemistry, p.24) are mainly what govern their difference and where they belong within the matrix of the sea. Cold, salty water sinks; warmer, fresher water rises

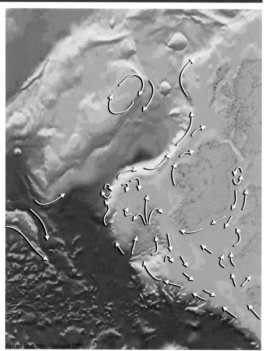

Ireland's 'local' currents take their main thrust from the south.
(Marine Institute)

and there can be great overturnings and exchanges around the year. Beneath a surface layer kept well mixed by wind-waves, there are seasonal boundaries between warm and cold water and, even deeper, permanent thermoclines at the interface with cold waters of great oceanic depth. Indeed, there are five layers generally recognised by oceanographers:

1. surface water to a depth of 150–300 m
2. central water that makes up the lower half of water above the permanent thermocline
3. intermediate water below the permanent thermocline and above the deep and bottom waters
4. deep water below the intermediate water but not usually in contact with the bottom
5. deep and bottom waters

It is wrong to imagine the deeps as invariably still and undisturbed, or necessarily isolated biologically from the water above. The existence of severe seabed currents, or benthic storms, has been detected at 2,400 m on the North Feni Ridge, west of Scotland, and these seem quite capable of whirling sediments up through the water column.

In general, the temperature falls as the depth increases, with a particularly rapid drop at the thermocline. From there to the sea floor, the temperature decreases more slowly, reaching between 1–4 °C near the bottom. In some regions, colder and deeper water rises to the surface, lowering the surface water temperature. The constancy of the permanent thermocline is much more marked in the tropics than in the temperate ocean, where layering is often produced by local and seasonal stratification. During the winter, for example, the west and south of Ireland are washed by deep Atlantic water, at maximum saltiness, well mixed by storms and several degrees warmer than the shallower Irish Sea. In late spring and summer, however, as the weather calms and the mixed layer absorbs the sun's heat, a band of warmer, less saline, lighter water surrounds the west and south coasts, setting up a marked layering of wide areas of sea. This stratification, with differences of several degrees between the layers of water, takes on special importance in the supply of phytoplankton, the ocean's primary food source, discussed in Chapter 5. Salinity differences shape other water masses in Ireland's near seas. On the Malin Shelf, north of Ireland and west of Scotland, the main body of salty Atlantic water meets a flow of lower salinity pouring out of the Irish Sea, and inshore of this lies coastal water further diluted by run-off from the land. The three water masses can have very different temperatures. As said above, sea surface temperatures, both to the west and south of Ireland, are several degrees warmer in winter than those in the Irish Sea: the shelf waters have a deeper mass and borrow warmth from water derived from the North Atlantic Current. The shallow Irish Sea loses heat more rapidly and the coastal freshwater run-off is colder again.

Fronts and boundaries

Temperature or salinity, and often both together, decide a vital characteristic of seawater, shaping its different masses and their physical behaviour: they fix its density (defined as its weight divided by its volume, or grammes per cubic centimetre). The saltier and colder the water, the higher its density and the more it is prone to sink; the warmer the water, the more it expands and rises. This decides much of the layering of the ocean (where the pressure of deep water also adds to density) and also creates vertical or sloping boundaries between the different water masses. Where these meet, there are often 'fronts' of turbulent or swift-flowing water (not to be confused with the atmospheric 'fronts' of weather forecasts, which have to do with the boundaries of distinct masses of air).

The main front in the Atlantic region of these islands, persisting all year round, is at the Irish shelf to the south and west of the island, where the shallower water of the shelf, often mixed vertically by the tide, meets that of the deeper North Atlantic at around 150 m down. At Ireland itself, the so-called 'Islay front', named for the Scottish island, runs from Tiree in Scotland to Malin Head in County Donegal. It separates Atlantic water from the less saline flood emerging from the Irish Sea and deflects the latter into the Sea of the Hebrides. This persists even in winter, and the current along the front runs at times at 20 cm per second.

A front also occurs within the Irish Sea, where strong tides through St George's Channel at the south and the North Channel, and others in and out of Liverpool Bay and the Solway Firth, leave an area of almost permanent slack water off the Irish coast north of Dublin. The front is at the boundary of the fast-moving water, between the south coast of the Isle of Man and the coast of County Dublin, and is at its strongest in August, when the calm area becomes stratified horizontally between sun-warmed water and deeper, colder water. Late spring and summer produce several such fronts between mixed water and stratified water – the Celtic Sea front, for example, to the south of the Irish Sea, and the front at the edge of the continental shelf, west of Ireland. These break down with the onset of winter cooling and the mixing induced by the first Atlantic storms.

The Great Ocean Conveyor

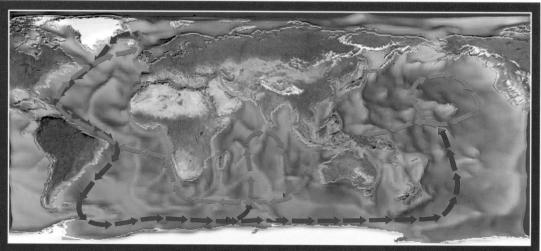

The Great Ocean Conveyor carries water around the planet and between the surface and the deeps. Red: warm surface current; Blue: deep cold current. (Illustration: Jack Cook, Woods Hole Oceanographic Institution)

The interplay of temperature and saltiness – the thermohaline conditions of the water – and their impact on its density has major consequences on an oceanic, even global, scale. In the Mediterranean, the sun's intense evaporation produces a flood of highly saline deep water, pouring out at the bottom of the Strait of Gibraltar. In the western Atlantic, at the Caribbean, water evaporated by the trade winds sails on across the narrow neck of Central America and falls as rain in the Pacific, helping to make that ocean far less salty than the neighbouring Atlantic. Indeed, its lower density makes it half a metre higher than the Atlantic: this is what drives Pacific water into the Arctic through the Bering Strait, between Russia and Alaska.

At the far north of the Atlantic, in the Norwegian Sea, plummeting temperatures create the most spectacular phenomenon in ocean physics. As warm, salty water from the south approaches East Greenland, the wind-chill of winter storms reduces its temperature from perhaps 10 °C to 2 °C. This plunges the North Atlantic Current to a depth of 2 or 3 km, releasing its heat to the atmosphere in the process. Farther north, the formation of winter ice extracts fresh water from the sea, creating more briny, dense water to sink as it chills.

As much as 1,300 km³ per day descend from the Arctic Ocean to become North Atlantic Deep Water. Much of this is formed in the Norwegian Sea and carried southwards again over a ridge on the seabed between Iceland and Scotland. More is formed in the Labrador Sea, but at not such a great depth, and the two layers flow southwards together on the western side of the Atlantic. At the surface, more warm water (originating in the Gulf Stream) is drawn north to sink in its turn. This action, the Atlantic Meridional Overturning Circulation (Altantic MOC), becomes the main 'pump' of the Atlantic Heat Conveyor and the Great Ocean Conveyor that carries water between the world's oceans.

The new North Atlantic Deep Water may not surface again for some 1,000 years. Creeping southwards in the Atlantic, it gathers in some deep salty lenses of water spinning out from the Mediterranean at the Strait of Gibraltar and later meets even deeper bottom water formed in the Antarctic. Brushing that current's circumpolar current, it surges on slowly into the Indian Ocean and surfaces finally in the North Pacific. Here, no new deep water is formed: the Pacific is not salty enough. Instead, the upwelling water travels back to the Atlantic and around the Cape of Good Hope, as the surface layer of the global circulation, warming again as it nears the Equator.

The salinity of water reaching the level of Greenland is essential to the pump that keeps the circulation going. Long before such a mechanism was even imaginable, the arrival of winter warmth for Europe was recognised as a possibly precarious privilege. The link between the Gulf Stream and Europe's mild winters was first promulgated by an American naval commander, Matthew Fontaine Maury, in his *Physical Geography of the Sea,* published in 1855. If this transport of heat from the Gulf of Mexico did not take place, he proposed, 'the soft climates of both France and England would be as that of Labrador, severe in the extreme and icebound.' This prompted Jules Verne to write, in *20,000 Leagues Under the Sea* (1869): 'we must pray that this steadiness continues because . . . if its speed and direction were to change, the climates of Europe would undergo disturbances whose consequences are incalculable.'

A century later, deep drilling was to retrieve evidence of profound and rapid swings in climate recorded in cores of ancient Greenland ice. Other drills, twisting into the deep seabed, brought up shells of foraminifera that helped testify to the ocean's remarkable capacity to switch between glacial and inter-glacial states in decades or less. Some 15,000 years ago, at the first great thaw of the Ice Age, melting ice sheets across North America flooded the North Atlantic with icebergs and fresh water, reducing salinity and halting the sinking of North Atlantic Deep Water. The Gulf Stream moved south and temperatures in northwest Europe fell by 5 °C in just seven years, ultimately bringing a glacial cold snap (the Younger Dryas) back to Ireland that lasted for six to eight centuries. Even tropical seas were chilled, bringing polar foraminifera into the water of the Canary Current and burying them off Mauretania.

Conflicting evidence

Recent decades have seen apparently conflicting evidence about the formation of deep water north of the Greenland–Scotland Ridge and the consequent flow of ocean circulation, and also argument on whether a slowing or halting of the flow would be catastrophic for Europe. Scientists of the Woods Hole Oceanographic Institute in America have been leaders in warning that climate change could instigate a Little Ice Age in the North Atlantic like the one that, from the mid-sixteenth to the mid-eighteenth centuries, brought long, severe winters and cold, wet summers to Ireland and northwestern Europe. They point to the appearance of 'huge rivers of freshwater – the equivalent of a 10-foot-thick layer' that have invaded the North Atlantic over the past thirty years, even in subtropical latitudes.

Some findings of major changes in the flow of North Atlantic Deep Water have rested on short-term samples of an ocean system now realised to have big natural fluctuations; as the International Council for the Exploration of the Sea (ICES) points out: 'The ocean at any one location varies on many timescales – from hours and days, to decades, centuries and millennia.' Yet one alarming analysis showing that the flow had weakened by 30 per cent in a decade was based on just five research results spread over forty years. It was to combat this lack of data that twenty-three countries combined to sow the oceans with the ARGO network of more than 3,000 floats. Launched some 300 km apart, these drift below the surface, measuring temperature and salinity, and rise every ten days to transmit the data to satellites. Ireland has contributed a dozen of these floats, the first of which were launched in the Rockall Trough early in 2008. Another array of deep marine sensors, called RAPID-WATCH (Will the Atlantic Thermohaline Circulation Halt), in which the UK's Natural Environment Research Council (NERC) is involved, are to be installed in the Gulf Stream between Florida and the Canary Islands, to detect any significant change in its flow.

Only in recent years have oceanographers been able to moor instruments for long-term measurement in remote, often violent Arctic waters, some of them battered by icebergs calving from the glaciers of East Greenland. A decade-long trend in the Atlantic waters passing north across the Greenland–Scotland ridge has been one of warming and increasing salinity (the latter, perhaps, produced by higher evaporation). The highest temperature in 100 years was recorded in the Kola Section in the Barents Sea off northwestern Russia, and in 2007 the summer melt opened a long-wished-for shipping route – the Northwest Passage – connecting the Atlantic and Pacific oceans north of Canada. According to the Intergovernmental Panel on Climate Change (IPCC), the Arctic seems to be heading for an almost entirely ice-free summer by the latter part of this century, for the first time in at least a million years.

Thus the promise of new trade routes around the top of the world is mingled with apprehension of disaster at some distant date. Assurances from some modelling that it might take two centuries for freshwater dilution to stop the Conveyor pump (MOC) will be tested by the measurement of long-term trends. In 2008, the UK's Marine Climate Change Impacts Partnership (MCCIP) expressed a high-level scientific consensus: 'There is considered to be a less than 10 per cent chance of a collapse of the Atlantic Heat Conveyor this century.'

There have also been challenges to the idea, generally accepted in science, that the release of heat in the formation of North Atlantic Deep Water is the prime reason for western Europe's mild winters. Some climate scientists have suggested that even if the MOC slowed or stopped, the prevailing westerly winds would still blow heat stored in the Atlantic in summer to Europe in winter: indeed, the few degrees of warmth lost in the halting of the pump might well balance those gained from climate change. The chief influence on the pattern of climate in western Europe will, in this scenario, continue to be the powerful oceanic and atmospheric forces engaged in the North Atlantic Oscillation.

North Atlantic Oscillation

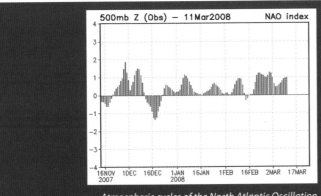

Atmospheric cycles of the North Atlantic Oscillation still have great influence on Ireland's seasonal climate. Early in 2008 it was mainly positive.
(Courtesy of NOAA Photo Library)

As one of the oldest weather patterns on record, the North Atlantic Oscillation (NAO) is still largely what decides whether Ireland's winters are warm, wet and windy or cool and dry. What oscillates in the NAO is sea level pressure of the atmospheric mass between Iceland and the Azores, islands on the same line of longitude but with two very different climates. In winter, the mass of air swings between Iceland's low pressure centre that generates so many Atlantic storms, and a high pressure centre over warm, sub-tropical waters between the Azores and Iberia.

When there is a very large and steady difference between barometer readings in the Azores and Iceland, the NAO is said to be 'positive' with 'a high seasonal index'. In this state, there are more and stronger winter storms travelling northeast across the Atlantic, bringing winds, higher waves and warm, wet air to Ireland but giving cold, dry winters to the Mediterranean. In a 'negative' NAO winter, the difference in pressure is small. There are fewer and weaker storms; warm, moist air is carried to the Mediterranean, and cold, dry, polar air from the north and east blows into northern Europe. But the NAO still accounts for only part of the variation in winter sea level pressure. The chaotic nature of atmospheric circulation means that even during periods of strongly positive or negative NAO winters, the atmospheric circulation is likely to produce local exceptions to the rule.

The variation of the NAO has sometimes been decades long; so, too, have been swings in the number and intensity of Atlantic hurricanes. Both are poorly understood and, along with fluctuations in the formation of North Atlantic Deep Water, reflect the interlocking of oceanic conditions with the atmosphere. In the late 1960s, for example, oceanographers became aware of what they were to call the Great Salinity Anomaly, a great pool of cold, fresh, polar water that appeared near the surface, off east Greenland. It was created by an unusually large discharge of ice as storms swirled around record low levels of pressure near Iceland, the northern cell of the NAO. The currents of the sub-polar gyre carried the pool anti-clockwise, first to the Labrador Sea, then on towards Newfoundland, then east towards Europe in the North Atlantic Current. In the mid 1970s, it reached the edge of the continental shelf beyond Rockall. Finally, by the early 1980s, its core, now somewhat reduced, was back off east Greenland. Because its water was too fresh to sink, it had acted as a sort of moving blanket, insulating different parts of the ocean from contact with the atmosphere as it moved around the gyre and successively delaying release of heat. Woods Hole oceanographers believe it may even have shut down the pump system for a year or two, bringing very cold winters to Europe.

Ocean chemistry: the planet's crucial brew

The passage of light into the ocean and thus the depth of its 'euphotic' zone (the part of the ocean that receives light) are governed by the concentration of organic and inorganic materials suspended or dissolved in the water column. To look over the side of a boat near the coast is to see perhaps a few tens of metres beneath the surface. In the open ocean or in the tropics, there are usually fewer nutrients to nourish plankton and fewer suspended particles. But even the clearest water holds a myriad of molecules from the planet's vast chemical laboratory.

More than eighty chemical elements are dissolved in seawater: a brew of gases, salts, minerals and isotopes exchanged with the planet's crust and atmosphere over millions of years. Even sea salt itself holds almost a dozen different substances. A mere half-dozen elements account for 99 per cent of all the dissolved salts, present as ions (electrically charged particles). The sodium chloride of table salt is not actually one of them: ions of sodium and chlorine are still separate and independent in the sea, along with those of sulphur, calcium, magnesium and potassium. Many of the elements are present in parts per billion and unfamiliar outside science. These trace substances, such as manganese, lead, gold, iron and iodine, are important to some biochemical reactions: iron, for instance, is an essential micronutrient for phytoplankton growth.

Salts circulate between Earth and its oceans by several routes. Volcanic eruptions supply sulphates and chlorides. Weathering of continental rocks dissolves sodium, calcium, potassium and magnesium, which are carried into rivers along with clay minerals such as silica and bicarbonate. Much of the solid material swept out to sea gets no farther than the rivers' offshore canyons, such as those off southwest Ireland, but great volumes of weathered particles are also carried as fine dust to the deep, open ocean. At the tectonic spreading zones, such as the Mid-Atlantic Ridge, cold seawater seeps down into hot, new volcanic rocks and is eventually expelled again through the 'black smokers', hydrothermal vents in the seabed discovered in the 1970s. In the process, the water loses some of its elements, such as magnesium and sulphur, but gains others such as lithium and rubidium and even silver, platinum and gold, if only as trace elements in parts per billion.

Despite the hectic physics of the ocean, it can present a surprisingly constant chemistry. The vast bulk of seawater has a salinity of between 3.1–3.8 per cent – 3.5 per cent is taken as the average – produced by billions of years of mixing and recirculation of the seas. This means that other processes must be taking a share of dissolved salts from the water. Some is deposited through reactions with the sediment. Others (e.g. silica, nitrate, calcium carbonate) are used in the making of marine organisms. Still more are returned to the land in aerosols from wind-blown spray, and evaporation at salt-pans on arid coasts. The constancy of the sea's saltiness is a measure of the remarkable planetary balance between the rate at which material is added to the oceans and its living ecosystems, and the rate of its recycling to the continents. When seabed sediments become rock under ocean pressure, and are uplifted to the landmass over millions of years through tectonic activity, their weathering completes the cycle of return to the sea.

Seawater also contains small amounts of dissolved gases (nitrogen, oxygen, carbon dioxide, hydrogen and trace gases). The warmer and saltier the water, the less it can absorb, and the surface layer is normally saturated with gases such as oxygen and nitrogen, releasing them as fast as they are dissolved. Once water sinks below the ocean surface, dissolved gases can no longer exchange with the atmosphere. Some of them – nitrogen and rare inert gases – stay much as they are, their molecules slowly diffusing through the water by physical processes. But others, such as oxygen and carbon dioxide, enter into the chemistry and biology of the ocean in ways that change their concentrations.

Surface of the Sea

The layering of the ocean can be on a mighty scale, its structure determined by wind, temperature and saltiness. But the surface of the sea, dancing to the light, is also a layer of its own – a skin perhaps 1 mm thick. Indeed, it holds sub-layers measured in microns, or millionths of a metre, with different ecological, physical and chemical properties.

As climate warms, this surface micro-layer is under close study. It is where the ocean makes exchanges with the atmosphere and where gases produced by plankton become aerosols that can fill the sky with clouds (see p.28). It is also an ecosystem increasingly vulnerable to pollution by persistent man-made chemicals toxic to marine life.

The main source of the natural substances is, of course, the water column below. Rising air bubbles collect all manner of organic materials, such as oils, fats and buoyant proteins produced by plankton and the decay of dead organisms, and these can appear as thin films or slicks on the surface. But this upper organic film also concentrates a whole range of man-made poisons to levels up to 500 times greater than exist in the ocean below. They include: pesticides; polychlorinated biphenyls (PCBs); organotin compounds; petroleum hydrocarbons and heavy metals. Thus, their concentration is predictably highest near urban and industrialised coasts, harbours and estuaries. This is what threatens the surface micro-layer as an essential microhabitat for an immense range of ocean micro-organisms (known collectively as *neuston*), together with larvae and fish eggs. Pollution has extended even to the polar seas, where simpler marine food-webs are, if anything, more easily damaged.

The great carbon question

If salinity, and its effect on water density, is the key to overturning and circulation of the oceans, the sea's role as a sponge for carbon is now crucial in the process of climate change. As the fourth most abundant element in the universe (next to hydrogen, helium and oxygen) and the basic building block of all life on Earth, carbon is continuously cycled through the planet, from the gases of its atmosphere to the molten mantle churning beneath its crust. Part of its cycle takes millions of years, as carbon in ocean-floor limestone sediments is drawn down into the mantle at the collision and sinking of tectonic plates and returned to the atmosphere in volcanic eruptions as carbon dioxide. The biological cycling of carbon is vastly more rapid: the amount of carbon taken up by plants in photosynthesis and released back to the atmosphere by respiration each year is 1,000 times greater than the amount that is moved geologically. But much of it is also stored in vegetation and soils, for a slower release through harvesting, cultivation and decay.

The vast ocean surface shows a busy exchange of gases between the water and the air. Oxygen, nitrogen, hydrogen and carbon dioxide, along with trace gases, are all dissolved through the surface in amounts decided by the water's temperature and salinity. Carbon dioxide dissolves readily, especially at the ocean's colder reaches, and a great deal is carried down and held in the slow-moving deep water formed in the North Atlantic. A huge amount of CO_2 is also absorbed from the atmosphere in the spring growth of plant plankton (see Chapter 5) and then almost immediately passed on into the ocean food chain as the tiny animals of zooplankton start eating it. They also take it from the sea to form shells of calcium carbonate, and this is generally the form in which residual organic carbon accumulates in seabed sediments and, under pressure, becomes limestone.

In the natural processes by which the Earth's carbon is recycled and held in balance, tens of billions of tonnes a year circulate between the atmosphere, rocks and oceans and the myriad life forms of land and sea. Human activity sends about an extra 5.5 billion tonnes into the atmosphere as carbon dioxide, having extracted fossil fuels from the organic sediments of coal and oil, and released carbon in forest clearance and soil disturbance. This has driven more and more gas into the ocean. Since the beginning of the industrial age (around 1800), the amount of CO_2 in the atmosphere has increased from 280 parts per million (ppm) to 380 ppm. The seas have absorbed at least half of this, and it would take tens of thousands of years for their waters to return to pre-industrial condition.

An acid ocean: the risks

The progressive acidification of the ocean through absorption of CO_2 from the atmosphere has so far shown up as a small but distinct decrease in the pH of surface water – the measure of acidity or alkalinity. A neutral medium has a pH of 7 (acidity increases as the pH numbers get smaller), so the estimated fall from 8.25 to 8.14 between 1751 and 2004 is still a decrease in alkalinity. But a progressive swing below 7 could, as many scientists have warned, have dire implications for marine life. An acid sea threatens the very structures of myriad organisms. To make shells, plates and skeletons from calcium and its salts, the seawater has to be supersaturated with calcium and carbonate ions – otherwise seemingly tough substances will start to dissolve again.

Some calcium-based structures spring at once to mind as vulnerable to an acidifying sea: the fragile globes of sea urchins; the plates of starfish; or the biscuity armour of crabs and lobsters that has to be reformed at each moult. As predators and scavengers, these are keystone species on the seabed. Most molluscs, too, are potential victims, from oysters and a hundred other bivalves to the myriad forms of sea snail. They are especially at risk in their first settlement from larvae, when building of a shell begins.

Much of the impact of acidification will be at a microscopic scale but nonetheless hugely significant. In the world of plankton, which helps to regulate the ocean's carbon cycle as well as being vital to its food-web, several groups of plants and animals are calcifying organisms. Among them are the single-celled coccolithophores, reckoned to be the most productive phytoplankton on Earth (their skeletons, drifting down to an ancient seabed when these islands were in tropical waters, made the chalk of the white cliffs of Dover and Antrim). Coral, too, is calcareous, and an acidifying sea threatens not only the tropical reefs (already seriously damaged by sun-bleaching) but the newly discovered cold-water reefs in the deeps to the southwest of Ireland.

CO_2 absorbed from the air is held initially in the ocean's surface fathoms and takes centuries to diffuse to deep water. This concentrates its effects in the most productive layer of marine life, and not only on its calcifying organisms. For all animals that breathe seawater – not merely fish, but the larger invertebrates and some of the zooplankton – acidification may have other consequences. They take up oxygen and lose respired CO_2 through their gills, a process which makes them more likely to absorb increased levels of CO_2 than would air-breathing animals. Acidification of their internal tissues and fluids could affect the ability of their blood to carry oxygen, with big implications for growth and reproduction. But, as with so much of the concern about the impact of rising CO_2 on the chemistry and biology of the ocean, political awareness has come late, and specific field research is in its infancy.

In confronting the crisis of climate change, however, some scientists and technologists seek to persuade the ocean to soak up even more carbon and bury it safely in the deeps. CarboOcean, a European research project, sees the ocean's uptake as 'the most important manageable driving agent for climate change' and is trying to assess its limits as a sink for man-made CO_2. Some schemes would attempt direct injection of the liquid gas to the floor of ocean basins where, in theory, it could remain trapped within the deep water of the Ocean Conveyor for perhaps 1,000 years. Others propose burial deep within seabed sediments where high pressures and low temperatures would hold it in frozen lattices. Still more plans would take a more roundabout approach, promoting the growth of phytoplankton by fertilising the ocean surface with iron, an essential micronutrient, or urea, a nitrogen-based fertiliser. This, it is suggested, would remove more carbon from the atmosphere through the plankton's photosynthesis, and then, in the death of the plant cells, the sinking particles would be locked away for centuries. Oceanographers counter, however, that most such organic carbon remains in the upper ocean or is returned to the atmosphere within a year; attempting either to fertilise the ocean surface, or to bury CO_2 at the abyssal seabed, risks profound interference with ecosystems that are still only partly understood. The signatories to the London Convention, the international treaty governing ocean dumping, agreed in 2007 that large-scale 'fertilisation' is not justifiable, given the current gaps in knowledge.

Seeding the sky: ocean, clouds and raindrops

Day to day and hour to hour, the passage of cloud and precipitation provides Ireland not merely with forty shades of green but a thousand different skies and shades of light: it is a constant pulse of liveliness and change. To live by an Atlantic shore is to absorb (at times, almost literally) the interchange of moisture between ocean and sky. We may never actually see how water is lifted from the waves; just its return in darkly silver curtains drawn across the islands. But that there is continuity, transformation, and replenishment of substance, we do not doubt for a moment. In the new weight of Atlantic rain, the building intensity of its more extreme downpours, the role of an ocean in climate change takes on an extra reality.

Our mammalian blood makes us feel the temperate sea as cold, but the ocean's planetary capacity to absorb heat from the atmosphere, store it, or release it in gaseous water vapour, all at a majestically gradual pace, helps to provide a climate we appreciate as relatively stable. The inertia of temperature in the ocean's surface layer calms the atmospheric flows so energised by heat and locks them into patterns in which the circulation of one is partner to the other. The role of solar heat in evaporation of the sea is obvious; but the friction of winds, too, not only sets the course of currents, but also evaporates water that falls elsewhere as rain, transferring heat to the atmosphere in the process.

Between evaporation and precipitation comes condensation: the process that conjures the shifting forms of clouds. The basic mechanics are familiar: warm, humid air cools as it rises, its vapour condensing into millions of water droplets. They spread out in wispy cirrus in the stratosphere or rise in billowing columns of cumulus, shaped by the meeting of unstable masses of cold and warm air. Each droplet needs to build around an airborne particle or aerosol, and the 'clear' sky is full of particles to serve as cloud condensation nuclei. Nature itself emits vast quantities of myriad kinds and sizes: from erupting volcanoes and forest fires; the belchings of ruminant beasts; the fine-as-dust siftings of pollens and spores: the terpenes released in the scent of pines and lemons. The list is endless and ever more arcane. To such motley flotsam is added our own smoke and fumes, vapour trails, air-fresheners, deodorants and so on. Most particles are back to earth in a week or less; the heavier ones still dry, the lighter ones, measured in nanometres – the thickness of a hair at most – and with a water-soluble fraction, becoming the seeds of cloud vapour buoyed up on swirling eddies of wind. Only as the droplets collide and fatten do they gain the weight to fall as rain.

The remote ocean, too, offers particles to the sky as cloud condensation nuclei. Salt from spray is an obvious mineral contribution, but quite another chemical has taken on a fascinating aura as a possible feedback agent helping to control the planet's climate. Dimethyl sulphide (DMS) is a gaseous compound released by short-lived, microscopic plant plankton as the cells die or are eaten by zooplankton at the surface of the ocean. In the air it is oxidised to form aerosol particles and these are carried up to form clouds of small droplets that persist for long periods without releasing rain. The 'albedo' or whiteness of their upper surface reflects sunlight back to space.

Plankton blooms (see Chapter 5) can cover thousands of square kilometres, and those of a key species, *Emiliana huxleyii*, have produced concentrations of DMS in the northeast Atlantic up to ten times higher than in the surrounding waters. But production of the compound seems to be even more widespread in the ocean. Oceanographers in Spain, analysing data from around the world, have found

The ocean is the cloud-maker, seeding Ireland's maritime skies. (Michael Viney)

that, during sunny periods, marine organisms in the open ocean release more DMS regardless of latitude, temperature or plankton biomass. Thus, the exposure of algae to harmful intensities of ultraviolet radiation seems to be controlled by a negative feedback loop. This is a climatic effect of the sort proposed by James Lovelock in his momentous theory of Earth as Gaia, a self-regulating biosphere maintaining stable conditions fit for life. 'But for the algal production of dimethyl sulphide,' he believes, 'clouds over the world's oceans would be less dense and the world would be a hotter place. This is true for even the North Atlantic, in spite of the huge production of cloud condensation nuclei on the land surfaces around it.'

In 2006, scientists from twenty European institutes joined research cruises from Galway aboard the Marine Institute's *Celtic Explorer* in one of the world's largest studies of plankton aerosol production and its impact on climate. In a project led by Colin O'Dowd of NUI Galway, analysis of the plankton's output, together with data from the university's atmospheric monitoring station at Mace Head, near Carna, County Galway, and NASA's satellite sensors, will help construct prediction models for plankton's role in a warming world.

Beans, Bottles and Buoys

Although not marine organisms, the 'sea beans' picked up on Ireland's Atlantic tidelines have long had a role in oceanographic speculation. Chief among them are tropical drift fruits and seeds, the 'peregrine disseminules', as botanists put it, of jungle vines and other pod-bearing plants growing in the West Indies and Central America. Their arrival on European coasts has been discussed for at least four centuries, with the first Irish record of the glossy brown sea heart (*Entada gigas*) dating to 1696. 'It is very easie to conceive,' wrote the botanist Hans Sloane soon after, 'that growing in Jamaica in the woods, they may fall from the Trees into the Rivers, or by any other way conveyed by them into the sea.' He posited a westerly trade wind 'for at least two parts of three of the Whole Year, so that the Beans being brought North by the Currents from the Gulf of Florida, are put into these Westerly Winds' way and may be supported by this means at last to arrive in [Ireland and] Scotland.'

Sloane's theory, written when the currents of the oceans were scarcely understood, is strikingly accurate. Perhaps a score of tropical plants have seeds capable of staying afloat for the transatlantic journey, which may take some fifteen months. In the 1980s, experiments with glass bottles showed that these take between 200 and 300 days to cross from Newfoundland or Nova Scotia to Europe. In 2007, a buoy washed up in County Sligo and traced back to Wedgeport in Nova Scotia had taken 221 days for the journey – thus, as the Sligo ecologist Don Cotton computed it, travelling 4,270 km at an average 19.3 km an hour.

The occasional coconut (*Cocos nucifera*) arrives on western shores, still in its fibrous husk and sometimes barnacled, or bored by marine molluscs, and, along with *Entada*, the commonest seeds are the far smaller, dark brown horse-eye bean (*Mucuna sloanei*), named for its conspicuous black hilum; the similar sea-purse (*Dioclea reflexa*); the grey acorn-like nickar nut (*Caesalpina bonduc*).

A tideline collection of transatlantic seeds: at the rear, a coconut (right) and a tropical box-nut, still in their husks, and a variety of sea-beans.

CHAPTER 3

Land Beneath the Sea

No one can live beside the sea and not wonder at times, with a child's curiosity, how the view to the horizon would look with all the water gone. There are plenty of maps of seabed contours, but few that offer the detail the imagination craves: the sculpture and relief of hidden heights, valleys and plains. Sidescan sonar, the echo-sounding technology introduced in the late 1960s, has been used to survey about 10 per cent of the world's deep oceans, but brushing thousands of square kilometres with wide swathes of bouncing echoes is still a costly operation. Away from national economic zones and oil/gas exploration, much of the deep Atlantic is still mapped by contour lines that join points of known soundings in rough approximations of the dark ocean floor.

Plotting the surface of the seabed can be important to fishermen, biologists and submariners, but it does not always produce the data of most economic value. These lie deeper again, in the mineral-bearing bedrock and oil-filled domes of the continental shelf, and are unlocked by analysing echoes from seismic guns that fire bursts of air into the ocean. These sometimes reveal, in passing, palaeo-landscapes shaped by the dramatically different sea level of the last Ice Age. In the 1980s, for example, the Geological Survey of Ireland detected ancient shorelines immured beneath seabed sediments at up to 130 m below present sea level. There are buried cliffs southwest of the Aran Islands, buried river channels off the southwest and east coasts, carved by the rush of water from melting glaciers.

The birth of the Atlantic was set in train about 180 million years ago, when the supercontinent of Pangaea, surrounded by ocean, began to split along the line of even older sutures joining crustal plates on the surface of Earth. The European and North American plates began to drift away from each other, on a split north to south, pushed apart by a slow flow of magma from the rift now called the Mid-Atlantic Ridge. The flow has had its eruptive periods and 'hot spots' – pushing Iceland up, for example, as an island of volcanoes. Lava from associated fissures surged across the northeast of Ireland about 55 million years ago. But today, the spread of Atlantic basalt from the central rift ridge is a relatively cold process, levering Europe and America apart by no more than an extra couple of centimetres a year: perhaps 20–25 km in a million years. A similar rift in the East Pacific creates new sea floor much faster and more explosively. Here are the 'black smoker' chimneys built of hydrothermal minerals

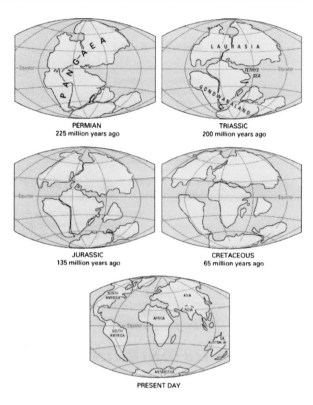

PERMIAN
225 million years ago

TRIASSIC
200 million years ago

JURASSIC
135 million years ago

CRETACEOUS
65 million years ago

PRESENT DAY

The making of Earth's oceans: tectonic snapshots from the first break-up of the supercontinent Pangaea to the spread of the modern Atlantic.

and communities of animal life thriving in boiling hot springs below thousands of metres of ocean. In neither the Atlantic nor the Pacific is the surface of the Earth expanding: far from the rifts, the creep of 'old' rock is dragged down at deep ocean trenches for recycling in the planet's mantle. In the Atlantic there are only two small trenches, the Puerto Rico Trench and the South Sandwich Trench off the tip of South America. The entire Pacific, on the other hand, is rimmed with deep trenches, which are leading old rock back under the continental plates in the process called subduction.

Most of the deep ocean floor is covered by reddish-brown clays, accumulating perhaps 1–10 mm per millennium from particles carried from the continents by water, wind or ice. They are generated slowly from the weathering and erosion of rocks, or dramatically in the ashy eruptions of volcanoes. Massive amounts of debris were carried into the ocean by icebergs during the retreat of the ice ages. Submarine volcanoes have added their own material, and a final, light seasoning arrives in the constant rain of cosmogenic dust from space.

Where the deep ocean floor is swept by strong currents, supersaturated water can precipitate crusts or nodules of mineral sediments. The fluffy seabed oozes (familiar from underwater filming) form at shallower depths, where ocean productivity is higher. Here the clay mixes with 'marine snow' – the skeletal particles of dead plankton and the other organic detritus sifting down through the water column. Near the continents, where more of the sediment is shed from the land and is subject to stronger water movements, oozes are uncommon. Even so, the higher production of phytoplankton, nourished by mineral upwellings and a more rapid return of organic detritus to the seabed, means that about half of all organic carbon burial occurs at the continental margins.

The Mid-Atlantic Ridge

Any tour of the great open seabed to the west of these islands finds a compelling boundary in the Mid-Atlantic Ridge – the huge underwater mountain range some 1,440 km from Ireland and far beyond the farthest point of national territorial markers. British and Irish trawlers fish there and scientists of both states join in international exploration of its secrets. The zip-fastener profile of the ridge, as it snakes down the centre of Atlantic maps, gives little idea of its dramatic scale and complexity on the way from Iceland to the deeps far to the southwest of South Africa. The ridge itself rises to less than 2,700 m below the ocean surface. But running down its crest is a wide rift valley that can be another 1,800 m deep and up to 50 km wide – even more of an abyss than America's Grand Canyon. Lying across it are volcanic ridges and transverse fractures where blocks of crust are sliding past each other. Here, too, are small, circular volcanoes that have added to the spread of basalt pushing out to east and west.

For hundreds of kilometres to either side of the Mid-Atlantic Ridge, the basement rock of the ocean is a sheet of basalt 4–6 km thick, overlaid by up to 2 km of sediment. But the Abyssal Plain, as it is called, is far from flat. There are old volcanoes and trenches; hills and valleys sculpted from the sediments by deep currents and boulders dropped by icebergs from successive glacial periods. As the plain arrives at the cliffs and slopes of the continental shelf, it meets huge wedges of sediment formed by submarine landslides. These were built up from sporadic flows of mud and glacial debris and deep layers of the ocean's pelagic sediments: an interleaving layer-cake potentially rich in oil and gas.

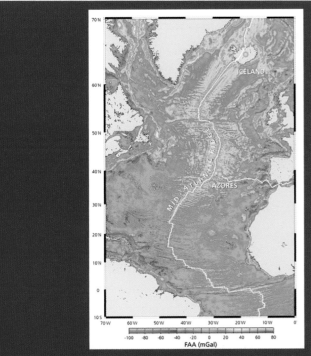

A bathymetric portrait of the Mid-Atlantic Ridge. (Map produced by Jennifer Georgen in a MIT/WHOI Joint Programme, with data from David Sandwell of the Scripps Institution of Oceanography and Walter Smith, NOAA)

Rifting of Earth's crust is a violent affair, as the ragged edge of the continental shelf west of Ireland and Scotland makes clear. It is flanked by a huge outlying chunk of rifted continental crust, the Rockall Bank, and a chain of sedimentary basins where the crust has markedly thinned. Only off the southwest of Ireland, beyond the Porcupine Ridge, does the shelf pitch more directly to the Porcupine Abyssal Plain, a sea floor 4,000 m down and millions of years younger than the ancient rocks it adjoins. The shelf itself, between 100 m and 200 m underwater, has a gentle gradient and a low relief of sedimentary banks, reefs and rocky outcrops no more dramatic than that of Ireland's terrestrial midlands. But this is scarred by the canyons of big rivers and other turbidity currents that notch the edge of the shelf and pour their sediments over it. Fans of debris at its base are studded with the bigger, heavier rocks, and vigorous currents continually swirl through this tumbled apron of the continental rise.

Travelling out from Ireland, the edge of the inner shelf can arrive surprisingly quickly: a mere 30 km off the north coast of Mayo and 60 km off southwest Kerry. In between, the shelf stretches out for 240 km due west of Galway city. The mountains, valleys and canyons beyond compose a terrain known only by touch, as it were, from the bouncing of fishing trawls and the echoes of sonar tapping from side to side like a blind man's cane.

The area of North Atlantic seabed, designated by Ireland as its economic terrain (see Box: Sharing out the sea floor, p.41), is roughly triangular. Its northerly boundary, on a line from Lough Foyle, goes

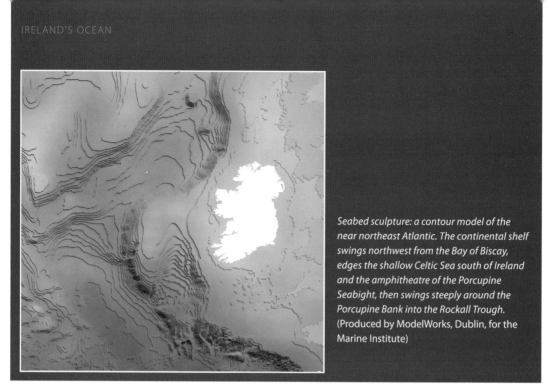

Seabed sculpture: a contour model of the near northeast Atlantic. The continental shelf swings northwest from the Bay of Biscay, edges the shallow Celtic Sea south of Ireland and the amphitheatre of the Porcupine Seabight, then swings steeply around the Porcupine Bank into the Rockall Trough. (Produced by ModelWorks, Dublin, for the Marine Institute)

from a point 7° W 55° N to another at 25° W 57° 30' N. From there, it steps back southeast to a point some 240 km south of Ireland, at 12° W and almost 47° N, then slants northeastward across the Celtic Sea and into the Irish Sea to roughly 54° N and 5° 20'W at Carlingford Lough. It contains most of the Rockall Trough, the southern half of its plateau along with most of the Hatton Basin, the Porcupine Seabight and part of the Abyssal Plain beyond, together with some 200,000 km² of continental shelf – in all, an area about ten times that of the Irish state.

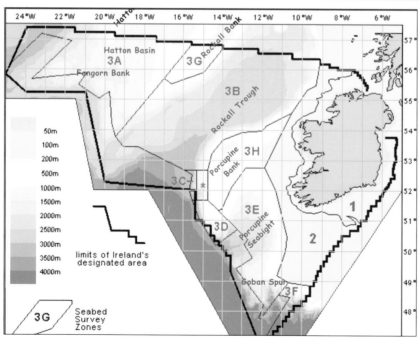

The banks and troughs of Ireland's Exclusive Economic Zone (EEZ).
(Geological Survey of Ireland)

The nearest and shallowest valleys of Ireland's share of the shelf begin in the northwest with some of the Donegal Basin, west of Scotland. Then there is the Erris Trough, off northwest Mayo, and the Slyne Trough off Galway, both around 1,000 m deep. At the southwest, 200 km off the farthest peninsulas of Kerry and Cork, the basin of the Porcupine Seabight is a dramatic sunken amphitheatre, 320 km across and 2,000m deep. It opens westwards on to the Porcupine Abyssal Plain and is bounded by three shallow, steep-sided platforms: to the east the Irish continental shelf; to the north the Slyne Ridge; to the west the Porcupine Ridge. Its basic platform is metamorphic rock about 1,000 million years old, overlaid by successions of sedimentary rocks such as sandstone and siltstone.

South of the Porcupine Seabight is the Goban Spur – a high plateau on the edge of the continental shelf – with a smooth, flat-topped platform and a series of tilted faults sloping westward in a rough piece of seabed that plunges to more than 4,000 m. The Porcupine Ridge is another high plateau, about 300 km long, that shallows northwards to the Porcupine Bank, with water depths of 200 m or less. Southwest of it, where the continental crust meets the oceanic crust on the Porcupine Abyssal Plain, lies the edge of the Irish National Seabed.

The Great Rockall Trough

To peer (metaphorically) from the western edge of the Porcupine Ridge is to gaze out into the great Rockall Trough: far bigger in area than the Irish Sea and a major feature of the deep-water landscape shared by Ireland and the UK. It is bounded at the north by an underwater ridge off Scotland that acts as a barrier between relatively warm Atlantic waters and the cold water of the Norwegian Basin and Faroe Islands. The ridge's existence and the marked temperature changes it caused were discovered by

The wave-worn granite cone of Rockall.

Wyville Thomson on one of his exploratory cruises on HMS *Porcupine*, and it was later given his name. From here, the trough sweeps down past the Hebrides and the Irish ridges of Erris and Slyne and opens wide in the south to the Porcupine Abyssal Plain. The eastern rim of the trough is scalloped with channels and wide canyons that pour debris down to form lobes and fans on its floor, as much as 2,000 m below. Its far western wall slopes up to the Rockall Bank. This is part of the plateau that, at the north, pushes up the tiny storm-swept granite cone of Rockall; at about 25 m in diameter, it is claimed by the UK as the domain of a Scottish shire. But the status of the surrounding ocean floor is disputed between Ireland, the UK, Denmark (for the Faroe Islands), and Iceland. Farther west still, the Rockall plateau dips to the Hatton Basin and rises again to the Hatton Bank before the final slope to the great Iceland Basin, east of the Mid-Atlantic Ridge.

The Rockall Trough's sedimentary floor, about 5 km thick, is scoured by powerful currents that constantly erode the slopes, moulding their debris into ridges, fans and flows of gravel. In the middle

Shipwrecks around Ireland, mapped by the National Seabed Survey. (Geological Survey of Ireland)

RV Celtic Explorer, *the high-technology research vessel built for the Marine Institute, played a key role in the mapping operations of the National Seabed Survey.* (Courtesy of the Marine Institute/David Brannigan)

is a giant, elongated mound of sediment with a surface sculpted by the northward-flowing current into waves as big as terrestrial sand dunes. This is the Feni Drift, the oldest formation of its kind anywhere in the northeast Atlantic.

In 1996, the sloping margins of the trough were the target of Ireland's first deep-water survey using GLORIA (Geological LOng Range Inclined Asdic), the sidescan sonar mapping tool that can chart more than 10,000 km² of seabed in a day. The survey mapped some 200,000 km² of sea floor, mostly the steep walls of the eastern slope of the trough. A prime purpose was to discover the contours that seemed most prone to collapse, along with the paths that any flow of sediment might take. Where piled-up sediment is soft, a seismic shudder, either geologically natural or resulting from oil/gas exploration, can precipitate what oceanographer Peter Herring, from Southampton Oceanography Centre, has called 'an underwater avalanche of unimaginable proportions', travelling for hundreds of kilometres and affecting seabed life for decades. Even a lesser slump or slide could have dramatic consequences for seabed installations. This 1996 reconnaissance survey (the Atlantic Irish Regional Survey, or AIRS) was carried out by the Dublin Institute for Advanced Studies, University College Dublin and the GSI, and funded largely under the Republic's government programme for fisheries research. It gave valuable experience in readiness for the Irish National Seabed Survey (INSS), launched in 2000 and managed jointly by the GSI and the Marine Institute.

The span of this survey was enormous, ranging from inshore bays to ocean depths hundreds of kilometres distant. In Donegal Bay, for example, seaward of the fishing port of Killybegs, it identified more than 100 wrecks and discovered a glacial moraine more than 40 km long (fishermen knew it already as a 'fast', at which point they would raise their nets). But in mapping some 890,000 km² of seabed, the survey charted a landscape of vast relief, not only for its surface topography and texture but its sedimentary layers and deepest geology.

A piece of the seabed from the Rockall Trough delivered aboard a survey ship. Such 'ground truthing' sampling of sands, sediments and rock-cores, taken from more than 200 locations, helped in analysing the multibeam sonar images of different sea-floor habitats.
(Courtesy of Geological Survey of Ireland)

Such intensive exploration of the ocean floor is less than forty years old. It began with the Deep Sea Drilling Project, initiated by the US in 1968. Prompted by the then revelatory theory of plate tectonics and sea-floor spreading, it helped to confirm it: the basalt flowing out from the great crustal fractures had kept a record of Earth's magnetic reversals in rock of different ages. In 1981, as the world-famous drillship *Glomar Challenger* was reaching the end of her useful life, 150 of the leading earth scientists set out a new blueprint for drilling even deeper and into more difficult rock, but still with the main objective of understanding the tectonic processes that shape oceans and continents. Among the discoveries of the Ocean Drilling Programme (ODP) was a buried, living world of microbes, feeding in deep-sea sediments and crust hundreds of metres below the sea floor. Irish scientists first became involved through the European Science Foundation Consortium for Ocean Drilling (ECOD), a co-operative venture by twelve European nations set up in 1986 within the framework of the ODP. As new partners in 2000, they were able to send Irish researchers on drilling programmes and make new proposals for Irish waters, notably for exploring the carbonate mounds of the Porcupine Seabight.

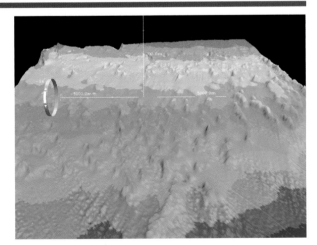

A group of cold-water coral mounds on the western Rockall Bank in images by the multibeam echo sounder.
(Courtesy of Geological Survey of Ireland)

A thousand mounds

Clusters of mounds of carbonate (limestone) mud on the seabed have been a most dramatic find in recent exploration of the deep Atlantic. Along the southern margins of the Rockall Trough and in the Porcupine Seabight, they number more than a thousand and vary greatly in size and shape – conical or ridged-shaped, and sometimes with very steep sides. They range from groups of small, individual mounds up to 5 m high and 75 m across to clusters or provinces of larger mounds

Among the international survey vessels chartered to assist in the National Seabed Survey were the SV Bligh. *and the SV* Siren. *(Courtesy of Geological Survey of Ireland)*

making alignments up to 15 km long and rising 300 m above the surrounding sea floor. Others, almost equally big, are buried in sediment. In 2002, the INSS mapped a mound on the Rockall Bank and the western slope of the Rockall Trough, in depths of up to 1,000 m, that is up to 350 m high. It is the largest discovered in the North Atlantic so far, surpassing even those of the Norwegian shelf.

The mounds vary greatly in composition and there are two contrasting hypotheses about their origin and evolution. One sees their growth as initially shaped by the external working of water masses and successive accumulations of debris from thickets of cold-water corals (see Chapter 4). The other explanation links the genesis of many of them to seepage of methane and other hydrocarbon compounds through cracks in the sea floor, causing local fertilisation of the bottom water.

The initial discoveries west of Ireland, by petroleum geologists prospecting with sub-sea-floor seismic imaging in the early 1990s, were followed by three EU-funded major research projects involving Irish scientists: GEOMOUND, ECOMOUND and ACES. The immediate concern of the first two was the origin and evolution of the carbonate mounds, and that of the third, their ecology and conservation, discussed in Chapter 4.

The mounds are quite different from the undersea mountains – usually defunct volcanoes – known as seamounts. In the classifications of bathymetry, seamounts have to rise above 1,000 m from the sea floor. Mountains between 500 m and 1,000 m are called knolls and those below 500 m are mere hills. Some seamounts broke the surface to become islands, such as those of Hawaii, the Azores and Bermuda.

There are perhaps 1,000 seamounts in the Atlantic, but new ones are being discovered and named all the time: among those on the southwestern edge of the Rockall Bank, and thus at the far boundary of Ireland's seabed survey, are Eriador, Rohan and Gondor – names borrowed from Tolkien's *Lord of the Rings*. Outside the map are Franklin and Marietta (farther to the north between Rockall and the Iceland Basin), and many more rise to either side of the Mid-Atlantic Ridge as it swerves down towards the Azores. While Ireland's share of ocean seabed is generally sparse in such volcanic topography, the special ecosystems of seamounts and lesser heights have come to figure increasingly in the hunt for new deep-water species of commercial food fish.

The Celtic and Irish Seas

The grand cirque of the Porcupine Seabight is the Atlantic's gateway to the Celtic Sea, which covers some 75,000 km² of the continental shelf south of Ireland. South of this basin, the ocean rears up more directly from the depths of the Abyssal Plain on a slope dissected by steep-walled canyons: King Arthur, Whittard, Shamrock, Black Mud Canyon. At the rim of the shelf, the sea shallows to a mere 160 m above a seabed that is, indeed, often darkly muddy. Much of it was dry land during the lowering of sea level in the last Ice Age, but that landscape has been long eroded, and the ocean now sweeps the approaches to the Irish Sea and English Channel with some of the fiercest waves in the world.

At the northeast of the Celtic Sea, approaching St George's Channel, the seabed is relatively flat and featureless, but to the southwest are long, parallel ridges of sand pointing to the open ocean. Great Sole, Cockburn, Jones and Labadie Banks were born in the early post-glacial turmoil of eroding tides and currents. Their crests lie between 90–100 m below the surface and the troughs between them are some 55 m deeper. Despite its name, the Great Sole Bank is most important to fishermen as a spawning area for hake, a fish that has flourished in the wider Celtic Sea. The Irish portion of the seabed stretches from a point some 240 km south of the island to another about 45 km southeast of Carnsore Point, at the corner with the Irish Sea. Wedged into this territorial corner is the North Celtic Sea Basin ('the Celtic Deep' to fishermen), some 120 km long and dipping an extra 40 m below the seabed. In this tectonic hollow lies the oil-bearing sedimentary rock exploited in the Kinsale Gas Field.

Beyond its imaginary boundary at St George's Channel, on a line from Carnsore Point, County Wexford, to St David's Head in Pembrokeshire, the Irish Sea is often less than 60 m deep, but its turbulent history in and after the last Ice Age has left its 47,000 km² of seabed marked with quite dramatic highs and lows. The deepest point is found in the narrow North Channel, only 20 km wide, between County Antrim and the Mull of Kintyre, where the powerful passage of tides from the open Atlantic scours the bottom to the bedrock at a depth of almost 275 m, and the even deeper chasm of the Beaufort Dyke still guards its rusting cache of discarded British munitions. The Celtic Trough continues south of it, running down the middle of the Irish Sea west of the Isle of Man. This was eroded in the period of low sea level and filled with glacial debris and sediments to the modern depth of 80–120 m. To the northeast of the Isle of Man, by contrast, depths of mostly less than 55 m slope up to the great sandbanks of the English west coast estuaries and the cockle beds of Morecambe Bay.

The ice-age legacy

An abundance of gravel and sand is the legacy of the ice ages: from the seaward flow of debris as glaciers melted, subsequent reworking by currents and waves, and from fresh erosion of soft cliffs of glacial boulder clay such as those at Ireland's southeastern corner. On the shallow coastal shelf of the western Irish Sea, some 20 km wide, there is a chain of twelve sandbanks between Dublin Bay and Carnsore Point. They include the Kish Bank off south County Dublin, the Codling Bank off north Wicklow and the Arklow Bank (the site of Ireland's first offshore wind farm). They are part of a resource of aggregates estimated in a late twentieth-century survey by the GSI as several million cubic metres of gravel and perhaps 100 times that of sand, in places more than 100 m thick. But the banks serve as important barriers to coastal erosion and important refuges for sea life. In 2005, they became part of a study by the Irish Sea Marine Aggregates Initiative (IMAGIN), a science-led consortium of expert organisations drawn from Ireland and Wales and funded by the EU. It has provided both governments with a framework for allowing dredging that is ecologically sustainable and does the least harm.

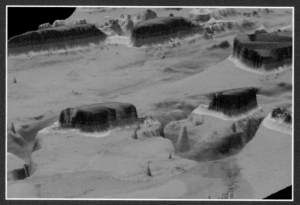

Clew Bay, County Mayo, above and below.
At the thawing of the last Ice Age, the bay was left studded with
drumlins: great mounds of debris heaped beneath the ice sheet.
Today, many are visible as islands, but sonar mapping has revealed
dozens of others surviving beneath the waves.
(Courtesy of Geological Survey of Ireland)

The southern Irish Sea and the waters off the southeast and northwest of Ireland hold the greatest volumes of sand and gravel, with smaller, unproven reserves in and offshore of a few bays in the west. Finding new and usable resources was one purpose of INFOMAR, the programme of inshore mapping that succeeded the deep-water scope of the INSS. Along with the multibeam sonar of the big Marine Institute research vessels, airborne lasers have been charting the intricacies of shallow and complicated bays.

The mapping began in 2006 with surveys of bays in the south and west with valuable aquaculture and fish-spawning waters. Ecological priorities extended also to a piece of seabed off the Dingle Peninsula the size of County Limerick, part of the 'Biologically Sensitive Area' acknowledged by the EU for its special importance to Irish Sea fisheries. One purpose was to map safe areas for bottom trawling without damaging gear or seabed reefs. Indeed, INFOMAR is producing three kinds of maps: the hydrographic, showing in 3D relief all the sandbars, reefs, canyons and cliffs; the sedimentary, showing the make-up of the seabed; and biological maps of habitats rich in marine flora and fauna.

The dramatic discoveries of cold-water coral reefs on the deep slopes of the Rockall Trough and Porcupine Seabight gave the far-flung explorations of the INSS a certain glamour these more domestic surveys may seem to lack. But the seabed of inshore Ireland is becoming a busy arena: as aquaculture expands, as wind farms, marinas and wave-energy machines seek new moorings, and inshore fishing itself is brought into balance with natural resources. From the tideline to the shelf edge, we are beginning to need to know Ireland's ocean as if with all the water gone.

Sharing out the Sea Floor

The dramatic planting of a Russian flag on the seabed at the North Pole by a Mir submersible in August 2007 was a symbolic bid by that nation to stake a claim to a major share of the potential undersea oil, gas and mineral riches of the Arctic. It was also a move in the long-standing saga of sharing out economic rights over the ocean floor, in which the INSS became a strikingly confident exercise.

The Third United Nations Conference on the Law of the Sea, initiated in 1973, took nine years to reach the Convention on the Law of the Sea (UNCLOS) that has now been ratified by 155 countries (the US still hangs fire, on issues of national sovereignty). Under Article 76 of this treaty, a state can assert rights over the sea floor far beyond the standard 'Exclusive Economic Zone' (EEZ) extending to 200 nautical miles from its coast. For this to happen, the claim must be based on geological criteria for a 'natural prolongation' of its continental shelf, to a limit of 350 miles from its territorial waters.

To date, Ireland's delineation and mapping of a vast wedge of the Atlantic, including some 200,000 km^2 of the shelf, is one of eight claims submitted to the scientific sub-committee of the UNCLOS commission. Arriving in 2005, Ireland's claim was preceded by submissions from the Russian Federation, Brazil and Australia and followed by New Zealand, Norway and France. In 2006, there was also a joint submission by France, Spain, Ireland and the UK, claiming a small area in the Bay of Biscay about the size of Ireland.

The Republic is also involved in claims disputing rights to the seabed around Rockall – the bare, wave-swept peak rearing up from an underwater plateau at the north of the Rockall Trough. It could be argued for as an extension of Ireland, the UK or even Iceland and Denmark's Faroe Islands. No controversy, however, appears to challenge Ireland's broader seabed claim. The deadline for claims under UNCLOS is 2009 and Article 76 holds that the commission's findings will be 'final and binding'.

Meanwhile, the concept of the Exclusive Economic Zone (EEZ) (moderated, of course, from its 200-mile extent where states share adjoining waters, as in the Irish Sea or English Channel) was given binding UN recognition in 1982. It includes fisheries as a national marine resource (unlike the wider UNCLOS seabed rights), but access to the fisheries of Ireland's EEZ, like that of other EU members, was surrendered into management by the Community's Common Fisheries Policy.

The sea rod Laminaria hyperborea. (© Aoife Guiry/Algaebase).

CHAPTER 4

Life on the Seabed

The best rock pools of one's young and enquiring life have a habit of sticking in the mind. Ireland's dramatic coastlines offer some of the most memorable in Europe: with one, perhaps, shaded by a great boulder of Donegal granite, where a snakelocks anemone spread tentacles of emerald neon, or another on a sea-fretted terrace of the Burren, where little purple urchins each carved a snug-fitting cup in the limestone, itself full of fossilised seabed life from an ocean 3 million years old.

It is in rock pools that we get a first, easy glimpse of the immense diversity of invertebrate life on the ocean seabed. Even an averagely populated pool is likely to hold many examples of the kinds of animals that also live on the ocean floor (the benthos) in hundreds of metres of water: flatworms, anemones, starfish, crustaceans, sponges, snails, hydroids and so on, all with different body forms and lifestyles. They are successors to the great explosion of multi-celled life forms that took over the ocean in the Cambrian period, more than 500 million years ago. But however advanced and varied in complexity, they live with the same constraints of water chemistry and pressure, available light or its absence, variation in temperature, and problems of locomotion in a world of three dimensions, where up and down is a dance between gravity and buoyancy.

The evolutionary path of seabed animals forked markedly between radially symmetrical forms that capture food from all directions, and animals with a front and rear. Radial creatures are not necessarily immobile: while most sea anemones tend to stay in one place, starfish and sea urchin range widely as predators and grazers. But mobile seabed animals need to process information as they go, which usually leads to feelers and antennae at the front, near a head that monitors stimuli and a mouth that takes in food. The sponges have evolved – if not, perhaps, very far – to another invertebrate form: neither radial nor having front and rear, but extracting food from water pumped through a bag-like body cavity.

Perhaps even more so than life ashore, the creatures of the seabed are keenly concerned with defence. They protect soft bodies with thick shells or, like the hermit crab, take refuge in shells left vacant by others. They arm themselves with hedgehog prickles, like the sea urchin, or with toxins, like the sea anemone. In the crowded, incredibly diverse and competitive shallows of the tropics, virtually all sponges on a coral reef are toxic; most of those in Irish waters face a less intense array of predators and have far less need of poisons. The brilliant colours of many seabed creatures, such as the nudibranchs (essentially soft snails without shells), are often warnings of toxicity, though this message would seem to lose its function in the pitch-black deeps.

Seaweeds at anchor

On the seabed, as on land, plants can take the form of crusts or thin green sheets spread over a substrate, but most seaweeds, or algae, branch out like terrestrial plants and reach up to make the most of the light they need for photosynthesis. Their anchorage, however, is usually a holdfast – sometimes, as with most of the kelps, a strong, claw-like structure glued to the rock – and, unlike the soil-penetrating roots of plants ashore, the holdfast plays no part in providing nutrients to build stems and leaves, which are gathered from minerals dissolved in the surrounding water. Water offers support that air does not provide on land, but also exerts the violent pressures of currents, swells and tides, so that seaweed stems (or stipes) can still need great strength as well as flexibility. Their blades may be broad, like those of the kelps, buoyed up by specialised floats and coated with slippery mucus to minimise friction. Or the plants may be dwarfed and mounded with blades divided finely into filaments, the better to disperse the surge of waves.

Seaweeds are also classified by the colour of the pigments they use for photosynthesis – colour which generally varies according to the degree of shade or depth in which they grow. They are sorted into three groups: the green seaweeds (Chlorophyta); brown (Phaeophyta) and red (Photophyta). All three have chlorophyll in their cells, but in the brown and red algae, this is masked by pigments that absorb light at different wavelengths. Red algae, for example, use the pigment phycoerythrin, which reflects red light and absorbs blue light. This penetrates water to a greater depth and so extends the area of seabed that can support algal growth.

The global census of algal species is still a work in progress, but an approximate database would offer 1,200 green seaweeds, 2,000 brown seaweeds and 6,000 red seaweeds. If we count the larger marine species attached to rocks, the roster for Britain and Ireland so far stands at 642; Ireland alone can list 501 and almost three-quarters of these can be found growing, in remarkable density and diversity, on the fretted granite coast of south Connemara. Here, the shelter of a maze of bays, a mild climate and pure, highly aerated oceanic water help the plants to use a wide range of habitats.

There are about eighty green seaweeds in Irish coastal waters, most of them growing on rocky shores and ranging from a few millimetres to a full metre in length. The more common ones have evocative common names such as gutweed (*Enteromorpha intestinales*), sea lettuce (*Ulva lactuca*) or velvet horn (*Codium tomentosum*). Like other seaweeeds, they can attract specialist predators: velvet horn, for example, spreading felted, tubular branches, is the favourite food of a bright emerald sea slug (*Elysia viridis*).

The intertidal and sub-tidal rim of the ocean is rich in brown seaweeds, restricted generally to temperate and cold seas. Ireland's 147 species range from modest wracks to the long blades of the kelps in their forest beneath the tide. It is among the wracks of the shore that one first notices the marked zonation of seaweeds in the slope towards the lowest of low tides. At the highest level, the short, branching, channelled wrack (*Pelvetia canaliculata*) absorbs its food from a sea experienced more often as spray than as submerging water. Just below it, comes the spiral wrack (*Fucus spiralis*). Then, on the broad slope of the middle shore, either or both of the knotted wrack (*Ascophyllum nodosum*) and the bladder wrack (*Fucus vesiculosus*) are found, both of which are lifted in an incoming tide by the gas-filled swellings in their fronds. The wide fringe of toothed wrack (*Fucus serratus*) at the lowest rocks is often covered with tiny animals – hydroids, bryozoans and coiled, spirorbid worms – all trusting on a quick return of water.

The succession of the wracks is shaped largely by different tolerances of exposure to the sun's heat and drying winds, and these factors also affect the seaweeds exposed only at the lower ranges of the tides. The broad and filmy fronds of kelps such as dabberlocks (*Alaria esculenta*) and oarweed (*Laminaria digitata*) flop down into the water, while just below them, *Laminaria hyperborea* can risk damage by leaving its stipe erect at the bottom of the lowest spring tides.

Kelp forests

In the kelp forest, the 'sea rod' Laminaria hyperborea flows tirelessly with the churning energies of swells and tides. (© Aoife Guiry/Algaebase).

The kelps are the biggest brown seaweeds and Ireland's five indigenous species add *Saccorhiza polyschides* (furbelows) and *Laminaria saccharina* (the 'sugar' kelp) to those mentioned above. They form canopied forests below tidal level; the distance these extend from the shore is decided by the slope of the seabed and the penetration of light, which in turn can depend on the density of plankton or suspended silt. In the murkier estuarial regions of the Irish Sea or the North Sea, the limit may be a few metres below low water, but in clear oceanic water off the west and north coasts of Ireland, kelps can grow in depths of 50–60 m, in light at a mere 5 per cent of surface intensity.

Laminaria hyperborea, the typical sea rod washed up on western tidelines after winter storms, is supremely adapted to handle the churning energies of waves and tides: its frond is deeply fingered to diffuse the rush of water and its rounded stipe bends with the flow and straightens again with a tireless elasticity. Even so, most of the living kelp is shed annually into the water, decomposed by bacteria and then eaten by suspension-feeders such as mussels, sponges and anemones: in some cases, up to 60 per cent of carbon found in coastal invertebrates has been produced originally by kelp. Spores are a further and substantial part of its production: a *Laminaria digitata* plant has been estimated to produce 6,000 million spores per year.

A rich fauna of invertebrates – mobile polychaetes, crustaceans and echinoderms – shelters in the branching holdfasts of the kelp beds, and more are supported among the tufted seaweeds clinging to the stipes. The constantly shifting fronds carry few settlers – crusts of sea mats (lacy colonies of minute, plankton-feeding 'moss animals' or bryozoans) and whiskery coatings of hydroids. Few species graze on the kelp itself: the blue-rayed limpet (*Ansates pellucida*) and sea urchins such as *Echinus esculentus* and *Psammechinus miliaris* are among notable exceptions. This may be because *Laminaria* tissue lacks the level of nitrogen and phosphorus that is found in phytoplankton. But the rocky forest floor is dense with sponges, bivalves, barnacles, sea cucumbers, feather stars and sea squirts, together with their predators, including large decapods such as lobster and crab. Kelp forests are, indeed, one of the most ecologically dynamic and biologically diverse habitats on the planet, along with acting as a nursery and feeding ground for many kinds of fish.

Dulse, (Palmaria palmata), *the chewable red seaweed, grows on the stems of Laminaria.*
(© M. D. Guiry/Algaebase)

Chondrus crispus, *carrageen moss, takes its own grip of rock or reef.*
(© M. D. Guiry/Algaebase)

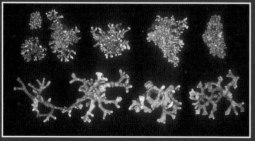

Sprigs of 'coral' from Galway Bay: the seaweed Lithothamnion corallioides, the common species in Ireland's beds of maerl.
(© M. D. Guiry/Algaebase)

The understorey of plants, adapted to shade, is mostly of densely leafy red and brown seaweeds, among them the chewable dulse (*Palmaria palmata*) that grows on *Laminaria* stipes (the edible red carrageen moss – *Chondrus crispus* – however, sticks its disc of a holdfast to rocks beneath the kelp or to reefs in shallower water). As kelp thins out in deeper water, red and brown seaweeds form their own band of growth until, perhaps as deep as 200 m, a final red plant – perhaps the filmy, bright crimson fronds of dock-leaved Delesseria (*Delessaria sanguinea*) – reaches up for the last of the light.

Of Ireland's 274 red seaweeds, there is a special ecological significance to the species that go to make up 'maerl' (a word borrowed from Brittany, where its extraction for spreading on land is long established). They are hard to tell apart on appearance, but among the rarer species, *Lithophyllum dentatum* – found off Cork, Galway and Mayo – is lobed like a petrified human brain. The cell walls of maerl seaweeds are calcified: building small, rigid, unattached plants or rhodoliths, each like a tiny sprig or nodule of hard coral. The brittle branches are no more than 10 mm in diameter and grow slowly – perhaps 1 mm a year. Alive, they are bright pink, like their algal relatives that form rosy crusts on rock; dead, their colour fades but the stone-like structure remains, so that a thin layer of live maerl may overlay deep deposits of dead skeletons. These accumulate on gravel or coarse sands in bays or inlets with a strong tidal flow, and currents may also sift broken fragments away to form sun-bleached 'coral beaches' ashore, as in south Connemara.

Live maerl has been found at more than 30 m deep, as in the exceptionally clear water off the Aran Islands, but most beds are in shallower water, up to low-tide level. The density and variety of animals burrowing into them – crabs, sea urchins, brittlestars and so on – has been termed 'spectacular' in studies for the Marine Institute. The bed's rigid matrix also shelters many soft, leafy seaweeds that use maerl for shelter and support – a flora exceptionally rich in species and contributing greatly to the notably high algal biodiversity of western Ireland. In late summer, some beds in clear water may have leafy plants of the very rare and beautiful red seaweed, *Halymenia latifolia*.

Sponges: the shape-shifters

Sponges (Porifera) are some of the ocean's most ubiquitous and primitive colonial animals, quite distinct from any other phylum and found from the low shore to the greatest depths. Their cells lack distinct tissues or organs and a confusing versatility of reproduction had them judged as plants until the eighteenth century. They reproduce both sexually and asexually. Most are hermaphrodite and produce both sperm and eggs, but there is usually cross-fertilisation: sperm is discharged through the vent, or osculum, and inhaled by another sponge. On tropical coral reefs, a fog of sponge sperm can be seen periodically, produced to time with the spring tides of lunar cycles, but this has yet to be captured on camera among the deep-water corals of the Atlantic. Asexual reproduction takes place by budding or fragmentation. A famous experiment showed the sponge's ability to regenerate: forced through a fine mesh, the separated cells regrouped and developed into several new sponges.

Glass sponge found at a depth of more than 500 m on the Lophelia reefs.
(NOAA Photo Library/Liz Baird)

The animals filter out planktonic and particulate food, some processing water equal to their body weight every 5 seconds. It is 'inhaled' through pores, moved on by flagella through a system of canals into the animal's central cavity, then expelled at high velocity through one or perhaps many vents. While sponges lack organs, they have distinct types of cells, grouped for special functions. Those that capture food by means of the flagellae absorb and digest it. Others, moving like amoeba, pass nutrients on through the body. So extremely fine is the sponge's filtering that it can remove some 90 per cent of suspended bacteria, and this has found a new relevance in Irish research for 'bioactive' compounds in the sea (see p.191).

The actual shape of the sponge can vary widely, from thin crusts on exposed overhangs and caves, to solid, round or lobed cushions; some are shaped like Ali Baba jars, others have hard papillae, like candles on a cake. Many are quite small – the largest of the erect types is about 15 cm high – but the cushions can range from a minuscule 1 cm to a full 1 m. Individual species can vary in colour and shape from one habitat to another, depending on water depth, speed of currents, available space and other factors.

Sponges are currently grouped into three classes:

- **Calcarea,** with calcium carbonate spicules, and found in shallow water, are generally pale in colour and grow away from light
- **Hexactinellida,** with siliceous spicules which have six rays, are commonly known as glass sponges, and found in deep water
- **Demospongiae,** with siliceous spicules and/or horny fibres of spongin, are found in shallow or deep water, often brightly coloured and in well-lighted places. They include the great bulk of the species in British and Irish waters. (The bathroom sponge, from the Mediterranean, consists only of spongin without the scratchy siliceous spicules)

The diversity and abundance of sponges in some locations in the northeast Atlantic rival that of tropical reef systems. One study off the coast of northern Norway took grab samples from an area of less than 3 m^2 , yielding 4,000 sponge specimens belonging to 206 species, 26 of which were not described. In 2006, a team of research divers led by Bernard Picton, the curator of invertebrates at the Ulster Museum, brought the roster of sponges on the rich reefs and cliffs of Rathlin Island to 128 – almost one-third of those known from Ireland and Britain. They included 28 species new to science, mostly of the crusting kind.

The species around Ireland, more than forty of which are common, range in colour and shade from white to grey and black, and beige to dark brown. Several are yellow, or orange or shades of red; one is blue, another green. Their variety finds an extreme in a species such as the common, bright yellow boring sponge, *Cliona celata*. Secreting acid, it bores into limestone and other calcareous substrates such as empty oyster shells. It lines a network of tunnels with its own cells, and all that can be seen on the surface of rock or shell are tiny yellow blobs which draw in and expel water. Given the right conditions, the sponge eventually emerges from rock to become its other forms, most spectacularly a massive, lobed sponge that can be ridged, or develop chimneys, and can reach 100 cm across and 50 cm high. Such growths ornament the narrows of Ireland's Strangford Lough, where tides rich in plankton surge in at dramatic speed. Here, too, the grey elephant's ear sponge (*Pachymatisma johnstonia*) grows to a convincingly huge size.

Turbulent waters hasten the flow of water (and thus of food) through the sponge, so that even in the roughest conditions of overhangs and gullies, the crusting sponges of the Demospongiae flourish. One of these, the green breadcrumb sponge *Halichondria panicea*, also shapes itself according to habitat, expanding to cushions and even branching forms in the plankton-rich waters of Lough Hyne on the coast of west Cork. In its common setting, under big waves on an open coast, it forms a low crust and grows many volcano-like vents to exhale a great throughput of water. In sheltered locations it may grow to a cushion up to 20 cm thick and, in tidal rapids, can cover rocky walls in mats several metres long.

All the above species belong to the Demospongiae. The Calcarea, with a skeletal network of limy spicules, are restricted to shallow water or the lower shore, either on rock or in clusters on kelp. A typical species is the purse sponge (*Grantia compressa*), like a tiny biscuit-coloured hot water bottle. The few known glass sponges, Hexactinellida, usually live in deep water. Some look and feel like small cups of rock; others are like empty cages of netting, or vases with a mesh on top (this, perhaps, to stop large animals climbing inside). Their skeleton of spicules is silicon-based – hence the 'glass' of their common group name.

With their sharp internal spicules and an often unpalatable chemistry, most sponges have relatively few predators. Some sea slugs and starfish prey on certain species, but other sea slugs and some fish seem actively to avoid the animals, or to take small bites from many different species. Others, like many nudibranchs, have evolved mechanisms to deal with toxins, incorporating them into special appendages and using them in their own defence. Many Porifera nonetheless have a rich associated fauna, such as worms, sandhoppers and crabs. *Suberitus ficus*, common on our western and southern coasts, is known straightforwardly as the hermit crab sponge, covering the shells used by the crabs and providing them with camouflage. It also attaches to rocks, shipwrecks, and certain scallops, but as a crab's passenger it gradually breaks down the protective shell and becomes a cloak for the growing crustacean.

Cnidaria: the tribe of tentacles

The plant or flower-like shapes of so many seabed animals made the early identification and classification (taxonomy) of a multitude of species a slow and often hesitant affair. There could be profound differences in appearance between groups of species that actually shared a basic body plan and an essentially similar life cycle. The sea anemone, for example, belongs to the phylum (or supergroup) of the cnidarians, as do hydroids, the colonial hydrozoans such as the Portuguese man-of-war, the true jellyfish, the corals, the sea fans and sea pens. Thus, the big Portuguese man-of-war and tiny, feathery growths encrusting the snail shells lived in by hermit crabs come from the same sub-folder of marine designs.

The name Cnidaria (pronounced 'kinnidaria') came originally from the Greek for nettle – *knide* – and the fact that nettles sting suggests the first inclusive characteristic: most cnidarians have stinging capsules that are activated when chemically or mechanically stimulated. What they all have in common, however, is a basic cup-shaped radial body plan which has a ring of tentacles and a mouth-cum-anus in the middle. Most of them also share a particular life cycle, exemplified by jellyfish. The 'fish' in the name immediately conjures its free-swimming, sexually active form called the medusa, the cup-body now 'upside-down' and trailing stinging tentacles. The medusa produces egg-cells which hatch into planulae (larvae) which float with the other drifting organisms in the plankton (see Chapter 5). After a time, the planulae turn into adults as polyps – cup-shaped, tentacled creatures that attach themselves to the seabed. In due course, a polyp produces detachable buds, like a stack of inverted saucers, which lift off as pulsing medusae to begin the cycle again. Not all Cnidarians follow every stage, and its species are classified by the form in which they spend most of their lives. Hydroids, anemones and corals live mainly as seabed polyps; jellyfish and siphonophores (colonial jellyfish, such as the Portuguese man-of-war) as medusae. As mobile, pelagic creatures, these will be described in a later chapter.

Hydroids

Hydroids are quite often like flowering plants, others like hairy moss, and some like tiny, leafless bushes. Few reach more than 4 cm high and many appear as hairy growths on piers and rocks. They may live as solitary polyps, or take on colonial, branching forms, in which some polyps are specialised for feeding (gastrozoids) and others for reproduction (gonozoids). Most are carnivorous, extending rings of tentacles, some short, some long, with stinging nematocysts to immobilise passing shrimp, worms or copepods. In reproduction, many species release free-swimming medusae; in others the medusae remain attached, but may be swept away into the plankton. In both, the sex cells generate gametes that unite to become larvae, swimming for a time as part of the zooplankton then dropping to the bottom to become polyps again. Some bud into new colonies; others grow into solitary animals.

Hydroids are found in submerged caves, on horse mussel reefs, in the holdfasts and on the fronds of kelp beds, on the seabed and rock faces beyond the kelp zone, on cold-water coral reefs, and in the basins and troughs off the west coast. Those at or near the shore are usually not much more than a few centimetres high. Some fasten to brown seaweeds and kelp. One, *Hydractinia echinata,* encrusts the shells of hermit crabs *(Pagurus bernhardus),* its feeding polyps covering the shells in a pink haze. Hydroid and crab live in symbiosis, the hydroid taking particles from the crab's meals, the crab perhaps protected by tentacled polyps that are thought to be associated with defence. In any event, the hydroid's larvae – produced unusually by shedding eggs and sperm into the water – crawl about to settle, for preference, on shells containing living crabs.

More than forty hydroid species are found around these islands, most of them widespread, common and sometimes brightly coloured. The tiny *Garveia nutans* is bright orange; *Sertularia gayi* bright yellow. Colonies of the tough-stemmed *Tubularia larynx,* adapted to strong tidal streams, can have a sea-pink prettiness when attached to rocks and piers; however, *Tubularia indivisa* (oaten pipes hydroid), growing to 18 cm or more, can clog the nets of fish cages moored in estuary mouths, when it may be known as 'bull's wool'.

The feathery or 'fir-tree' types of hydroids, 5–10 cm high, are particularly abundant from the shallow waters to about 50 m deep. Beyond that, bushy kinds predominate. Past 70 m, species tend to be far fewer, more fern-like, and reach greater heights: some to 20 or 30 cm. Most hydroids rise from hard surfaces, but the dramatic and solitary *Corymorpha nutans* lives on bottoms with sand and gravel, down to some 100 m. At 10 cm tall and resembling a frail, attenuated sea anemone with an almost transparent stalk, it belongs to a subclass of hydroids, Athecata, with polyps unprotected by a sheath. Its whorl of long tentacles bend like a nodding flower ('nutans' means nodding). *Corymorpha nutans* is grazed by the nudibranch *Cumanotus beaumonti* as one of many predators on hydroids. Among them are sea slugs; these are immune to the toxins in hydroid stinging cells and, as with the sponges, pass them into their own skin as an extra defence against predators of their own.

In their furry, plant-like forms, hydroids can be confused with bryozoans, otherwise called sea-mats or moss animals, a dozen species of which can occur on a single rock. These are small animals, or zooids, that share out colonial functions such as feeding, reproduction, anchoring to the substrate, or picking off other invertebrates and larvae that might smother the colony. Their forms can include gelatinous and calcified crusts as well as tufted and branching colonies resembling dried seaweed, and it can take a microscope to sort them out reliably.

Sea anemones

Nothing more graphically illustrates the ocean's gift of life than the transformation of an intertidal sea anemone as the water returns and swirls above it. From a mere blob of coloured jelly on the rock, it expands into a flower-like organism of often exceptional beauty. But anemones at every depth are carnivorous animals, with a mouth at the centre of the disc and stinging cells in the circles of tentacles that find such graceful form.

Within the enormous phylum of Cnidaria, sea anemones belong to the class Anthozoa, along with corals, sea fans and sea pens. They are at the evolutionary peak of cnidarian evolution, being highly specialised polyps with no medusa stage. While some species are familiar from exploration of the intertidal zone, they exemplify the discovery that life goes all the way down. The lovely dahlia anemone (*Urticina felina*) of crevices in rocky shores is still abundant, and even bigger, at 200 m, having passed through several colour morphs on the way. The far larger deeplet sea anemone (*Bolocera tuediae*), extending glassy tentacles to a spread of 30 cm, starts appearing at 10 m but is just as happy at 2,000 m, attached to solid objects in the sediment. On deep soft bottoms, the burrowing tube anemones, Ceriantharia, retract very long tentacles into cylinders made of mucus and particles of sediment.

The dahlia anemone (Urticina felina).
(Courtesy of Marine Institute)

Anemones use stinging tentacles to seize and paralyse prey and bring it to their mouths. Worms, invertebrate larvae, molluscs and crustacea are all part of their opportunistic diet. Our largest, the plumose anemone (*Metridium senile*), has a column perhaps 30 cm high, topped by hundreds of thin tentacles in dense, creamy plumes as an adaptation for feeding on fish eggs and other zooplankton. Some anemones use their tentacles to set up moving currents and catch food particles with the help of a sticky secretion.

But stinging tentacles can also become weapons against other anemones for territorial reasons. Put a number of big snakelocks anemones (*Anemonia viridis*) into an aquarium and each will use purple-tipped tentacles in a slow-motion duel, to gain its own feeding space. Some species have other weapons, such as stinging threads discharged through the mouth (acontia), and wart-like beads (acrorhagi*)* that are batteries of stinging cells, packed with powerful nematocysts. The latter are the weapons of the familiar deep red beadlet anemone (*Actinia equina*), so common around our shores – common and numerous but always spaced well apart: in the hazardous conditions of the intertidal zone, a secure and suitable space is an especially important resource. But even in the more stable habitats of deeper water, aggression and defence can become a corollary of reproduction.

Sea anemones reproduce in two ways. They are separately sexed: the sperm shed by males is absorbed by females, which then shed planktonic larvae. For a minority of anemones, this is the only means of reproduction. Another minority is tied exclusively to cloning from internal buds. Probably most anemones combine the two in some form: *A. viridis*, for example, splits down the middle into two halves. In his New Naturalist book, *Seashore*, Peter Hayward describes how cloned beadlets seem to recognise each other and 'an unrelated beadlet placed in the territory of a clone will be attacked and driven out'. Cloned colonies, budded off from a single original animal, maintain a perpetual defence at the perimeter of their patch. Cambridge geneticist Steve Jones draws an evolutionary moral from the variations in anemone clone behaviour: 'Some are aggressive, while others are calmer but respond at once to attack. Some clones do not fight back, but instead throw more soldiers into the front line as their members are killed. Colonies are able to settle only next to those against whom they have some chance in a fight. In time, a resentful truce emerges and battle starts only when a newcomer arrives.' Such conduct in a 'brainless' society, he suggests, shows that all animals have a life beyond the simple prescriptions of their DNA: 'A little dose of judgement or reason comes into play even in animals very low in the scale of nature.'

Sea anemones often remain in the same place for several days, weeks or even months. They can move around in two ways: by creeping on their pedal disc (so slowly that the movement can only be ascertained by a change of position in aquariums, or observed by time-lapse photography) or they can inflate and let tides and currents sweep them off to a new location. A third option is exercised by the cloak anemone (*Adamsia palliata*, *A. carciniopodos*), yet another organism like the sponge *Suberitus ficus,* to seek a symbiotic transport on shells occupied by hermit crabs. It attaches itself to the underside of the shell so that its short tentacles are well placed to catch particles dropped by the crab. In return the crab is protected by the anemone's nematocysts. Indeed, Norway's Frank Emil Moen, with long diving experience in the fiords, insists that 'the hermit crab, if threatened, communicates with the sea anemone. If a diver or a fish comes too close, it will shake its abdomen, and this serves as a signal for the anemone to discharge the acontia.' The base of the anemone extends into two lobes which wrap around the shell to meet on the top. As the crab grows, the anemone also secretes a chitinous membrane from its base to build an extension for it and prolong the crab's tenancy.

Some anemones also have a symbiotic relationship with single-celled algae, zooxanthellae, best known for their photosynthetic role in coral reefs. Zooxanthellae are found in the gastrodermal cells of the anemones, as in the cells of other invertebrates such as clams and sea slugs that use the photo-synthetic products from the zooxanthellae as their carbohydrates; the zooxanthellae use the nutrients of the waste of the anemone. The algae account for the strong green tint in the tentacles of many specimens of *A. viridis*.

Anemones have few predators: chiefly, the sea slugs. The grey sea slug (*Aeolidia papillosa*), for example, common in shallow water, feeds on a wide range of anemones and uses their undischarged nematocysts, transported to the ends of their cerrata, as a defence. For the burrowing anemones, the cerianths, withdrawal into their tubes may be the safer option. The most common around these islands is the star-shaped *Peachia cylindrica* which burrows in sand or gravel on seabeds at depths down to 100 m. The beautiful *Aureliania heterocera*, the imperial anemone, like a crimson or white rose with crimson flecks, is a burrowing species of deeper water and therefore rarely seen, but it has been found on the northeast and west coasts of Ireland.

Far more accessible, and remarkable for its dense aggregations, especially on vertical rock faces

The jewel anemone (Corynactis viridis).
(Nigel Motyer)

and in the shade of Laminaria, is the brilliantly coloured jewel anemone (*Corynactis viridis*), just 1 cm in diameter and 1.5 cm high. It is often bright green, with a bright red knob to each tentacle, but is also white or pink. Even tinier as individuals, the encrusting anemones that carpet rocks and shells and even sponges and other marine life need close inspection to see their beauty. The semi-translucent, pinkish-brown encrusting anemone (*Epizoanthus couchii*) is one of those found from low-water mark out to 100 m deep, adhering to rock or shells. Since its minuscule polyps contract at the slightest disturbance and it fights for space with other encrusting organisms, it is scarcely very prominent. Even the splendid dahlia anemone, glowing in the colours of Venetian glass, can contract and 'disappear', since it decorates its column with shell-fragments, gravel and algae that provide an impressive camouflage.

Dead man's fingers and other corals

On surge-swept walls of underwater cliffs and caves, already a tapestry of colourful organisms, another group of cnidarians joins the anemones and hydroids. Soft corals (Anthozoa) can grow beside sponges and look very like them, with similar protuberances and colours. Dead man's fingers (*Alcyonium*

Bright-orange soft corals of Alcyonium digitatum – *'dead man's fingers' – delight scuba divers off Ireland's west coast.*
(Nigel Motyer)

Thickets of pink Lophelia pertusa *crown cold-water coral reefs in the deeps off Ireland's west coast.*
(© MARUM / www.marum.de)

digitatum) often forms dense colonies, generally white around the coasts of Britain but almost all of them orange on Ireland's west coast and sometimes with the smaller, red-fingered *A. glomeratum* for contrast. This is one of the so-called Lusitanian species, native to the warm waters around Spain and Portugal, but brought north in the flow of plankton carried in the Shelf-edge Current.

On rocks and boulders down to 100 m live solitary 'true' or hard corals, which look like small sea anemones but have a dense, calcareous skeleton in which the cup-shaped polyp is anchored. The common Devonshire cup coral (*Caryophyllia smithii*) is another southern species found on the south and west coasts of Ireland but also as far north as Shetland. Usually solitary, variable in colour and no bigger than an egg-cup, it extends rings of transparent, knobbed tentacles from a zigzag-patterned rim. In western deeps, the stony *Lophelia pertusa* is the main builder of the celebrated cold-water coral reefs revealed for the first time in the late twentieth century. Its calcareous cups – usually white, pink or yellowish and about 5–10 mm in diameter – are secreted by the polyps on branches that grow about 6 mm a year. This is a little faster than many tropical stone corals, despite their different way of gaining food from the sea.

The cold-water coral archipelago of the northeast Atlantic is part of a global phenomenon, and a continuum of reef-building which also embraces the tropical corals. The tropical species are symbiotic with plants that use sunlight and photosynthesis in shallow water, but the cold-water reefs are built by only a few coral species, mostly living in darkness and depending for food on particles – marine snow and zooplankton – transported in strong deep-water currents. Away from the large reefs, *L. pertusa* colonies occur on soft bottoms in groups that are no more than 10 m in diameter and often much smaller. Its frequent companion in the reefs is the smaller coral, *Madrepora oculata*, with shorter cups, and a solitary cup coral, *Caryophyllia sarsiae,* often attaches abundantly to the colonial species.

Coral reefs

'The water is gin-clear. The lights on the submersible allowed me to view 10 to 15 metres across the top of the reef. For as far as I could see, there extend huge white coral colonies, occasionally broken by a line of yellowish sponges or a break in the coral surface that throws a dark shadow. The corals really do look a little like giant cauliflowers. Among the luminous white coral, hundreds of points of lights shine back at me, the reflective eyes of shrimps and lobsters.'

(Andre Freiwald, after visiting a coral reef at Sula Ridge, 300 m down in Norwegian waters)

'The reefs' diversity makes them the Irish equivalent of a rainforest.'

(Anthony Grehan, NUI Galway)

Nothing has shown more dramatically how mysterious the ocean remains than revelations about the coral reefs growing in its depths. The discovery of their abundance, geographical spread and ecological richness has quite overturned the accepted idea that coral reefs were confined to the shallow, sun-warmed waters of the tropics. Cold-water corals are nourished by different means, but serve in much the same way to shelter and sustain teeming communities of invertebrates and fish. They are, in various terms – 'biogenic islands'; 'ecological hotspots'; 'oceanic oases' – cities, even, of the deep. In this, they take their place with worm and mussel reefs of shallow waters as habitats, greatly benefiting other organisms and therefore creating areas of high biodiversity and biomass.

The main species of the reef-forming, cold-water corals, *Lophelia pertusa*, was described by Linnaeus in 1758 and its existence to the west of Ireland had been known since broken chunks appeared in the first deep-water dredgings of the late 1800s. That it grew into reefs became obvious from the debris that surfaced in trawling and dredging a century later. But the presence of hundreds of reefs, stretching in a great arc on the continental slope from Spain to Scotland and around to Norway, became evident only with the development of high resolution mapping devices such as multibeam echo sounder. Similar explorations were finding reefs also off the American east coast, but nowhere in the Atlantic have they proved more abundant, larger or more diverse in species than off Ireland. Here, the oldest dead coral branches have been dated at some 2.6 million years old.

The beauty of coral in the hand.
(Courtesy of Geological Survey of Ireland)

Deep coral in close-up from the ROV camera.
(Courtesy of Marine Institute)

Most of the corals grow in abundant thickets on carbonate mounds on the seabed at depths between 500–1,000 m. *Lophelia*, however, needs a hard substrate to settle on and individual colonies are found growing on rocks released by melting icebergs. These dropstones may have fallen on to existing mounds or, after settling in a plain of sediment, seeded the mounds the corals built by themselves. As a colony develops, neighbouring branches often join together, strengthening the whole framework; however, attacked by erosion, branches break off and fall providing a new substrate to be recolonised. In this way, coral both traps sediment from currents and rises on a stratum of dead branches. Boring animals such as sponges help to reduce this layer to rubble; thus, the *L. pertusa* colonies join to build reefs, with the more fragile coral *Madrepora oculata* helping to fill gaps in the construction.

A brilliant gorgonian, a soft coral fan, grows near the base of a cold-water coral mound.
(© MARUM/www.marum.de)

Here and there in the stony thickets, fans of soft coral known as gorgonians wave gently in the currents. Their trunks and branches were among the first cold-water corals to be snared by fishermen. Edward Forbes described this in his *Natural History of the European Seas* (1859): 'The great tree *Alcyonium* [now *Paragorgia arborea*], a branched zoophyte of leathery texture, is a very wonderful and characteristic production of the abysses of the Boreal Seas. The lines of the fishermen, when fishing for the redfish, or uër, become entangled in its branches, and draw up fragments of considerable dimensions, so large, indeed, that the people of the country believe it to grow to the size of forest-trees, an exaggeration in all probability, but nevertheless one founded in unusual magnitude.'

Anchored by its holdfast, a *Paragorgia* colony may grow over several centuries as high as 5 m, supported by a protein skeleton, with the polyps growing from a softer rind.

How do the deep corals feed? On the tropical reefs that form in sunlit, shallow water, corals grow in symbiotic partnership with microscopic algae (zooxanthellae) that live among the polyps. The algae's photosynthesis shares sugars and oxygen with the corals, while the zooxanthellae receive carbon dioxide and nutrients from their hosts. Cold-water corals, however, growing in water temperatures as low as 4 °C, have no such partner. They take their food directly from organic particles and zooplankton in the currents swirling around the tops of the reefs.

The rich diversity of the coral reef. The Crinoidea – feather stars or sea lilies – are primitive echinoderms and beautiful members of the deep coral reef community.
(Courtesy of Geological Survey of Ireland)

Teeming species of the reefs

These reefs provide niches and food for hundreds of different kinds of animal. By 2004, as sampling and video built up the knowledge of European scientific teams, a study for ICES listed 1,317 species associated with the reefs including sponges, hydroids, bristle worms, crustaceans, molluscs, echinoderms, bryozoans, nematodes, comb jellies and many invertebrate species new to science or showing new adaptations to the habitat. In one example, the large worm *Eunice norvegica* tucks its parchment-like tube into the lattice of the reef, whereupon new coral forms protectively around it.

A microscopic image of a large (approximately 10 cm) Eunice norvegica *worm found living within mucus tubes woven through* Lophelia *coral. The iridescence is from light refraction on the cuticle secreted by the worm.*
(Courtesy of NOAA Photo Library/Scott France)

More than twenty kinds of fish have been watched on camera at the reefs. They include such familiar mid-water species as cod (*Gadus morhua*), ling (*Molva molva*) and haddock (*Melanogrammus aeglefinus);* and highly valued seabed fish such as halibut (*Hippoglossus hippoglossus*), lemon sole (*Microstomus kitt*) and anglerfish (*Lophius piscatorius*), along with characteristic sharks and other species more typical of deep waters.

The Darwin Mounds, on the south flank of the Wyville Thomson Ridge, support dense populations of single-celled protozoans, xenophyophores, especially on their downstream 'tails'. These are remarkable organisms known for a century but only recently investigated. Most single-celled organisms are microscopic in size, but these giant protozoans are pancake-like creatures up to 25 cm across. Their name stems from the Greek for 'bearer of foreign bodies', for xenophyophores build shells or tests by cementing together all manner of handy sea-floor debris, both organic and mineral. They were once thought rare, because so few specimens survived being brought to the surface in any identifiable form. How they feed or grow is still unknown, but now they are recognised as dominating whole areas of the seabed across the globe, sometimes at densities of more than 2,000 per 100 m². Whatever their true ecological role, they seem to provide a habitat for an increase in the local diversity of species.

Sea fans

On the deep-water reefs, soft and flexible corals called sea fans or gorgonians can reach a great age and the size of small trees, but far smaller colonies grow in inshore waters. On the deeper rocks and stones, *Eunicella verrucosa* spreads intricate salmon-pink branches across the current (sometimes white branches, as in Galway and Donegal Bays). Off southwest England, sea fans sometimes occur in 'forests' but in most places individuals are widely separated. They seem to reproduce infrequently and large specimens may be as much as forty years old. Their slow growth – a mere 10 mm a year – make them vulnerable to collection for the tourist trade, and *Eunicella* is now a protected species in Britain (but not, so far, in Ireland). The only other sea fan found in these waters is the small northern sea fan *Swiftia pallida* (white or greyish and sometimes tinged pink), newly found on the west coast of Scotland and the southwest Irish coast at the Kenmare River. It forms slender colonies, no more than 20 cm tall and with little branching, on rocks and boulders at depths of 18–60 m.

Sea pens

These colonial cnidarians are the only hard corals adapted for life on soft bottoms. When their popular name was coined, the use of a sharpened quill for writing was still familiar. Each animal consists of a central chalky limb or stem which supports it and anchors it to the seabed. Fine feather-like barbs grow from this stem and carry colonies of polyps. They are suspension-feeders, living on plankton and organic particles trapped by the polyp tentacles.

Three sea pen species are well known from Irish coastal waters, their beauty often noted in habitats of deep, soft mud. The largest is the tall, white *Funiculina quadrangularis,* living at depths to 2,000 m off the north and west coasts. The much smaller slender sea pen, *Virgularia mirabilis*, up to 60 cm and very slender, can withdraw into the mud when disturbed and is often abundant in deep, man-made harbours (it has also been found in Valentia Harbour in County Kerry). It is luminescent in the dark: a characteristic shared, when disturbed, by the stout, red colonies of the phosphorescent sea pen (*Pennatula phosphorea*), its frequent companion off western coasts.

Annelida: the worms

To the diver's eye, the sediments of deeper water can often seem as inert as bare rock, but the rippled texture of the seabed presents a frozen picture of sand and gravel in constant rearrangement by benthic currents and the passage of storm-driven swells. In this semi-fluid, shifting world, where even anemones live in tubes, the burrowing and tube-dwelling worms come into their own. The images of television programmes such as the BBC's *Blue Planet* have helped to reveal the often exquisite beauty of their underwater forms. Some of the bristle worms, the polychaetes, living in clean sand, extend food-gathering tentacles to feed on microalgae at the surface. Others are carnivores, feeding on small invertebrates, but most of the sedentary species of the family are nourished by organic deposits. Their food-processing and burrowing activity (bioturbation) returns nutrients and minerals to the sea.

Marine worms are divided into several phyla: flatworms (Platyhelminthes); ribbon worms (Nemertina); roundworms (Nematoda); segmented worms (Annelida); cactus or penis worms (Priapula); spoon worms (Echiura); peanut worms (Sipuncula), gutless worms (Pogonophora) and tube worms (Phoronida). Most flatworms are parasitic on animals or fish, but among them are the free-living turbellarians, often tiny and leaf-like, whose carnivorous diet includes a wide range of invertebrates. The largest in Irish waters is the candy-striped flatworm (*Prostheceraeus vittatus)*, which can grow to 5 cm, living under stones and seaweed and among colonies of sea squirt.

At another extreme of size are some ribbon worms (Nemertina) that – literally at a stretch – are among the longest marine invertebrates in the world. Among those around these islands are the bootlace worm *(Lineus longissimus)* that has been seen at 10 m long (and only 5 mm wide), crawling on rocks among mussels and barnacles. *Tubulanus annulatus,* the football jersey worm (with red and white stripes and rings) extends to a more modest 75 cm. It is sometimes found intertidally beneath stones, amongst Laminaria holdfasts or on sand or mud near low water level.

The most abundant marine animals by far are the infinitesimal, free-living nematode worms, usually 0.5–3 mm in length and easily numbering 1 million in a square metre of seabed: they form a big part of the celebrated biodiversity of the Rockall Trough, where most of them are certainly new to science. The 800 species identified so far in the North Sea are a small fraction of some 4,000 species described worldwide. They are selective algal feeders and consumers of detritus and bacteria and their role in the nitrogen cycle is substantial.

The segmented worms or annelids are better known as earthworms (Oligochaeta), leeches (Hirundinea) and bristle worms (Polychaeta); the latter are almost exclusively marine dwelling, while the

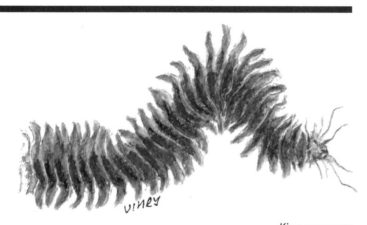

King ragworm.

other two only have a few marine representatives (marine Oligochaeta are known as sludge worms and are found in muddy deposits with vast numbers in polluted estuaries). A third group, the beard worms (Pogonophora), have been added to Annelidae. As large, segmented worms the polychaetes, or bristle worms, are the most familiar; but, between mobile and sedentary species, the phylum is divided into a multitude of families.

Among the mobile species are the scale worms (Aphroditidae) of which the large sea mouse (*Aphrodita aculeata*), up to 20 cm, is sometimes washed up on Munster beaches. This curious, oval-shaped animal, with iridescent green and gold bristles, is thought to be carnivorous, feeding even on ragworms among its own kind. It lives in the sediment, or under rocks or seaweed on the lower shore; it lives in shallow water and at depths of 170 m; other members of the family are much smaller, generally not more than 5 cm.

Among the large and carnivorous bristle worms, the ragworms are familiar to shore anglers digging for bait, but they are found from the muddy sands of estuaries right out to the deep ocean. On the lower shore and in the shallows, ragworms live in U-shaped burrows, but in deeper water they join the free-living or 'errant' bristle worms, with well-developed eyes and antennae. Their bristles, extending from the segments like pairs of rudimentary legs, are a help in locomotion, and ragworms can be both large and fiercely colourful. *Nereis diversicolor*, for example, is often green and yellow with tints of orange and red, and the king rag, *Nereis virens*, is green, iridescentpurple and yellow and can reach an exceptional 90 cm in length.

Most of the sedentary, suspension-feeding polychaetes live in tubes in sand or mud and often

Tube worms in Killary Harbour.
(Courtesy of Marine Institute/J. White)

extend flower-like crowns to filter food and absorb oxygen. The peacock worm (*Sabella pavonina*), for example, extends a crown like an incredibly dainty feather duster from a tube that may extend for 10 cm above the surface; it looks more like an anemone than a worm. But the group includes some tiny species with very distinct habits: one, the horseshoe worm (*Phoronis hippocrepia*), common in western and southern bays, bores a home in limestone or even the shells of oysters, periwinkles and mussels; others create calcareous coils on seaweed or stones.

The honeycomb worm (*Sabellaria alveolata*) creates shelter for many other organisms by building tubes of sand grains and shell fragments in cumulative, tightly-packed colonies that do, indeed, resemble gritty masses of honeycomb. The worm reaches its northern limit in Britain and Ireland, but otherwise extends southwards to the Mediterranean and Morocco. At its northern reaches, *Sabellaria* reefs are found mainly on shores with a hard substrate scoured by a brisk wave action that brings a good supply of sand grains. A notable reef off Wicklow Head, in a Special Area of Conservation, is 0.5 m thick and home to a rich diversity of associated animals including molluscs, brittlestars and sea squirts. Three of its species – a bryozoan, an amphipod and a polychaete – are rarities in Irish waters.

Another small phylum of sedentary worms can have exceptional impact on the seabed by their vigorous deep burrowing, especially where they live at high densities. The 18-cm echiuran, or spoon worm (*Maxmuelleria lankesteri*), common in fine sands and mud, lives in a U-shaped burrow, one end of which opens at the top of a cone of ejected sediment up to 30 cm high and 40 cm across. Its burrow may extend more than 80 cm below the surface, with up to 2 m between the burrow openings. In the Irish Sea, it has stirred up radionuclides originating in Sellafield's nuclear reprocessing plant. In the Atlantic deeps, an echiuran proboscis caught on camera suggested a buried animal at least 1 m long.

Worms will also burrow into bones – even, as recently found, into the bones of dead whales descended to the deep sea floor. The newly described phylum of Osedax digest the marrow-fat of the bones by using bacteria living within the worms' tissues. This suggests solutions to digestive mysteries existing even in well-known species. The tube-dwelling pogonophorans of deep water, for example, enjoyed uniqueness as the only known multicellular, non-parasitic animals without digestive organs; gutless wonders, indeed. The celebrated tube worms found at hydrothermal vents in the mid-Pacific and lacking mouth, gut or anus, were originally grouped with the pogonophorans, but on discovery of their symbiotic bacteria have become a separate phylum, the Vestimentifera. Some similar species are found in sulphur environments at cold seeps in the Atlantic.

Classification: Order in Diversity

Just to talk about the immense diversity of life in the sea demands some framework of order. Relating one species to another, one family of species to the next, has been a perennial human challenge in exploring the rest of nature, and it is impossible to consider all the marine species without some sort of classification system.

One way of relating species is by the characteristics they share – a task complicated at once in the ocean by animals that look like plants, and vice versa, and others that have evolved from the same basic body plan, but which now look incredibly unalike in form and have totally different lifestyles (the squid and oyster, for example, are both molluscs). The differences have developed from evolutionary chance, adaptation and selection, all of which tend towards an increasing complexity.

Organisms are gathered into groups by the closeness of their overall evolutionary relation-ships, and then the species are ordered into an ascending hierarchy: genus, family, order, class, phylum and kingdom. Thus the ocean's common mussel, *Mytilus edulis*, belongs to the genus *Mytilus* in the family Mytilidae, in the order Fillibranchia, the class Bivalvia, the phylum Mollusca and the kingdom Animalia.

In any overview of the groups, such as the one presented here, the sequence of the phyla (plural of phylum) is always followed in the same way, beginning with the algae and ending with the chordata. That the latter phylum includes sea squirts stuck to rocks, and freely-moving fish and other vertebrate animals – including humans and birds – shows the subtle reach of the science of taxonomy. In this introductory account, some minor phyla and classes have been left out, and species have been chosen mainly to demonstrate their distinctive character and ecological role.

Molluscs: variations on a theme

Even with their great variations in form, most animals in the different ocean phyla have some rough resemblance to each other. Echinoderms – sea urchins, starfish and the rest – all show a radial symmetry; shrimps, crabs and barnacles have the segments, appendages and calcareous or chitinous armour of crustaceans. With the molluscs, however, forms and lifestyles have evolved down so many pathways in so many different environments that they could almost populate an ocean by themselves. Oysters and mussels are molluscs, yes, but so are snails and sea slugs, octopuses and even the giant squid (*Architeuthis dux*).

The common limpet (Patella vulgata).
(Courtesy of Marine Institute)

Periwinkles (Littorina littorea).
(Courtesy of Marine Institute)

Dogwhelks (Nucella lapillus).
(Courtesy of *Marine Institute*)

What molluscs have in common is a simple and distinctive basic ground plan that combines a radial symmetry with a bilateral one. They may crawl, bore, burrow, hop or dash about in the water column, but the original body-system they evolved put all their vital organs in a hump on their upper surface (protected by a mantle or shell), with the head in front, and their muscles in a 'foot' underneath. Later came complexities and adaptive refinements (tentacles, gills, jet propulsion, the bivalves' feeding chamber) but no group among the molluscs descended from any other, and tracing the evolutionary pathways of the various animals has been an enduring fascination of marine biology.

Of the eight classes of molluscs, the two largest groups on the seabed – the gastropods and the bivalves – account for most of the empty shells washed ashore on our beaches. They include, for example, more than 100 species of bivalves, from the near-microscopic to shells the size of one's hand. Among myriad gastropods, they also offer limpets and sea snails that can be seen alive among the inter-tidal rocks and seaweed. The group name of limpets – archaeogastropods – marks their affinity to the ancient and primal mollusc design, but this makes them far from simple animals. The apparent immobil-ity of the common limpet (*Patella vulgata*) is mislead-ing: when the tide returns it wanders abroad to graze on microalgae in perhaps a square metre around its home and returns unerringly, whatever the turmoil of the waves, to the same tight-fitting scar that it has ground into the surface of the rock. Despite close study, the precise navigational cues it uses (probably chemical) have still to be discovered.

Ireland's coastal sea snails can be tiny, even smaller than the three-spotted cowrie (*Trivia monacha*), the *finicín* of Connemara. Of our eight or so species of periwinkle only one, the dark, edible periwinkle (*Littorina littorea*), is big enough to eat. But the species range from colourful, conical top shells, the spiralling tower shell (*Turritella communis*) and the pelican's foot shell (*Aporrhais pespelicani*), through to the large whelks of offshore water. Their stout, usually whitish, shells often arrive at the tideline. Those of both the common whelk (*Buccinum undatum*) and the red whelk (*Neptunea antiqua)* reach about 10 cm, but the former shows a striking adaptation to living with particular predators: its shell is far more heavily armoured on Atlantic coasts, where it encounters the powerful claws of the big brown crab (*Cancer pagurus),* than it is in the Irish Sea. Here too, it lives in relatively shallow water, while the red whelk ranges out to depths of 1,200 m. The prey of whelks includes marine worms and bivalves, and the much smaller dogwhelk (*Nucella lapillus*), common on rocky coasts, is an assiduous predator of mussels. Like the other sea snails the dogwhelk has a radula (a horny, tooth-bearing ribbon of a 'tongue', unique to molluscs), that can file through a shell, even if this takes several hours. The snail exudes enzymes to soften the shell for attack and also, perhaps, to render its prey insensible. Its own shell, in white, grey or yellow, can vary markedly in shape between exposed and sheltered shores, and, as potential prey itself, may have an especially narrow opening as a defence against crabs.

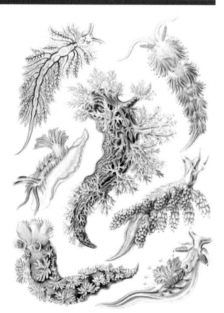

Nudibranchia, from Ernst Haeckel's Art Forms of Nature, 1904.

Beautiful sea slugs

The gastropods include sea slugs (Nudibranchia) with or without a vestigial shell, or with a much-reduced shell contained in the body. One of the last is the sea hare (*Aplysia punctata*), a quite large animal (20 cm) that has been known along the west coast for more than a century, named for its erect head flaps and sometimes feared as poisonous from the cloud of purple ink it ejects when disturbed.

Translucent and voluminous appendages of various shapes (called cerata), often finger-like and tipped or spotted with brilliant colours, are typical of sea slugs and can give them bizarre and beautiful forms quite unlike those of their terrestrial cousins. Combined with the graceful rippling of the mantle as they glide over the seabed, their frequent, glowing beauty has captivated marine scientists. As one British authority on their order, T. E. Thompson, suggested: 'They are to the molluscs what the butterflies are to the arthropods, or the orchids to other flowering plants.' The nudibranch webpages of the Ulster Museum's encyclopaedic website, www.habitas.org. uk, offer a striking gallery: *Coryphella gracilis*, *Doto fragilis*, *Eubranchus farrani*, *Thecacera pennigera* and many more.

Sea slugs in more muted shades gain camouflage among seaweeds and seabed surfaces; the largest of the Irish nudibranchs, *Tritonia hombergii*, for example, is a pinkish-brown and so covered with cerata that it can look like the crusty back of an edible crab. It is found all around the coast, using its radula to rasp at the soft coral of dead man's fingers. Most sea slugs feed on hydroids, often as exclusive to their species as are the food plants of caterpillars ashore. Carnivorous nudibranchs that habitually prey on toxic invertebrates can transfer the poison they absorb to the tips of their tentacles as a defence against their own predators, and it is these species that have the brightest colours as a warning. The top size for the eighty or so species of sea slug around Ireland is about 20 cm; most are far smaller and some less than 1 cm. They are hermaphrodite and often mate in chains, linking male ends with female ends. Ribbons or beaded strings of spawn wound among hydroids are often a good sign of their presence.

Bivalves

The twin, rounded shells of the bivalves are usually mirror images of each other, sprung open on a hinge by a tough, elastic ligament. This form of mollusc has arisen from a 'hole' in the original design – more exactly, the cavity left between the animal's visceral hump and the overlying mantle or shell. As gills evolved, this cavity became a respiratory chamber. It also enabled the powerful jet propulsion of squids and cuttlefish. As the mantle crept out in twin lobes to enclose the bivalve, the cavity became a complicated but most efficient feeding chamber, filtering and digesting phytoplankton in water drawn in by the gills.

The common mussel (Mytilus edulis). (Don Cotton)

Ireland has more than 100 bivalves, some as small as 1 mm in diameter, living between the middle shore and some 200 m deep. Among the debris of seashells that tumble in to our tidelines are ark shells, mussels, fan and file shells, scallops and oysters. They live on the surface of the seabed or attached to rock, and the cockles, razors, venus, carpet, trough, otter, wedge and tellin shells are burrowers into sand, gravel or mud. Most bivalves are burrowers, using the powerful muscles of the foot to draw the shell into the sediment. Razor fish (*Ensis* spp.) have long, smooth, streamlined shells for rapid retreat within their permanent vertical burrows. The oval and fragile sand gaper (*Mya arenaria*), consumed by the million in America as the soft-shell clam, has siphons extending perhaps 40 cm to a keyhole-shaped opening at the surface of sand or mud. Cockles, on the other hand, in their ribbed and globular shells, live only in the top few centimetres of sand. Here too, and shaped not unlike a cockle, burrows the speckled carpet clam (*Tapes decussata*), called *palourde* by the French, much sought after for the shellfish market.

Many of the bivalves living on rocks or on the seabed are immobile and accumulate in dense colonies. The common mussel (*Mytilus edulis*) encrusts the rock of exposed Atlantic shores in a blue-black mosaic or carpets the gravel of estuaries. It is anchored by strong byssus threads secreted from a gland, and when predatory dogwhelks attack dense beds of mussels they may find these used against them tying them down and trapping them.

On some inshore seabeds of mud or muddy sand, another and much larger colonial mussel not only filters the water column but creates some of the most remarkable sublittoral communities of northwest Europe. The horse mussel (*Modiolus modiolus*) lives initially with most of its shell buried in the sediment and secured by deeply anchored byssus. If it survives the early assault by crabs and starfish, it may live for forty years or more and, as generations pass, the accumulation of dead shells, sand and faeces builds reefs that can rise several metres from the seabed.

Hundreds of species may finally be counted in the reef community; among them sponges, ascidians, soft corals, anemones, tubeworms, brittlestars, urchins, starfish, barnacles, crabs and other decapods, whelks and other gastropods. A dense growth of leafy seaweeds, hydroids and bryozoans can create an ideal settling area for the spat (spawn) of scallops – as in the sheltered waters of Strangford Lough, County Down, Ireland's prime location of fully developed *Modiolus* reefs. Here, uncontrolled dredging for the valuable queen scallop *(Aequipecten opercularis)* has caused severe and indiscriminate destruction (see Box: Strangford Lough, p.85).

Elsewhere around these islands, large expanses of muddy gravel are covered in scattered clumps of half-buried *Modiolus*. Where currents are very strong, large areas of sediment may be bound together by more or less completely buried reefs, creating waves or mounds with steep faces up to 1 m high and many metres long and extending over hundreds of hectares.

Much of the soft Irish coast was once fringed with extensive beds of the common European flat oyster (*Ostrea edulis*). Before human predation, it built massive, cemented reefs like those of *Modiolus*, but it survives today only in some western bays, in Lough Swilly and Lough Foyle, and on the offshore seabed. It can live for fifteen years or more, and the upper shell often appears at tidelines: rounded, thick and gnarled and often riddled with holes bored by the sponge *Cliona celata*. Gross overfishing and the native oyster's vulnerability to predators and parasites led to the cultivation of imported oyster species with larger shells: the Pacific oyster (*Crassostrea gigas*) can grow to 18 cm; the European only to 11 cm.

In contrast to the anchored, eyeless lives of mussels and oysters, the scallops' freedom to hop away from predators and even to swim can come as a surprise. All scallops begin life attached by byssus threads, but the two largest Irish species, the king scallop (*Pecten maximus*) and the smaller queen scallop, are among those that become free as they grow. They work themselves into a sandy bottom, lying on their deeply cupped right side, with the flat valve on top like a lid. The approach of a predatory starfish is detected by a row of elaborate eyes, shining like ball bearings among the tentacles fringing the gape of the scallop's shell. A young scallop may swim away, gulping water into its valves and squirting it out near the hinge in a jerky jet propulsion. For a large scallop the movement becomes a hop along the sea floor, the animal bouncing on its hinges.

King scallops are typically inshore species and up to the 1970s they were harvested in sheltered Irish bays. From then on the scallop fleet had to range farther afield, eventually reaching waters nearer to British and French coasts than those of Ireland.

Among the more oddly shaped bivalves, the fan shell (*Atrina fragilis*) is also one of the largest found in Europe. Its elongated triangle of a shell, like a partly closed fan, sits vertically and immobile in the seabed at depths of up to 400 m, anchored by byssus threads to small stones deep in sandy mud or gravel and projecting just above the surface. At perhaps 30 cm long, it has become a trophy of collectors (it is protected in Britain), but its scarcity around these islands is more probably due to trawling: the shell is so fragile that predatory fish such as rays can easily break it. Bivalves can also be tough enough to bore holes. The wrinkled borer (*Hiatella arctica*) is common down to about 50 m, using its valves to penetrate soft rock or other shells. The great shipworm (*Teredo navalis*) on the other hand, bores permanent, chalk-lined tubes into the wood of piers, boat hulls and drifting beams – an operational design that inspired the cutting shields of today's tunnelling machines.

Cephalopods: the clever chameleons

Of all the transformations of marine evolution, few are as fascinating as the development of molluscs from their simpler forms into animals such as the octopus, cuttlefish and squid. Some cephalopods are giants of the deep that do battle with sperm whales, while the ordinary octopuses of Irish waters can learn some things as quickly as cats or dogs. The cephalopods have the most complex brains of any invertebrates.

Blaschka model of an octopus (see also p.102).
(Courtesy of Natural History Museum)

Squid. (Courtesy of NOAA Photo Library)

Octopuses are still molluscs (the plural is right: 'octopus' is Greek, not Latin) even though they have entirely lost the shell of the original mollusc design, while in squid and cuttlefish the shell is internal and changed into an organ of buoyancy. The molluscan foot has divided into suckered tentacles surrounding the mouth, and the jaws now form a strong, parrot-like beak that can crush the shells of crabs and bivalves. Cephalopods are carnivorous and the squid has become totally pelagic, using the convulsive pump of its mantle cavity and siphon for water-powered jet propulsion at up to 40 kph. The jet can be directed by aiming the siphon funnel, a precision equally valued by the cuttlefish as it hunts above the seabed.

Nearly all the squid landed in Ireland are a by-catch of other fisheries and mainly of two species: the long-finned squid (*Loligo forbesii*) and the common squid (*L. vulgaris*). They live in deep water at the edge of the continental shelf and make seasonal inshore forays. Both have a mantle of up to 60 cm and are noticeably different only in the arrangement of suckers on their ten arms. With them in the catches may be the European common squid (*Alloteuthis subulata*) – a very common coastal species much smaller than *Loligo* and with a slender, pointed tail – and any of three species of flying squid. These use their jet propulsion to escape predators, becoming airborne for as far as 50 m. The very large, oceanic squid *Ommastrephes bartrami*, with a mantle of up to 75 cm, uses webs between its tentacles to aid its flight.

Recent landings of *Architeuthis dux*, the giant squid of abyssal depths, have brought both science and sympathy to what was once the ultimate demon of the deep, wielding tentacles like giant hosepipes in the drawings for lurid marine adventure stories. Rarely seen whole before the advent of modern bottom trawling, increasing numbers (but still small), have been caught in nets or found dead. As the biggest of all invertebrates, with unblinking eyes the size of hubcaps, they have fought the largest predators, often turning up in the bellies of sperm whales, such as those landed and flensed at the Norwegian whaling station near Belmullet, County Mayo, in the early twentieth century. Sperm whales scarred by serrated sucker edges have suggested that far bigger specimens of *Architeuthis* exist in the deep than have ever been seen ashore.

The largest specimen of giant squid on record had a mantle of 5 m, with an extra 13 m of tentacles, but those on the Irish list (beginning with a beached animal at Dingle in 1673) have been

far smaller: in Inishbofin in 1875, in County Clare in 1880, in the belly of sperm whales in Belmullet in 1910 and 1913, and in Clare in 1918. In 1995, for example, three were caught in bottom trawls, west of Aran and on the Porcupine Bank, at depths of around 300 m. They all measured about 6 m overall, and weighed a mere 27 kg or so, compared with the tonne of the record-holder. Specimens up to 10 m long have been captured along the Norwegian coast. A model of a giant squid

A giant squid (Architeuthis), *ultimate demon of the deep.*

is on display in the Oceanworld Aquarium in Dingle, County Kerry.

Of similar form, but a totally different scale and habitat, the cuttlefish is sometimes glimpsed inshore, swimming over sand or eelgrass. 'People often argue about the cuttlefish,' wrote Séamas Mac an Iomaire in 1938, 'some saying they're young squid and more saying they're not, that they're a class unto themselves, that they're not bound to the squid or *láir bhán* by ties of kinship or affection.' But the cuttlefish noted along his Connemara coast seem not to have been the common European species *Sepia officinalis*, with a mantle perhaps 45 cm long. The '*cudal méarach*' was 'only about two inches long' – perhaps the dainty elegant cuttlefish (*Sepia elegans*) – and 'the *cudal sceitheach* ("spewing" cuttlefish) is smaller than that and it lets off his ink every now and then'. That may have been the tiny 5-cm little cuttlefish (*Sepiola atlantica*). It was remarkable to find such animals with common names in Irish. Yet these comical-looking miniatures, with their large and innocent eyes, do have a new popular sobriquet: to fishermen trawling for prawns on the Porcupine Bank and catching (and discarding) sepiolids by the thousand, they are 'Mickey Mouse squids'.

The key to the cuttlefish's lifestyle is its internalised shell – the oval 'bone', white, brittle and feather-light – that sometimes drifts ashore to our southern and eastern tidelines as a remnant of its owner. When its pores are filled with water, it anchors the cuttlefish to the seabed, its usual hiding place by day. Pumped out and gas-filled, it gives the animal neutral buoyancy, ready to hunt above the benthos with muscular squirts of water. Cuttlefish also excel remarkably in the exercise of changing colour at will, a capacity shared with squid and octopuses. Used for camouflage, this can find them suitably brown over kelp and creamy over sand, but in the throes of courtship their colours and patterns shimmer and flicker in rapid and dazzling sequences. The most arresting cuttlefish display, seen also at times in the octopus, occurs when the animal is preparing to lunge at prey, and is distinctive enough to have a name: 'Passing Cloud'. The animal's body blanches, and thick black bands travel rapidly forward over its dorsal surface to the tips of the tentacles, perhaps to blur perception of its shape or motion at the moment of attack.

The colour changes of cephalopods are achieved by the expansion, contraction and, when needed, pulsation of millions of chromatophores – multicellular organs under neuromuscular control. They act on central cells full of pigment in different colours and combine with iridescent elements to produce an astonishing range of visual effects. In octopuses, the changes are famously linked to mood and emotion. 'An octopus in good form,' writes Cambridge's Martin Wells, a notable student of their nervous systems, 'has a look of alert intelligence not shared by other marine animals. It changes colour, skin patterns and skin texture continuously, the more so if it is interested in what is going on around it.' He describes the great agility of octopuses out of water ('eight arms can loop over the side of a bucket quicker than two arms can put them back') and warns of the likelihood of bites. There are other hazards in trying to pull an octopus from its rocky lair: 'If the objects grasped include you and the sea floor . . . quite a small octopus could hold a snorkeler underwater'. But the animal is open to more amiable relationships, quickly learning to take food directly from a diver's hand and remember the particular silhouette of its benefactor.

The common European octopus (*Octopus vulgaris*) has a distinctly warty body. It is usually about 70 cm overall but can grow substantially bigger, and has two rows of stout suckers on its tentacles. It is found mainly off Ireland's south coast, whereas the lesser (or curled) octopus (*Eledone cirrhosa*) and North Atlantic octopus (*Bathypolypus arcticus*) are found all around the island. The first reaches some 50 cm overall, with single rows of suckers, dwells generally among rocks and is sometimes stranded in spring tide pools; the second lives mainly on sand or mud and is no bigger than an adult's palm. But both can also be found in considerable depths, and *B. arcticus*, ranging down to 600 m, lacks an ink sac, as do most deep-sea octopuses.

Just as the biggest giant squid has yet to put in an appearance, the full abyssal variety of the cephalopods – soft-bodied, bright-eyed and hard to catch – is probably a long way from being known. Scientists from Southampton and Aberdeen recently studied the distribution of deep-water species in the northeast Atlantic, helped by almost 600 specimens collected from commercial and research trawls. Among thirty-six different species, cuttlefish and squid were most abundant at the shallower depths (150–500 m). In the real deeps, the dominant species are octopuses. They have no use for ink sacs, but have cirri – finger-like structures – on their arms as well as suckers: all the better to grip the prey they seize in the dark. In the summer of 2008 a trawler from Fenit, fishing southwest of the Aran Islands, hauled up the remains of *Haliphron atlanticus,* one of the world's largest octopuses, with eyes 10 cm across – 'rather like ET', it seemed to Kevin Flannery, the Dingle marine biologist who identified the animal. Rarely retrieved intact because of its jelly-like tissue, it is thought to reach a length of 4 m and a weight of 75 kg.

Crustacea: life in armour

Acorn barnacles (Semibalanus balanoides).
(Courtesy of Marine Institute)

Most of the planet's living species, including insects, spiders, centipedes, shrimps and crabs, belong to the phylum Arthropoda. Picturing any of them evokes a flexible, segmented body and jointed limbs; they have an external skeleton with a rigid cuticle of chitin or calcium. In the ocean, most arthropods belong to the 50,000-odd species of crustaceans, with two pairs of antennae and appendages on the trunk for feeding, walking or swimming.

Such seemingly simple characteristics do not, needless to say, rule out the usual dazzling diversity of body shapes, appendages and lifestyles. The tiny sea spiders preying on the hydroids of Ireland's coastal shallows (as many as ten species in Galway Bay and Strangford Lough) are unmistakably marine versions of their arthropod equivalents ashore. But can the acorn barnacle (*Semibalanus balanoides*), glued to a rock or the hide of a humpback whale beneath a tent of shell, really be a crustacean? For centuries it had to be a mollusc, like the limpet, but the nineteenth-century Irish surgeon and naturalist John Vaughan Thompson watched the development of plank-tonic animals that, while minute, were unmistakably crustaceans. Once fixed to a hard surface, their six pairs of thoracic appendages extend, not to walk, but to comb phytoplankton from the water. The feathery appearance of these cirri prompted an early confusion of natural history, in which a stalked barnacle, *Lepas anatifera*, washing ashore on driftwood and fish boxes, became the 'goose' barnacle. Another stalked species, *Lepas fascularis*, secretes a spongy white float on which to drift.

Crustaceans come far smaller (some live between sand grains) and their lifestyles include burrowing shrimps and ambling hermit crabs. But the more familiar forms are marked by rapid movement, sometimes helped by the flap of a tail fan, as in the backward flick of shrimps and prawns and the balletic dances of the lobster. Among the decapods, prawns and shrimps are thin, light and swim; big crabs and lobsters walk in heavy armour (made relatively light by the water's buoyancy) and their foremost appendages become powerful pincers, shaped to crush, cut and tear. Their growth demands repeated moults of the carapace, which is cast off as a colourless, ghostly simulacrum (like the empty spiders one finds in dusty corners): the pigments that give crabs and lobsters their colour are in their tissue, not their shells. Thus, the empty carapaces of crabs that drift ashore belonged to dead animals and have nothing to do with their moulting while alive.

There are crabs that swim, with hind legs flattened to a pair of paddles, and one of these, the velvet swimming crab (*Necora puber*), makes an unlikely appearance among the three crabs (of forty or so Irish species) to have a commercial value. With a fleecy back but aggressive temper, it is the main predator of cuttlefish. As a by-catch in crab pots, it is marketed in a steady 300 tonnes a year, but first preference remains the edible crab (*Cancer pagurus*), with a reddish-brown carapace that may reach 20 cm across. It has been retrieved as far offshore as the Rockall Bank, in depths of more than 300 m, but finds more molluscs to eat in much shallower water.

Common Shore crab (Carcinus maenus).
(Courtesy of Marine Institute)

The intensive fishing of the brown crab has focused research on their recruitment to the two main stocks off Ireland: one to the north, the other off the southeast. Their moulting and mating takes place in summer in shallow waters, but is followed by a spawning migration of the females that may take them for hundreds of kilometres across the seabed. The females of many crab species undertake such travels to release their offspring in areas that give them the best chance of development. Just why females from the northern stock should journey westwards to the edge of the continental shelf, moving at up to 2 km per day is still unclear. Those of the southeastern stock move southwest with the coastal current, and one notably covered 136 km into the Celtic Sea after 287 days at liberty.

The spider crab (*Maja brachydactela*) is the third commercial crab species, at the northern limit of its range in Ireland and Scotland, but probably increasing in abundance and extending its range as the climate warms. It is found in especially high numbers in the Tralee and Brandon Bays of County Kerry. Here, indeed, they seem to stay throughout the year, and since the 1980s have been fished with up to 10,000 pots for the French and Spanish markets. The crabs are distinguished by spectacular mating gatherings in early summer, when moulting females are surrounded by males, sometimes in a large mound of several hundred animals. The conjunction of mating and moulting is standard behaviour for crabs. A male seeks out a female preparing to moult her shell and carries her under his body, perhaps for days, until her moulting makes copulation possible. Then he protects her for the time in which her shell is hardening. She burrows in the sand, scooping out a large cavity in which to lay her eggs and attach them beneath her legs, nursing them for several months before releasing them as larvae into the plankton.

In the common shore crab (*Carcinus maenus*), the prime predator of intertidal life, a deep green colour marks actively growing animals with frequent moults, while the reddish carapaces of those beneath the tide are of large, mature crabs with long intervals between re-shelling. Hermit crabs, on the other hand, such as the young *Pagurus bernhardus* found in some of our rock pools, fit a naked abdomen, already soft and twisted, into a sequence of empty snail shells (only the abdomen or tail is naked, the rest is armoured). These are thoroughly examined and tested for weight and size, since the crab has to drag its shelter behind it. As it grows, it must move out from the tidal pools into deeper water in search of its ultimate dwelling, the whelk. Where these shells are in short supply, the crab may evict a damaged or dying whelk to take over its habitation.

Lobsters great and small

The lobster most readily identified with Ireland is not usually called a lobster at all, but a Dublin Bay prawn, langoustine or scampi. *Nephrops norvegicus* is, nonetheless, a small lobster with kidney-shaped eyes, capable of growing to an overall 25 cm and coloured bright orange even before it is cooked. Also unlike its big blue relative, the European lobster (*Homarus gammarus*), it spends most of its time in unlined burrows carved in mud the consistency of chocolate mousse. The holes are spaced in colonies and defended with aggressive territorialism.

The Dublin Bay prawn, from mud like chocolate mousse.

Its special habitat occurs in still, deep water from Iceland to Morocco, including grounds west of the Aran Islands and even out on the Porcupine Bank. But the main seabed of the fishery (the second most valuable in Ireland, after mackerel) is in sheltered, muddy shallows of the northwest Irish Sea. Berried females rarely emerge from their burrows, so they are largely undisturbed by the 'tickler' chains that trawlers drag ahead of their nets: thus, most Dublin Bay prawns are the larger male lobster.

A word at this point about the true prawns, swimming nervously with eyes out on stalks, or prancing on their rear legs and pointing at the world a sharply jagged unicorn's horn, called the rostrum: the common prawn (*Palaemon serratus*) is the largest of the main family (a group of eight, some more transparent than others) and thus the main one caught commercially as 'shrimp', but is actually common only on the west and south coasts, from Connemara, County Galway, to Carnsore Point, County Wexford. It feeds on fragments of seaweed and small worms and, being preyed on by almost all fish, changes colour to match its background. There are several other families of prawns in Irish waters, some much smaller, and while few live in depths greater than 100 m, others can still be found down to 1,000 m or more. Virtually all migrate to deeper water in autumn and return to the shallows in summer. Species of small prawn, their rostra reduced to a small spine, are generally called shrimps, of which the

In the Porcupine Seabight, the squat lobster is the most common walking crustacean.
(Courtesy of Geological Survey of Ireland)

European lobster (Homarus gammarus).
(Courtesy of Marine Institute)

best-known family are the Crangonidae. The common shrimp (*Crangon crangon*) lives buried in sand from the middle shore down to 150 m, feeding on polychaete worms, molluscs, and other crustaceans.

The European lobster (*Hommarus gammarus*) is at the other end of the scale. Reaching 50 cm in length and weighing about 5 kg at perhaps 20 years old, its inky-blue carapace is then often encrusted with barnacles (there have been venerable monsters: a Cornish lobster in the *Guinness Book of Records* had an overall length of 1.26 m and weighed 9.6 kg). The animal is a solitary creature, eyes swivelling on movable stalks as it scavenges or hunts slow-moving molluscs, worms and urchins, and feeding most heavily in the summer. Those living on the outer continental shelf, down to about 150 m, migrate inshore in summer to find warmer water for growth, moulting and egg-laying, while the lobsters living inshore stay put all year round. This actually helps the offshore lobsters to grow faster and moult more often, because very cold bottom temperatures endured by the inshore lobsters in winter hold back their growth. On the other hand, inshore lobsters have a wider choice of individual shelters, notably sandy crevices under deep shelves of rock, while those living far offshore must often double up in holes in muddy sediment.

Their summer pairing is like that of crabs in its juncture of female moulting and mating, but the eggs are not extruded for a year or so and the one deposit of sperm stored by the female may be used to fertilise two successive batches. They stay attached to the lobster's underside as 'berries' and hatch in the following summer. Through their four free-swimming larval stages they live as light-sensitive plankton, rising in the water column by day and sinking again at night. Having settled and burrowed and moulted into foraging juveniles, their growth can demand up to a further ten moults in the first year, each leaving them even more vulnerable to bottom-feeding fish.

The red-brown spiny lobster or crawfish (*Palinurus elephas*), often fished with 'cray nets' on the west coast, is much the same size as *Homarus*, but lacks its huge pinching claws; the very long antennae and many nodules and spines on its carapace are other distinctions. It prefers rocky ground in warmer (and generally deeper) water, where it is generally gregarious and sedentary, moving out only at night to feed or reproduce.

The crawfish or spiny lobster (Palinurus elephas) *on a colony of deadman's fingers.* (Nigel Motyer)

Between crabs and lobsters, in appearance, are the squat lobsters (also called mud shrimps) that, tucking their abdomen under their thorax, have somewhat crab-like proportions. Living under rocks and stones from the lower shore to depths of 150 m, they are rarely seen except by divers and in fishermen's nets, but are prized as seafood when they are found. The most commonly encountered in Irish waters is the greeny-brown *Galathea squamifera*, with a body of perhaps 5 cm and rather longer, spiny pincers. The orange and blue *Galathea strigosa* is twice the size and the most aggressive in the group. With *G. squamifera*, it has been studied in Lough Hyne and in the Irish Sea.

Echinodermata: fashioned by five

In the phylum of Echinodermata the number five becomes an almost mystical principle of design. They are divided into five classes and all have five (or multiples of five) sections radiating symmetri-

Echinus esculentus, the largest Irish urchin, feeds on kelp. (© M. D. Guiry/Algaebase)

cally from a central mouth. The rule of five is epitomised in the globular sea urchin, with a 'test', or exoskeleton of calcium carbonate, and covered with a thin layer of epidermal cells through which the urchin's movable spines (part of the skeleton) protrude. Between them extend hundreds of tiny tube feet in five double rows (hydraulically manipulated) that stick the urchin to a rock in the surge of a swell, or take it on slow, algae-browsing perambulations. All are controlled by a brainless network of nerves.

Largest of the three common species of globular urchin found along Irish coasts, down to depths of 100 m or more, is the edible sea urchin (*Echinus esculentus*), with a test the size of a grapefruit, some 10–12 cm in diameter. Internally, its striking feature is the 'Aristotle's lantern', a structure of five jaws with five teeth that, protruding from the mouth at the centre of the urchin's underside, can tear algae and grind encrusted organisms from the rock surface. So severe may be its grazing that large patches of rock are left coated only with a glowing, rose-red crust of coralline algae. The urchins' pinky-orange tests, washed in denuded of their spines, are often treasured as beautiful ornaments. What is

Purple sea urchin (Paracentrotus lividus). (Courtesy of Don Cotton)

edible in the living animal are the five-branched gonads or roe sacs (the sexes are separate) that develop in the spring breeding season to fill the roomy spaces in the test.

Irish fishing of urchins has been directed largely, however, to the much smaller purple sea urchin (*Paracentrotus lividus*), a warm-water Lusitanian species that colonised much of Ireland's west coast in modern times. It has been a notable resident of pools in the coast of the Burren and on the Aran Islands, using teeth and spines to grind close-fitting hollows in the soft limestone as an added protection from predators. It reaches only 7 cm, but its roes are a familiar seafood in France. Intensive fishery and export in the late twentieth century depleted many Irish populations, some past the point of renewal. The urchin is now, however, proving a successful species for aquaculture (see p.148).

The third common Irish urchin is the small shore or green sea urchin (*Psammechinus miliaris*). At about 5 cm in diameter, it prefers sheltered habitats under stones or in crevices and is found from the lower shore to 100 m, often camouflaged by pieces of seaweed trapped among the spines. Its Aristotelian teeth are omnivorous, sometimes chewing on barnacles and bivalves pulled apart with the help of its tubular, sucker-like feet.

A second group of sea urchins, the 'heart' or 'potato' urchins, lack these teeth, using their feet to find food particles instead as they burrow in sand and gravel. Their spines are mainly on the upper surface and directed backwards. Of five heart urchins in Irish waters, the commonest, *Echinocardium cordatum*, spends most of its life buried perhaps 30 cm deep in sandy sediment at depths down to 200 m or more, and is usually encountered after death as a fragile white test at the tideline. The largest, the purple heart urchin (*Spatangus purpureus*), goes even deeper (to 900 m) and can reach 12 cm in size.

A striking and little-known deep-water sea urchin, not usually found in less than 30 m of water, was found on the Mullet Peninsula in 1973. The pencil urchin (*Cidaris cidaris*) has a test 7 cm across and forty or more strong spines that are up to twice as long. Normally found in deep water off the west coast, it has been likened to a ball of wool with knitting needles stuck in it.

Starfish

Starfish and dahlia anemones feeding on guillemot eggs fallen from nesting cliffs in County Kerry. (Nigel Motyer)

A second class of echinoderms, the starfish (or asteroids) are commonly recognised in one orange animal with five plump fingers or rays, the common starfish (*Asterias rubens*). A determined and efficient predator, it uses the terminal suckers of its tube feet to prise apart the shells of mussels, oysters and other bivalves, and, through a gap perhaps less than 1 mm wide, inserts its stomach to begin an 'out of body' digestion. *Asterias* can reach remarkable concentrations: a gathering on the coast of Cornwall was 1.5 km long and 15 m wide and was judged to have cleared about 4,000 tonnes of young mussels in four months. A swarm with a far less familiar purpose was discovered in 2004 in the water beneath the ledges of a cliff in County Kerry. Above was a large colony of nesting seabirds, and the starfish were feeding on the fallen eggs of guillemots, in company with scavenging dahlia anemones.

But *Asterias* is one of more than twenty asteroids known in Irish waters, in a variety of colours: vivid purple, red, green, orange and yellow along with more subtle hues. They stand out among the anemones, hydroids and all the other plant-like shapes on the sea floor. Most are found in the shallow water (out to about 40 m deep), but some come up in fishermen's nets and one, *Bathybiaster vexillifer*, has been studied 2,200 m deep in the northern Rockall Trough, where it burrows into sediment in search of bristle worms. Starfish range in size from a tiny cushion star of 1.5 cm up to 40-cm giants with non-conforming numbers of rays – seven for *Luidia ciliaris*, a sand-dweller, and up to thirteen for the purple sunstar *Solaster endeca,* a notably aggressive predator on other echinoderms.

Like sea urchins, starfish have several hundred small tube feet on the underside of their bodies,

A feather star anchored to a dropstone in deep water. (Courtesy of Marine Institute)

used for walking and burrowing into the sand for prey; they are also used to wrench ajar the shells of mussels and oysters with a sustained, unrelenting suction from feet working in relays. The animal then extends its stomach through the open gap to envelop and digest the mollusc. In another physiological talent, starfish can regenerate a limb if one is broken off: either the severed limb generates a whole new animal or, more usually, a new limb replaces the broken one.

Crinoids, or feather stars, are the asteroids' exquisite relatives, extending delicate, jointed arms into the water like a bunch of ostrich feathers, with tube feet on the arms to collect drifting food particles. They fall into two groups that share the same 'upside-down' body plan compared with other echinoderms (their mouths are uppermost) but have different lifestyles. Stalked crinoids, the sea lilies, are attached to the bottom in deep water, while the feather stars of mainly shallow water can move about freely on the seabed and even swim. Caught on deep-water video, however, some species of sea lily, such as *Endoxocrinus parrae*, have shown surprising animation: not only do they wave their arms to shake off debris or dislodge little crabs and other food thieves, but, if threatened by grazing sea urchins, may detach the stalk near the base and crawl away at several centimetres per second, dragging the broken stem behind them.

Feather stars have a ring of short cirri underneath the central disc with which to fasten themselves to rocks or kelp. In Irish waters, *Antedon* feather stars wave ten arms, variously coloured in red, white and brown, and up to 10 cm long. *A. bifida* can be particularly abundant at the southwest and northeast corners of the island, where they may dominate whole areas of rock.

The brittle star echinoids (Ophiuroidea) have arms so long in proportion to the small, central disc that they resemble harvestmen spiders. They are found from the lower shore, among seaweeds, in crevices and under stones and out to 400 m deep, sometimes in crowded beds on gravel or burrowing into soft sediment. On muddy sand in Galway Bay, for example, the little brittle star *Amphiura filiformis* (a mere 1 cm across, but with arms ten times as long) has been counted at 700 per square metre. Where such great densities of animals are burrowing, the seabed can be changed ecologically, oxygenating the sediment and encouraging microbial activity – the bioturbation also met with in the burrowing of sedentary worms.

The cotton-spinner (Holothuria forskali), *a sea cucumber, was washed up on White Strand beach, Cahirciveen, County Kerry.* (Rosemary Hill)

In sometimes grotesque contrast to the delicacy of these starfish, the sea cucumbers (Holothuroidea) seem to lack the symmetry of other echinoids, but do, in fact, follow the quintessential structure, whether looking like short, curved cucumbers or rather large worms. Most live in the sublittoral shallows, and the largest are as likely to the near the lower shore and low tide mark as in deeper water, but there are species living as deep as 1,000 m.

The tentacles, which surround the mouth at one end, are modified tube-feet, knob-like in some species and in others up to 10 cm long and bushily branched. Unlike those of some tropical waters, the sea cucumbers around Britain and Ireland tend to be monochrome in dark, leathery skins. One large black sea cucumber up to 20 cm long, *Holothuria forskali*, common on the west coast of Ireland, is known as the cotton-spinner from a reflex which shoots out a mass of sticky white threads when roughly handled or attacked. This is one of the epifaunal cucumbers (living on the surface of the sea floor), but others burrow in sand, mud or gravel, their long tentacles floating up in the plant-like manner of hydroids. Of these, one, the sea gherkin *(Pawsonia saxicola),* has a pure white body, but keeps it tucked into rock crevices or beneath a boulder.

Tunicates

Sea squirts, like the sponges, are essentially bags for the filtering of water (their outer skin, or tunic, prompted their name). Yet they form a tiny class – no more than 3 per cent – in the phylum of Chordata, the rest of which are vertebrate animals such as fish, birds and people. This is because, swimming as tadpole-like larvae, they have a flexible tail in which there is a notochord (a skeletal tube, forerunner of the backbone) and dorsal nerve cord, two of the features that also mark out vertebrate animals. These persist in the free-swimming, pelagic forms of tunicates – the jelly-like salps – but disappear in the forms that settle on the seabed: the ascidians.

Tunicates come in a great variety of shapes, often resembling fungi, and when disturbed they contract and expel a jet of water (in the salps, this acts as a propellant). The sessile ascidians form part of the seabed carpet of animals from the intertidal zone to the deep sea. Among them, the common sea squirt (*Ciona intestinalis*) is a gelatinous vase up to 12 cm tall, found down to 500 m but growing also on ships' hulls, buoys and piers. The star ascidian (*Botryllus schlosseri*) is colonial: the individuals are grouped around exhalant openings in star-shaped patterns. Another colonial species, the light bulb sea squirt (*Clavelina lepadiformis),* forms a group of small transparent bulbs, encrusting stones and seaweed down to 50 m. In 2006, the discovery of an encrusting alien, *Didemnum*, in the Malahide Marina, County Dublin, and subsequently in Carlingford Lough, County Louth, and Galway Bay, raised serious alarm (see 'Underwater aliens' p.81).

The far seamounts

3D representation of seamounts.
(Courtesy of ICES)

The attraction of fish to such hotspots and their pursuit by deep-water trawlers has brought a new energy to the study of seamounts, the volcanic cones or ridges that tower up from the Abyssal Plain. Some of these mountains are 100 km across, and while most are at, or far beyond, the boundary of Ireland's seabed territory their role in the Atlantic ecosystem gives them much more than a distant importance. The OASIS project, funded by the EU, in which a team from NUI Galway is taking part, is studying two of them: the Sedlo Seamount, 180 km north of the Azores, has a summit 750 m below the surface; the Seine Seamount, the same distance northeast of Madeira, rises to within 170 m of the surface.

The collision of deep currents with the steep, rocky slopes of seamounts causes eddies and upwellings that lift nutrients from the seabed and diffuse them into the water column (the mountains have thus been called 'the stirring rods of the ocean'). This nourishes exceptional concentrations of plankton (see Chapter 5) and supports a food chain that builds up to predators such as swordfish (*Xiphias gladius*), tuna, sharks, squid, dolphins and attracts even seabirds wheeling above the waves. The seamounts' bare rock and boulders, a habitat rare in the abyssal ocean, provide hard perches for corals, sponges, sea anemones, ascidians and other suspension-feeders, many unique or endemic to each seamount and often new to science. Some are thought to live for a century or more. The fish communities too, can show adaptations to these special habitats of turbulent submarine water and generous food supply. Seamounts both disperse species into the ocean and provide oases or stepping stones for wide-ranging migratory fish, turtles and mammals.

Millions at home in the mud

The exceptional richness of species on the coral reefs and seamounts, and their strong and often beautiful contrast with grey and featureless sediment around them, can gravely underestimate the abundance and importance of marine life in deep-sea mud. This is, after all, the dominant habitat of the northeast Atlantic and indeed of the planet as a whole. Given the previously unsuspected wealth of organisms discovered by today's research, in which almost every sample of mud seems to contain new species, it is quite possible that deep-sea sediment is the home of most living creatures on Earth. The myriad animal marks on its surface – pits, burrows, mounds, tracks and casts, collectively known by the German word *Lebensspuren*, or 'life traces' – are evidence of teeming life below and of habitats created by the host of animals themselves.

There have been projections of up to 10 million species of seabed life, of which the mud-dwelling nematodes (simple, unsegmented worms, some a mere 1 mm long) may alone account for a substantial share of the planet's animal diversity. In the muds of the northeast Atlantic, they are joined by multitudes of copepods, single-celled foraminifera in their shells, infinitesimal shrimps and minute crustaceans of the order Tanaidacea. Moving up to larger invertebrates, a video study in the Rockall Trough showed an average of 1,700 individuals in 1 m^2 of mud, well over half of them polychaete worms. Sessile fauna also inhabit deep sea muds, including glass sponges (*Pheronema spp.*) the size of soccer balls, stalked anemones, hydroids and sea pens.

On the sediment surface in the deep northeast Atlantic, echinoderms are outstandingly the most common group of larger animals. Sea cucumbers have modified their forms in the deep sea, developing swimming fins or oral tentacles. They sometimes form herds that move together across the sediment, sucking up its smaller inhabitants as they graze. They have been counted at 7,000 per hectare, and with a throughput of 100 g of sediment per cucumber per day the animals are considerable bioturbators of the seabed. In the Rockall Trough, burrowing brittle stars have far outnumbered other megafaunal groups, including the sea urchins and starfish.

The density and distribution of species in the deep North Atlantic – not merely benthic animals, but fish as well – is hugely influenced by the seasonal crops of phytoplankton and the subsequent deposits of marine snow. Their annual variation may affect the seasonal growth and reproduction of a wide range of deep animals, including sponges, burrowing bivalves, spider and hermit crabs, and longer-term variation could account for dramatic changes in seabed populations. On the Porcupine Abyssal Plain, a single decade of the late twentieth century saw an increase in one species of sea cucumber (*Amperima rosea*) from 4 to 6,500 individuals per hectare.

The depth and temperature of water are also important, tending to sort species and communities in bands along the ocean slope. Just as similar species are graded in sequence down the seashore – most obviously in the seaweeds – such successions continue among related animals right down to the abyss. In the Porcupine Seabight, for example, where squat lobsters are the most common walking crustaceans, two closely related species occupy successive and quite narrow bands of depth. Where they overlap, a slight difference in design of their pincers seems to secure them a separate living. Crabs are comparatively rare in the deeps, but there are red crabs that penetrate down to 1,000 m and beyond. They share their bright colouring with the large prawns that prowl the seabed: at such depths, the water column screens out the red wavelength of light, so the colour becomes an effective camouflage.

Living light of deeps and night

Below 1,000 m (say, half-way down the slope of the Rockall Trough) the final darkness is pierced only by the intermittent flicker of bioluminescence, the living light of the deep. The intense spread of illuminable organisms is evoked in an observation by Alan Jamieson, a Scottish marine scientist working with ROVs (remotely operated underwater vehicles), that 'at depths beyond solar light penetration, thousands of bioluminescent events per second illuminate trawl gear, making it visible to fish.'

In almost all deep-sea fish and invertebrates, light serves to attract prey, to warn or confuse predators, to communicate within a shoal, to attract mates – or simply to find the way. Most of this intricate neon display is produced by luminous organs in the skin called photophores. These secrete a chemical compound, generically called luciferin, that glows when oxidised – a reaction activated by an enzyme, luciferase. Less often, the photophores hold colonies of phosphorescent bacteria. The chemically produced light is generally bluish, since this is the wavelength that travels farthest in water and to which marine vision is most sensitive. Many deep-sea species have rows of photophores; some have only a few that may be hidden by flaps of skin until the light is needed. The female deep-sea anglerfish uses light in the lure that dangles above her hidden crescent of a mouth, both to attract prey and to signal her presence to a mate.

Not all deep-sea light, however, is confined to the blue-green end of the spectrum. Research is finding more and more instances of the use of red-orange light, especially by predators. Most deep-sea fish are black or reddish in colour, reflecting little of blue light, and are thought to be unable to detect red light when it shines upon them. By using 'headlights' that are filtered or otherwise switched to the red end of the spectrum, predators can both find prey more easily and approach it undetected. The widely accepted idea that deep-water fish are generally 'blind' to red light has, however, been challenged by the discovery that some Pacific deep-sea siphonophores use flickering red fluorescent filaments to attract the fish they seek for prey, even at these thinly populated depths. Perhaps half of all jellyfish are bioluminescent in some form and, together with brightly luminous salps, produce some of the most bewitching images from the ocean.

Most cephalopods, the squids in particular, can also produce brilliant displays. The great deep-sea squid *Taningia danae* has photophores the size of lemons in the tips of two of its arms and flashes them rapidly when attacked by sperm whales, sharks or tuna. The tiny Atlantic squid *Heteroteuthis dispar*, on the other hand, which moves through a wide range of depths, has glands inside its mantle that offer two defensive options when attacked, according to the light level at the time: disappearance in a cloud of black ink, or in one of glowing, bioluminescent mucus. Some squid use bioluminescence for camouflage when in the mid-depths, balancing downwelling light with their own radiance in order to weaken their silhouettes; at even shallower depths, some species use it to blur their forms in filtering moonlight. For deep octopuses, the bioluminescence that dots their arms can be a lure for crustaceans, whose highly developed eyes seem to draw them to light. Their photophores can also enrich the already astonishing range of colour changes that distinguish octopus communications or states of mind.

Bioluminescence is by no means confined to the deeps – only to conditions that make it useful. Some dinoflagellate plankton, such as *Noctiluca scintillans*, may light up the night sea if stirred up, for example, in the bow-wave and wake of a boat. The display is produced more naturally in the predatory assault on *Noctiluca* by the teeming copepods of the zooplankton. Why should these tiny crustaceans be put off their food by prey that flashes when seized? Perhaps because, being transparent themselves, they do not want to be lit up for other predators, however briefly, by a chemical glow in their gut. On the other hand, the bioluminescence of mid-water shrimp such as the krill *Meganyctiphanes norvegica*, the most common in these waters, is attributed to their diet of bioluminescent dinoflagellates.

In the tiny brittle star *Amphipholis squamata*, often hidden under shells and stones in Irish waters, only its five arms are luminous, apparently shining most brightly as a lure to crustacean prey. Many other invertebrates use luminescence defensively. The sea pen *Pennatula phosphorea*, for example, sends slow waves of blue-green light to its extremities when disturbed – part of a package of deterrents that include stinging organelles (specialised structures within the cell) and chemicals that upset its main predator, the Dover sole. It can also, as a last resort, withdraw into a tube deep in the mud. The big and bristly parchment worm (*Chaetopterus variopedatus*), found all around Ireland, goes even further, retreating to the bottom of its tube while squirting a bright cloud of luminescent mucus into the surrounding water to confuse a potential attacker. Thus, bristle worm and deep-sea squid seem to have evolved, quite separately, a similar defence.

Underwater aliens

In January 2006, an angler fishing for codling on the Suir Estuary, County Waterford, reeled in an unfamiliar crab, clasping the hook with sharp white pincers protruding from hairy muffs. He had caught the first Chinese mitten crab (*Eriocheir sinensis*) ever recorded in Ireland. Ecologists hope it was a solitary specimen, a marine hitchhiker on a ship docked in the estuary's container port, for this particular crab, carried to a German river a century ago, has proved one of Europe's most undesirable aliens. In Europe it has undergone population explosions in millions, and a recent surge in reproduction in Britain has taken it up half a dozen rivers running into the Thames Estuary. It riddles soft banks with its burrows,

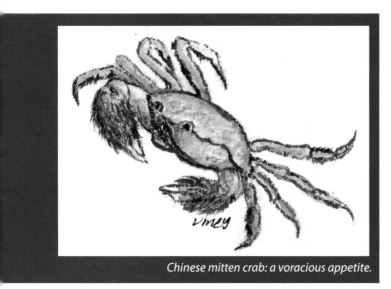

Chinese mitten crab: a voracious appetite.

migrates across land, and shows a voracious appetite for freshwater life, even leaping on fish in the night.

Compared with such evident menace, another alien discovered in Ireland the same year might seem to pose a mere nuisance. A colonial sea squirt, or ascidian, in the genus *Didemnum* spp. (no one has yet settled on a species) has been spreading disconcertingly in bays and harbours on both American coasts. It appeared in Europe in 1991 and in New Zealand in 2001. Since the first discovery in Malahide Marina in 2006, it has been found in Carlingford Lough and Galway Bay. Alarm has been raised by the Marine Institute and by the website 'www.invasivespeciesireland.com' that alerts the public to the 'most unwanted' aliens. *Didemnum* has become globally notorious for smothering man-made surfaces, but its large, mat-like colonies also invade rocky reefs and shellfish beds on gravelly bottoms. It drapes man-made marine structures – boat hulls, piers, oyster trestles, and so on – in long gelatinous beards like lobes of fungi.

Some mats smother in another way, by shutting out the sun. In its native waters around Japan and Korea, wireweed (*Sargassum muticum*) is a relatively small, innocuous, feathery seaweed. On sheltered shores around Europe, its fronds can grow quickly up to 16 m long, forming a dense, floating mass, borne up by bladders and casting deep shade on the seabed. It arrived in France, probably with imports of oyster spat some forty years ago and has since spread north to Norway and south to Spain. It was first discovered in Ireland in Strangford Lough in 1995 and then, after some years, in several western and southern bays. It spreads by fragments of fertile fronds and 'germlings' produced sexually, and is now expected to spread to all coasts of Ireland, growing vigorously each summer and shading out native algae where its mats are thickest.

Native species can also suffer alien competition for space and food. The Australasian barnacle *Elminius modestus* arrived in Britain's Chichester Harbour, close to the Portsmouth naval base, during the Second World War. It quickly became widespread in European waters and was first recorded on the west Cork coast, near Lough Hyne, in 1957. In 2003, a search of ninety Irish shores found the barnacle on almost half of them and commonest on those with shelter. In the exceptional shelter and warmth of Lough Hyne's northern basin, *Elminius* has become the dominant barnacle species. It reproduces some six times a year, compared with the single spawning of the native barnacle, *Semibalanus balanoides*; it also grows rapidly and can tolerate a wide temperature range, together with turbid water and reduced salinity.

These four species illustrate the many different ways in which alien species can become harmfully invasive outside their own ecosystems. Others among the thirty-five or so aliens known to be established around Ireland's coasts appear to pose no immediate ecological threat. But still more of menacing lifestyle are waiting in the wings. Ireland's leading authority on marine aliens, Dan Minchin, has particularly cited the slipper limpet (*Crepidula fornicata*), whose runaway, smothering lifestyle in European waters is to the coasts what the zebra mussel (*Dreissena polymorpha*) is to lakes and rivers; and the Asian shore crab (*Hemigrapsus penicillatus*), already in France and proving an invasive neighbour to Europe's native green shore crab. Both could reach Ireland with imports of half-grown oysters or other, perhaps experimental, shellfish species: the history of movements in the oyster industry offers dire examples of the importation of parasites and disease organisms.

Ships' ballast water pumped in at one port and out at another, transfers billions of tonnes of water each year, and with it thousands of marine species, including bacteria, eggs, juveniles or planktonic larvae. In 2004, a Ballast Water Convention 'to prevent, minimise and ultimately eliminate the transfer of harmful aquatic organisms and pathogens through the control and management of ships' ballast water and sediments,' was adopted by consensus of seventy-seven nations at a conference of the International Maritime Organisation. Its regulations only come into force, however, after thirty governments, with one-third of the world's shipping, have ratified it. By the end of 2007 only ten had done so, representing 3.6% of global shipping, among them Norway and Spain as the only Europeans. The move towards standard installation of ballast water treatment on newly built ships has also been delayed.

Sargassum muticum *growing in Galway Bay.*
(© M. D. Guiry/Algaebase)

Shelter and warmth give Lough Hyne an extraordinary diversity of species. (MarBef)

Lough Hyne:
The Biologists' Rock Pool

Almost since the Rev William Spotswood Green found Ireland's first recorded purple sea urchin in its clear and balmy shallows in 1886, Lough Hyne on the coast of west Cork has served as a pristine aquarium, or huge rock pool, for marine scientists. Almost 1 km², and linked to the Celtic Sea by a narrow tidal channel, it holds several thousand species of marine animals and plants in a wide range of exposed and sheltered environments: cliffs, beaches, boulders and salt marshes. Its exceptional value for the study of temperate ocean organisms brought designation as Europe's first Marine Nature Reserve in 1981. A resurgence of research activity from NUI Cork brought new field laboratories at the lake, now widely used by Irish and British universities and visiting scientists from across the world.

More than 50 m deep and sheltered by woodland and rocky promontories, the lough is stirred only by the strong tidal flow at its kelp-lined rapids. Its extraordinary biodiversity includes 73 kinds of sea slug, more than 100 sponges, 24 kinds of crab, and 18 species of anemone. Shelter and warmth have made it particularly hospitable to southern species: 2 Lusitanian gobies are among its 70-odd inshore fish, and the purple urchin has been one of the most studied species in the lough. Less welcome have been colonisation by the invasive seaweed *Sargassum muticum* and an Australasian barnacle, *Elminius modestus,* both of which have the potential of harming the lough's natural ecosystem.

Strangford Lough:
Special Area of Conservation

From the thrilling surge of the tide at the southern narrows to its placid lapping in the shallows at the far end, some 30 km north, Strangford Lough in County Down holds some of the richest marine life in northwest Europe. An arm of the western Irish Sea, it captures enormous quantities of plankton, and the forceful renewal from the open sea guarantees a year-round mixing of water. This has nourished brilliant carpets of seabed invertebrates and more than 2,000 species – almost three-quarters of all those found on the entire northern coast.

From cobbled depths of 60 m inside the narrows to the distant tidal mudflats imprinted each winter by great flocks of migrant waterfowl, the lough's sorting of sediments is exceptional. So also, until the later decades of the twentieth century, was the extent of the horse mussel *(Modiolus)* colonies, building solid mounds and reefs on soft mud bottoms. Protection of the reefs, and their overlay of more than 130 other species, was a prime reason for nomination of the lough as a Special Area of Conservation. Yet their progressive destruction by small local trawlers dredging for queen scallops went unchecked until almost all the reefs had been seriously damaged and an ecological change investigation by Queen's University found them 'not in favourable conservation status.'

Trawling and dredging were banned from the lough in 2003. Four years later came a proposed halt to all fishing (mainly potting for lobsters, crabs and *Nephrops)* within two small 'non-disturbance zones' to protect the last two relatively undamaged reefs of horse mussels.

Dublin Bay prawn (Nephrops norvegicus). (Courtesy of Exploris Aquarium, Portaferry)

A restoration plan agreed with the European Commission under the Habitats Directive made it clear that this might have to be achieved by artificial reseeding of the mussels' former range. As a northern species, however, *Modiolus* may be inherently at risk of long-term extinction at Strangford as sea temperatures warm with climate change.

The lough is still home, however, to many

Sunstar (Crossaster papposus). (Courtesy of NOAA Photo Library)

beautiful and unusual species. For example, at Exploris (Northern Ireland's aquarium) beside the entrance narrows, the lovely red sunstar *(Crossaster papposus)* can be seen – with up to eleven arms, the most of any starfish in Irish waters.

Moon jelly. (Nigel Motyer)

CHAPTER 5

Under the Microscope

The World of Plankton

Seasons transform the sea just as powerfully as they change the land. Spring wakes the phytoplankton, the drifting, microscopic plant life of the temperate ocean, just as it stirs the growth of grasses ashore. They are like fields of vegetation in the upper layer of the ocean. As a pale green clouds the navy blue of the deep Atlantic, satellites record the colour change sweeping north from Spain. The spring phytoplankton bloom is more intense and widespread in the North Atlantic than anywhere else in the world. Its burgeoning meadow supplies the energy for sea life, from the smallest animals of the zooplankton up to the largest whales. Indeed, its production of biomass can exceed the nourishment supplied by green leaves to animals and insects ashore – perhaps as much as 30 tonnes of food from a single hectare of sea.

In March, the water off Ireland's coasts is nearly as cold as it gets – an average of 10°C off the southwest and 7°C off the northeast. It is scantily seeded with spores of diatoms, some living in deeper water or even overwintering at the seabed. They are the earliest group of phytoplankton to wake and multiply as days lengthen and the sun gains in radiative power: they will be followed by other groups, the dinoflagellates and protozoans. The single cells of diatoms are a mere one thousandth of a millimetre in size, but to see them under a microscope is, in the classic image of Alistair Hardy, 'like looking at a group of crystal caskets filled with jewels.' The cell walls are made from dissolved silica drawn from the water, and while many indeed offer beautiful variations on a glassy pill-box, others forming chains resemble lacework, ribbons and legged insects.

The nutrients they require are taken up from the sea. Within each is a chloroplast: a matrix of molecules that captures the energy of sunlight and changes carbon dioxide and the elements in seawater into nucleic acids, proteins and sugars, and liberating oxygen in the process. Thus they help to regulate Earth's climate, producing roughly half the oxygen in our air and extracting huge amounts of carbon dioxide from the atmosphere, turning it into organic matter by photosynthesis.

Phytoplankton cells need not only light and carbon to photosynthesise, but also mineral nutrients such as nitrates (to make proteins), phosphorus (for enzymes) and trace elements such as iron. Like the silicon for their cell walls, these have risen from deep water next to the seabed, stirred and mixed by winter storms or in upwelling currents. Less naturally, and not always beneficially, nitrates flow out from rivers polluted by farm fertiliser and city waste.

Energised by food and light, the diatoms begin to divide into two in a rapid, exponential explosion, doubling their numbers in a day or two and multiplying perhaps ten thousandfold in a fortnight. As the water calms and warms into summer (about mid-July) they are joined in food production by billions of another phytoplankton group – the dinoflagellates, in a changing procession of species. Dinoflagellates have whip-like flagella that can propel them through the water towards the sunlight: indeed, some commute in the water column, spending their nights many metres deep to scavenge nutrients, only rising again after dawn. Their shapes are no less inventive than the lacy intricacy of diatoms: spiky spheres, stars, mandalas, and deep-etched crystal bowls. Some species are luminescent, such as the aptly named *Noctiluca* which can make the sea sparkle on summer nights (also, as Rachel Carson wrote memorably, 'causing fishes, squids or dolphins to fill the water with racing flames and clothe themselves in a ghostly radiance.'). But the summer blooms of other dinoflagellates can tint the sea with murky brown and yellow, and the term 'red tide' has come to be synonymous with the blooming of many toxic species. Known forms of phytoplankton now run into thousands and include many micro-organisms on the border between animals and plants. Some, the zooanthellae, live within other organisms as symbiotic partners and can be found in many marine invertebrates such as sponges, corals, jellyfish, and protists.

Protists are also called protozoans, a name that translates from the Greek as 'first animals'. Some of this family, such as the ciliates, foraminifera and radiolaria, can photosynthesise in their planktonic stage. Ciliates in various shapes have bunches of cilia like thistle fluff; foraminifera are

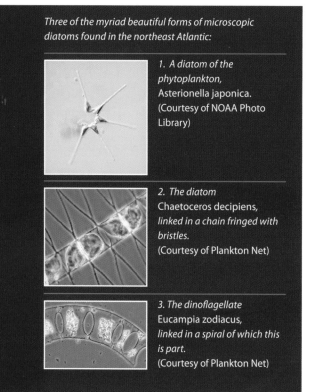

Three of the myriad beautiful forms of microscopic diatoms found in the northeast Atlantic:

1. A diatom of the phytoplankton, Asterionella japonica. (Courtesy of NOAA Photo Library)

2. The diatom Chaetoceros decipiens, linked in a chain fringed with bristles. (Courtesy of Plankton Net)

3. The dinoflagellate Eucampia zodiacus, linked in a spiral of which this is part. (Courtesy of Plankton Net)

variously shaped discs, from pinheads to several millimetres in size. Their form depends on the environment in which they live and so they can be used as markers of different water conditions. Radiolaria are aptly named: they suggest oddly shaped antennae or spiky satellites, ranging in size from 50µm (micrometres) to a few millimetres, and in colonial form to several centimetres. Other protists are the xenophyophores: large, unicellular creatures, in platters as big as 25 cm in diameter, found in profusion at some deep-water carbonate mounds (see p.58).

Swarms of nanoplankton

Completely new forms of phytoplankton in overwhelming numbers revealed themselves to science in the late twentieth century. The blue light of the new fluorescence microscope found swarms of unsuspected, glowing motes in seawater samples: hundreds of thousands in a single cubic centimetre. These were the picoplankton or nanoplankton, in sizes between one five-hundredth and one fiftieth the diameter of a human hair. They include cyanobacteria that are related to the blue-green algae, the oldest-known form of life, and are so abundant they are thought to account for half the photosynthesis of the ocean. In the same thimbleful of water could be several million even smaller bacteria, and tens of millions of viruses smaller again – invisible particles in a teeming soup of life. Bacteria live in the water column, in the guts of marine animals and even in the extreme conditions of hydrothermal vents in the deep ocean and the cold seeps of the mid-Atlantic rift valley, where they convert hydrogen sulphide into organic material for shrimps, mussels and clams. In the wider ocean they fulfil a triple role: they feed on, and break down, the organic detritus of the seabed; in the process, they release dissolved carbon into the water column; they are eaten by protozoan phytoplankton which in turn are eaten by zooplankton, thus setting up a 'microbial loop' of nutrients.

Along with dissolved minerals carried up from the depths, the spring bloom of phytoplankton needs a relatively calm and stable water column to keep the plants drifting within the glow of sunlight. As spring advances into summer on the Atlantic shelf, the sun's energy creates a sharp temperature boundary between a surface layer of some 35–40 m and the chilly depths below – at 70 m, a drop of perhaps 6 °C. This barrier is called a thermocline, and the process that creates it is stratification. The earlier in spring the calming seas allow stratification, the sooner the bloom of phytoplankton gets under way. At the same time, its effect is to seal off the warmer layer from replenishment of nutrients from below, so that the population explosion of phytoplankton, already under assault from predatory zooplankton, is slowly starved to a halt.

This interrupts the flow of food until the autumn, when falling temperatures allow the water column to mix again, fertilising fresh blooms of dinoflagellates before winter. Then storms disperse the plankton, and while patches may linger in shallow coastal waters, the luxuriant fields of micro-vegetation that covered large areas of the ocean have disappeared. The life of most phytoplankton organisms is, in any case, a brief one, measured in hours or days. Even without the turbulence of water to carry them down beyond the glow of sunlight, they die as tiny flakes of marine snow – the drifting descent of cells to the ocean floor.

The 'snowflakes' (actually more like clumps or strings) are not of dead phytoplankton alone, but of the tiny corpses of zooplankton and their faecal pellets, and dead picoplankton clustered into particles heavy enough to sink. The larger flakes may reach several centimetres across but still take weeks to reach the ocean floor. This perpetual snowfall is a familiar image in marine biology, but it has taken time-lapse photographs to show the dramatic, downward pulses of detritus that follow the massive blooms of phytoplankton in spring. In *Mapping the Deep* (2000), Robert Kunzig described the scene (recorded by a camera anchored on the floor of Ireland's Porcupine Seabight by Anthony Rice and colleagues at the British Institute of Oceanographic Sciences): 'The first pulse arrived in late June and spread out to form a small patch. Soon thereafter the pace quickened, as patch after patch rained in, covering the brown mud with overlapping tiles of dark green. The snow pooled in the furrows and pits dug by the sea-floor animals and it drifted up against the side of their mounds . . . By late July, the mud around the camera was fully carpeted in green.' This heaping plant debris, arriving still from the ocean surface, becomes the food of sea-floor animals, from brittle stars and burrowing worms to the infinitesimal bacteria. Their reprocessing of nutrients and minerals closely echoes what happens to dead plant foliage on land.

A local blooming

The seasonal timetable of phytoplankton blooms varies with the weather from year to year. But (as shown in Chapter 1) the ocean is also much more 'local' than we might suppose. Off the west of Ireland, it is governed by the interplay of water masses between the continental shelf and the wider ocean, mediated by the Shelf-edge Current. In the shallow Irish Sea, strong tidal streams control the mixing and temperature of the water. Despite plenty of nutrients, the spring bloom of phytoplankton arrives there a month later and declines two months earlier than in the open shelf areas to the north and south. Only in the sheltered and deeper northwest of the Irish Sea, between the coast of County Louth and the Isle of Man, does the water stratify to encourage a richer bloom.

Even on the Irish coasts that face the open Atlantic there are, so to speak, 'rooms within rooms' in the wide mass of the sea. The summer zone of stratification that slowly develops across the inshore shelf not only has a 'floor' above deeper, colder water, but an outer vertical boundary between the stratified water and the mixed ocean water beyond. Outside this thermal wall, or front, the summer phytoplankton are mostly small dinoflagellates; inside, there is both greater biomass and diversity of species. Even in this stratified zone, upwellings of colder, nutrient-rich water can break through the summer thermocline.

Upwellings can be deeply mysterious, lasting for several days or weeks. Sometimes they are a churning up of the water layers by strong but temporary local currents, as in the press of a spring tide (Cilian Roden, tracking the annual cycle of phytoplankton in the coastal waters of Connemara, found that all the spring and summer blooms were most developed at spring tides). Wind can also play a big part, pushing warm surface water aside so that cold water rises to take its place. But off the south coast, in particular, upwellings bring water from the seabed, 80–100 m down, producing patches of water near the coast that are several degrees colder than the water offshore. Here, the mechanism seems to lie in the westward-running coastal current of the Celtic Sea and its actions in turning the corner off Cape Clear to meet the waters of the western shelf. Its upwellings nourish a fresh burst of diatoms even in late summer, when dinoflagellates dominate elsewhere. They occur particularly near the gaunt lighthouse citadel of the Fastnet Rock and along the south coast of Cork towards Courtmac-sherry. As late as mid-August, the coves inside Roaringwater Bay can envelop the swimmer in shockingly cold water – less than 11°C, or up to 5°C colder than in a comparable bay in Connemara.

The upwellings can nourish dense blooms of phytoplankton, spreading in coloured patches near the sea surface. Wind-driven currents may carry these into bays, where their decay can use up the water's oxygen, suffocating fish and seabed animals. Some dinoflagellates form colonies that can foul beaches and fishing nets with a sticky, irritating foam. Others, far more seriously, produce potent toxins that travel through the food web, harming or killing the higher forms of life, such as seals and birds. Accumulating in filter-feeding shellfish, they can poison human consumers, producing diarrhoea or even severe symptoms of paralysis or amnesia. *Dinophysis* and *Alexandrium*, the two most troublesome toxic dinoflagellates species in Irish waters, form overwintering cysts (a dormant phase in the reproductive cycle) that accumulate on the seabed, ready to spread their cells when spring returns. A third dinoflagellate, *Protoperidinium crassipes*, once regarded as benign, was revealed by mussel experts to cause diarrhetic symptoms through azaspiracid poisoning.

Closing the bays

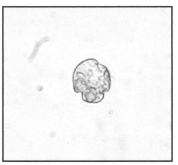

Karenia *under the microscope.*
(Marine Institute)

The problem of harmful algal blooms is common to much of the world and Ireland's Marine Institute is one of many national agencies that maintain a constant monitoring of shellfish for the presence of toxic species: several of the island's aquaculture bays have been closed to shellfish harvesting for months on end. But explosive blooms of some dinoflagellates can also cause massive damage to marine ecosystems and aquaculture by the simple profusion of their cells. One common 'red tide' species in the northeast Atlantic (and also around Japan) is *Karenia mikimotoi*, which can sometimes reach concentrations of several million cells per litre of water. They contain toxins, but also kill by suffocation and the exhaustion of the water's oxygen as they decay. In the summer of 2005, an exceptionally massive bloom of *Karenia*, lasting two months, devastated the marine life of many western Irish bays, from Cork to Donegal, killing small fish, farmed shellfish and seabed animals. Tidelines became littered with dead heart urchins, lugworms and other invertebrates.

Records of such events are piling up globally, but whether or not they have actually grown more common is still a matter of debate, since observation has intensified to match the growing importance of aquaculture. Some scientists link the apparent increase in blooms to pollution, and many of them, toxic or not, may well be fed by nitrogen and phosphate flowing out from rivers. Some small, enclosed sea inlets are suffering the same kind of eutrophication that overtook some of the larger Irish freshwater lakes, and plumes of over-enriched water, surging out from the estuaries, are carried along the coasts by local currents. Salmon farms in bays and inlets produce their own pollution (an estimated 35 kg of nitrogen and 5 kg of phosphorus per year per tonne of fish).

Climate change and local quirks of hydrography could also play a part in plankton blooms, and Cilian Roden has a further challenging proposition. He points to the gross overfishing of Ireland's oysters in the nineteenth century, which virtually extinguished the natural oyster beds that formed huge carpets of shells in many of the island's bays and estuaries. In Clew Bay, County Mayo, up to 6 million oysters a year were dredged and sent to Britain; the beds on the east coast, around Arklow, stretched for 50 km. Left alone, an oyster may live and spawn for decades; the many-layered and sculptured shells that are sometimes washed ashore come from veteran specimens. Oysters graze on phytoplankton, filtering it from the water, and their larvae join the teeming zooplankton that also feed on it. These are part of the predatory controls that regulate whole shallow-water ecosystems, and the loss of the oyster beds was a major, man-made change in the natural balance.

Zooplankton: the glass menagerie

In the ocean generally, the myriad animals of the zooplankton form a jostling glass menagerie of minute crustaceans, fish larvae, gelatinous medusae, comb jellies, salps, worms and snails. The great bulk of their numbers are tiny, shrimp-like crustaceans – copepods and krill. Most of the remainder are the 'meroplankton': animals, such as larvae of fish, molluscs or echinoderms, which swim as plankton for only part of their lives.

In the waters of the Irish shelf, copepods can account for more than nine-tenths of the dry weight of zooplankton: their numbers in the ocean are past any estimation. No bigger than a grain of rice, they stretch out long, fringed antennae to hold themselves steady in the water and use other, shorter ones to whisk single cells of phytoplankton into their mouths. This microscopic food seems not to interfere with their transparency, but some species carry bright red pigment: sieved out by the gill-rakers of a basking shark, copepods can fill its stomach with something very like tomato ketchup (Sir Alister Hardy – see below – cooked netfuls of *Calanus* copepods to make 'a pleasant shrimp paste'). Our waters also have krill, the euphausiid shrimps of zooplankton more familiar from polar oceans. While nowhere as plentiful as the krill of polar seas, they still provide food for the baleen whales and herring of the North Atlantic.

Several copepods are parasitic, sometimes fearsomely so to human eyes: a large hunting copepod, *Sphyrion lumpii*, is a parasite of the redfish and can be seen projecting from its host for 10 cm. Of some fifty species listed so far as parasites of common Irish fish, the most troublesome are those known as sea lice (*Lepeophtheirus salmonis* and *Caligus elongatus*), up to 16 mm long and the scourge of salmon farms with dense populations of fish.

As a primary prey of human food fish, the changing abundance of copepods and their drifting concentrations are of great concern to the fishing industry, and the importance of all zooplankton to the ocean's food web has made it the focus of exceptional scientific effort. The Continuous Plankton Recorder (CPR), set up by Britain's Sir Alister Hardy in 1931, is unique in marine biology for its monitoring of oceanic plankton in the North Atlantic and North Sea. On some regular sea routes of merchant ships it has maintained a virtually unbroken monthly coverage since 1948. Run now by the Sir Alister Hardy Foundation for Ocean Science in Plymouth, its network of volunteer ships from nine countries (England, Scotland, Norway, Denmark, Sweden, the Netherlands, Iceland, Canada and the US) have towed recorders for more than 4 million miles, collecting some 200,000 samples of plankton from all over the North Atlantic.

Towed at a standard depth of 7 m, the CPR traps phytoplankton and zooplankton on a moving band of silk gauze that is slowly wound into a tank of preserving formalin. In the laboratory, the gauze is cut into sections, each representing the plankton from 3 m³ of water taken during 18 km of tow. These

A plankton sampler towed at the sea surface.
(Marine Institute)

are all assessed for the 'greenness index' – a measure of the amount of chlorophyll present – and then up to 450 species are identified and counted on each alternate sample. The data then nourish an Atlas of plankton abundance and species. They have also shown that different water masses have different communities of plankton, both from south to north and from the open ocean to the continental shelf. The huge number of samples also helps to even out the effects of the vertical migration of many zooplankton species during the 24-hour period. Most commonly, these spend the day in deep water and rise at night to feed in warmer, food-rich water near the surface: a migration through perhaps 100 m of depth. They may all move up and down together in a narrow band, or spread at night through the whole water column: the net benefit from their behaviour is still being explored.

Plankton and climate change

Dramatic year-to-year variations in the abundance of zooplankton can occur throughout the Irish shelf and the Irish Sea, depending on swings in sea surface temperature, the stress of winds and changes in the North Atlantic Oscillation. This is the atmospheric phenomenon that powerfully influences the prevailing weather of the North Atlantic (see p.23). When strong westerly winds stir up and mix the ocean's surface layer, the turbulence can hold back the spring phytoplankton bloom and affect the subsequent abundance of copepods. The long-term dataset of the CPR has also shown, however, the mounting impact of climate change. Over the past forty years in the northeast Atlantic, cold-

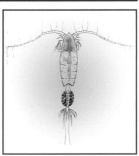

Calanus finmarchicus
(under the microscope),
a northern species in retreat.
(NOAA Photo Library)

water species of plankton – both phytoplankton and zooplankton – have retreated northwards and warm-water species have moved after them. And while climate change has given phytoplankton a longer growing season and greater abundance in the North Atlantic, a long-term decline in zooplankton has worrying implications for the ocean's pelagic life. Around Ireland it is most marked to the north and west of the island, but it is general to the North Atlantic: in 1996, the CPR survey showed an all-time low in recorded levels of zooplankton. The changes have especially affected the local abundance and distribution of two of the larger copepods, *Calanus finmarchicus* (a northern species) and *C. helgolandicus* (a southern species). *C. finmarchicus*, which has been far the more abundant of the two, overwinters in densely packed numbers in the cold water at 600 m off the edge of the continental shelf, and rises to the surface in early spring as the phytoplankton begins to reproduce.

The regime shift that is overtaking the ocean's primary production of food, the threat of toxic species to Ireland's burgeoning aquaculture, and the significance of plankton for the trend in climate – all have brought urgent study to the identification and tracking of phytoplankton populations and the ocean conditions that nourish them. Monitoring by sea is difficult and costly, and marine microbiologists of the Martin Ryan Institute at NUI Galway are involved in a different approach. The EU BICOLOR project has been seeking a way of using optical instruments to analyse the light in, and reflected from, the sea's surface so that it reveals the types and quantities of phytoplankton present, even without the colour change of an obvious algal bloom. Such detection could provide an early warning system of crucial value to the expanding industry.

Swimmers and drifters: jellies and others

The by-the-wind sailor (Velella velella)
(Courtesy of Bobby Gray)

The Greek word *planktos* (or 'wandering') has been used by scientists to gather into plankton all the drifting or floating creatures of the sea. But there is something incongruous in marshalling gelatinous animals, 1 m across, into the misty legions of microscopic life that 'plankton' means to most ordinary minds. Besides, the jellyfish, in their various classes and kinds, are taking on a rather new image in today's ocean. In a marine system gravely disrupted by overfishing, they have become, whatever their passivity, an ecological force to be reckoned with; even, in some instances, to be feared.

Between July and November of 1992, and again in 2006, the tidelines of the west coast became continuous, glittering ribbons of wrecked jellyfish medusae. These were not, however, the familiar glass paperweights and lampshades of *Aurelia* or *Chrysaora* jellyfish, but the small floats of the by-the-wind sailor (*Velella velella*). Millions of them marked out the highest reach of the tide and piled into dense drifts in gullies and pools. Such mass strandings were, as the *Irish Naturalists' Journal* noted, 'extraordinary occurrences'. But *Velella* arrives on Ireland's Atlantic shores in most years, with varying abundance and at random times of year. It is also among the more intriguing of the ocean's gelatinous coelenterates – the 'jellies', whose very substance can seem so simple.

Velella is technically not a jellyfish – that is, a single invertebrate animal. Like its giant pelagic relative, the Portuguese man-of-war (*Physalia physalis*), it is one of the siphonophores: each an elongated, joined-up colony of individual organisms, or zooids. The surface-drifters among them are well known and have popular names, but most types are found in depths where sheer fragility resists their retrieval in a plankton net. Trailing long curtains of fishing tentacles, lit up sporadically with bioluminescence (see p.80), they are among the most abundant and formidable carnivores in the sea.

One of the mid-water species is the pinky-white pearl-chain jellyfish, *Apolemia uvaria*, seen by divers off Ireland's southwest coast (and sometimes in pieces around the sea caves of County Clare). Its stem has a chain of polyps that may be more than 20 m long.

Compared with such a creature, *Velella* is a dainty miniature. Its float is a blue, gas-filled, oval disc perhaps less than 8 cm across. A triangular flap stands up from it, translucent, rainbow-tinted, and set diagonally across as a sail. Around the rim of the disc hangs a short skirt of stubby tentacles. These stabilise the disc against the pull of the wind, but they are also individual fishing zooids with stinging cells. They pass food to a central feeding zooid suspended underneath the float and this is set in a ring of reproductive zooids, also individuals in the colony. Little of this undercarriage, as a rule, survives its journey ashore. It may have been grazed off by one of its pelagic predators (such as the bubble-raft snail *Janthina* (see p.100) or indicate mortality at a good distance from land. In mass strandings on Cornish and Welsh coasts in 2002 – even more abundant than the earlier Irish event – some *Velella* arrived not only alive, but fit to release infant medusae (each a multiple offspring of a single fertilised egg).

One distinction of *Velella* has proved a perennial tease: why should millions of them have their sails mounted on a NW–SE axis across the float while millions more are set NE–SW? Blown before the wind, each axis pulls the float a different way: the first to the left by as much as 60°, the second to the right (the angle arises because water-drag and wind rotate the float, causing it to sail across the wind). While both forms occur commonly in the North Atlantic, left-sailers predominate in Irish waters, where westerly winds bring Velella northwards from tropical and sub-tropical seas (in a sample collected by the authors from Thallabawn strand in 1992, there were 228 left-sailers and 42 right-sailers). Among the millions of *Velella* cast up on America's Pacific coast, right-sailers are in the majority. This sorting of the species by prevailing winds presumably disperses it to a pattern and density that maximise its survival and reproduction.

Portuguese man-of-war with powerful stinging cells. (Islands in the Stream Expedition 2002. NOAA Office of Ocean Exploration)

In the Portuguese man-of-war, the colonial organisation of *Velella* is writ large. The iridescent, blue-and-pink float is a gas-filled balloon (mostly carbon monoxide) up to 30 cm long. The trailing tentacles, studded with notoriously powerful stinging cells, may stretch up to 20 m. Unlike *Velella*, the colony has some control over its movements by manipulating its crest, pumping it up or deflating it to affect the speed of drift. Returning a stranded *Physalia* to the sea (carefully, from a bucket), Rachel Carson was struck by its almost sentient exertions, 'visibly adjusting the shape and position of the sail as it scudded along before the wind.' Yet winds, currents and eddies still largely determine the voyages of the men-of-war, whether herding them together in the Gulf Stream or sweeping them ashore. In autumn 1968, around a thousand were stranded on beaches on Cape Clear Island off west Cork, in company with thousands of by-the-wind sailors.

The true jellyfish

The medusae of true jellyfish, the Scyphozoa, such as the moon jellies (*Aurelia aurita*) common across the world's oceans, are individual animals with no brain but an elementary nervous network. At the margin of the bell are spots sensitive to light and chemical 'scent'. Like sea anemones and coral polyps, jellyfish have a radial, flower-like plan that allows them to react to food or danger from any direction, and most share in the ability to sting, some very powerfully, with nematocysts on trailing tentacles. Oral arms – four to eight of them – carry food captured by the tentacles to the mouth centred on the underside.

Delivered to the tideline, moon jellies have usually lost both their four oral arms and the frill of short, thread-like tentacles that hang from the edge of the bell. Still prominent, however, are the four crescent-shaped purple spots clustered around the centre. Either way, these are the gonads or reproductive organs: ovaries in the female jellies, testes in the male. Sexual separation is another big difference from the hermaphroditic siphonophores – as, indeed, is a life cycle that settles most Scyphozoa on the seabed for part of their lives.

In the breeding season, sperm shed into the sea by the male are attracted to females and swim in through the mouth for internal fertilisation. When the eggs hatch, the young free-swimming planulae, powered by beating cilia, emerge by the same route to join the plankton. They shortly drift down to the seabed and attach themselves as hydroids, or polyps. In the following spring, they grow buds of tiny new medusae, like a stack of saucers that lift off to pulse upwards in the water column. The remarkable Maude Delap, rearing jellyfish in aquariums in her Valentia conservatory in the early 1900s, made a significant contribution in matching particular medusae to their polyps.

Moon jelly against the light: the pink rings are the reproductive organs. (Nigel Motyer)

Jellyfish have no gas-filled floats, but keep their neutral buoyancy (and thus their elegance) by regulating the chemistry of the bell. This has an outer skin and a lower layer that lines the digestive cavity. In between is a thick layer of gel, the mesoglea, reinforced with elastic fibres. Domed jellyfish swim in short bursts of jet propulsion: muscle at the edge of the bell contracts to squeeze the water through a narrowed aperture, while the fibres in the mesoglea pull it back to refill. In larger, flatter species, the umbrella is too wide to produce a jet, but the bell walls ripple to produce a gentler, more constant, rowing motion. The swifter pulses of jet-swimmers contact more prey but at a higher cost in energy; rowing produces vortices in the water that pulls a steady supply of small but nutritious zooplankton towards the trailing tentacles.

Among the five kinds of pelagic jellyfish found regularly and commonly in Irish waters, the moon jelly is least reliant on elaborate fishing tackle. Its

Compass jellyfish, of Art Deco opulence. (Nigel Motyer)

mouth-arms reach out to the edge of the bell to scrape off small planktonic creatures (baby barnacles and crabs among them) that have stuck to its mucus like insects to flypaper. The other four regular species have trailing organs which can cause human swimmers varying degrees of pain. A single tentacle can have hundreds or thousands of nematocysts embedded in the epidermis, each of which can uncoil a stinging thread that acts as a tiny harpoon. It is triggered through contact and injects a toxin designed to paralyse or kill small prey. Since pressure alone is what fires the harpoons, a freshly stranded jellyfish – or even pieces of tentacle – may need to be treated with caution.

The frequent strandings of moon jellies are often accompanied by the larger, more colourful compass jellyfish (*Chrysaora hysoscella*) whose radiating brown pattern gives it the opulence of an Art Deco lampshade. Maude Delap reared one from a planula in a bell jar, taking notes of its development and nutritional needs. It must have felt cramped by the end, since it grows to more than 30 cm, with long frilly mouth-arms and trailing tentacles that can sting like a nettle, especially if they brush the human eye.

About the same size or smaller, but deep blue to purple and with many long stinging tentacles is *Cyanea lamarckii*. Its more northerly relative, the lion's mane (*Cyanea capillata*) is one of the largest jellyfish in Irish waters, with a reddish-brown bell ranging up to 80 cm across and a formidable forest of very long, lion-coloured tentacles. It is a continuous rower, living on small fish, and can move at several kilometres per hour with the aid of ocean currents. It is particularly prevalent around Ireland and Britain and often washes ashore in pieces, as it did abundantly on County Dublin beaches in 2006. Both species of *Cyanea* are known to attract baby cod and whiting (perhaps 2 cm long) which seem able to treat the powerfully stinging tentacles as a sheltering structure.

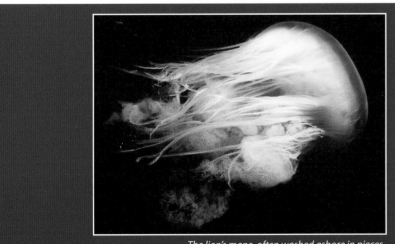

The lion's mane, often washed ashore in pieces.
(NOAA Photo Library)

The barrel jellyfish (*Rhizostoma octopus* or *pulmo*) – also known as the blubber or dustbin-lid jellyfish – is another very large, solid-looking species, occasionally reaching 90 cm across. It has no tentacles fringing its bell: the stinging cells are on the eight arms instead, which fuse together as the animal grows, into a lobed spongy structure like lung-tissue (hence, on occasion *pulmo*, but the eight arms currently favour *octopus* as the suffix). It is another jellyfish with companions: young horse mackerel swim with it, and a pelagic crustacean, the amphipod *Hyperia galba*, spends the summer tucked inside the umbrella.

The substantial *Rhizostoma* is the favourite prey of the great leatherback turtle (*Dermochelys coriacea*), which regularly migrates northwards to Irish waters in summer to feed. As part of the Irish Sea Leatherback Turtle Project (see p.167), the first major research into jellyfish populations off Ireland has studied the distribution of the five regular species, using shoreline surveys, counts from ships, and from low-flying aircraft. It covered almost 8,000 km² of the Celtic and Irish Seas. These shallowing waters of the continental shelf, with strong tidal flows, complex stratifications and areas of mixing, provide a mosaic of marine environments. One striking implication of the research is that the different jellyfish species can have specific distributions and that, to quote one paper from the project, 'their occurrence in particular areas is not as passive as once thought.' A dramatic example was the discovery of consistent, summer-to-summer hot spots of *Rhizostoma* in three bays: Rosslare Harbour in County Wexford, and Tremadog and Carmarthen Bays on the coast of Wales. Huge numbers of the jellyfish extend at times over tens of square kilometres and reach densities of one per square metre. Hardly surprisingly, the Welsh bays at least, are well known for the sighting of feeding leatherbacks.

The scientific team of the Turtle Project also took advantage of their survey flights above the Irish and Celtic Seas to note the abundance of another notable predator on jellyfish, the sunfish (*Mola mola*), widely regarded as a quite rare and solitary wanderer in these waters. The total spotted over the three summers was sixty-eight, which, though still modest, greatly outnumbered the leatherback turtles. The team have drawn attention to high levels of by-catch of sunfish by drift gillnets in the Mediterranean and swordfish longliners off California: a factor which may have greater ecological consequences than might be supposed.

Such aggregations of jellyfish have yet to be fully explained. Like all drifting coelenterates, jellyfish tend to be gathered by currents and gyres, sometimes into very large rafts, or into long lines where currents meet at a front. They may throng bays rich in their plankton food – but the same waves and winds can have brought both together. Alternatively, rafts may result from the concurrent hatching of medusae from mature seabed polyps – an occasional event especially noticeable in *Aurelia* in sheltered waters.

Far beyond such natural gatherings, jellyfish are sometimes reaching plague proportions in various parts of the world. Indeed, there have been serious warnings that the combined effects of climate change, overfishing and coastal eutrophication could cause some ecosystems to become dominated by them, even as relatively passive predators.

Carried north in millions, Pelagia noctiluca *enveloped an Irish salmon farm.*
(Nigel Motyer)

An elegant salp off an Irish coast.
(Nigel Motyer)

Jellyfish feed both on fish larvae and the zooplankton that nourishes them, and concern about their future abundance prompts closer study of their effect on the ocean's food chain.

The most dramatic examples of population explosions have been remote from Ireland. Among them, great blooms of the giant Japanese jellyfish (*Nemopilema nomurai*), 2 m across and 200 kg in weight, have been choking the nets of fishermen in the Sea of Japan. Off Namibia, in southwest Africa, in waters heavily fished for sardines and anchovies, the biomass of jellyfish is now estimated to exceed the total weight of commercial fish stocks.

In the northeast Atlantic, all projections warn of an increase in jellyfish, especially in years when high pressure zones centred on the Azores bring warmer water northwards. In the late autumn of 2007, under just such conditions, billions of *Pelagia noctiluca* (the purple stinger – a small, luminous and waspishly-stinging southern jellyfish) were carried to Irish waters. Some drifting flotillas were noted off western coasts, but the jellyfish were also carried into the Irish Sea in unprecedented numbers. Concentrated by currents and a change of winds, they formed a dense mass reportedly 10 m deep and covering more than 20 km² off Glenarm Bay, County Antrim. Here, they enveloped Northern Ireland's only salmon farm and caused the deaths of its entire stock of over 100,000 fish.

Even fragments of stinging species, or newly hatched medusae passing through the gills, can do substantial harm. Great mortalities were sustained by salmon farms in the Outer Hebrides in 2002, caused by clouds of three little-known and minuscule species of pelagic hydrozoan abundant in the ocean's middle depths. Such events have prompted a nine-nation project called EUROGEL, to explore 'key factors regulating the abundance and succession of jellyplankton species in European waters.' 'Jellyplankton' is shorthand for 'gelatinous zooplankton', a realm of ocean life which reaches far beyond the jellyfish forms familiar from beach strandings. Within the class of hydrozoans, the subclass of hydromedusae includes tiny (even microscopic), transparent, yet potentially toxic medusae. Their already bewildering variety is joined in warm and tropical waters, by a wide range of pelagic, gelatinous tunicates, or salps.

Luminescent comb jellies

Even in the North Atlantic, however, there are jellyfish-like animals sufficiently different to be classed separately; they do not have a polyp or medusa stage in their development, nor do they have stinging cells. These are the comb jellies of the phylum Ctenophora (literally meaning 'comb-bearing' from Greek *ktenos* for comb). They are generally spherical or elliptical, transparent or palely coloured, and propel themselves gently with eight rows of iridescent cilia, like combs, that run the length of the animal. They are also luminescent in darkness, and some will light up in bright blue or green when disturbed. Most are only a few centimetres in diameter, like the tentacled sea gooseberry *Pleurobranchia pileus*. This is sometimes so numerous around Ireland in autumn that it gets trapped in rock pools, where it may light up in 'elusive moonbeam flashes', to borrow from Rachel Carson's *The Edge of the Sea*.

Ctenophores as large as footballs have been found in the deep ocean. They are voracious carnivores, feeding on other drifting animals, especially copepods and other zooplankton. They have no brain but a network of nerve endings on their outer skin, and some catch their prey with sticky, trailing tentacles. Others, without tentacles (Nuda) swallow their prey whole, or cut it up with their cilia. *Beroe cucumis*, about 5 cm long, pinkish, and shaped somewhat like a bishop's mitre, is the only Nuda species found so far in Irish waters, where it feeds voraciously on other comb jellies.

Raft-makers: snails and barnacles

Janthina *drifts with its eggs beneath a raft of bubbles.* (Don Cotton)

Among the drift-animals of the ocean's surface arriving at Ireland's tidelines, snails and barnacles seem, at first, unlikely: how do they manage to float? The violet sea snail (*Janthina janthina*) creates its own raft, blowing bubbles of mucus that trap the wind and harden into something like cellophane. Suspended upside down (as we would see it), *Janthina* drifts in the hope of collision with its principal prey, the by-the-wind sailor (*Velella velella*). It protects itself meanwhile, by the countershading of its shell, the violet paling almost to white as seen from below. *Janthina* and *Velella* sometimes arrive ashore still in each other's company, though the snail's beautiful, fragile shell is now usually mysteriously empty and the *Velella* shorn of its suspended tentacles. Significant strandings of *Janthina* occurred on western shorelines in 2007.

The pelagic, drifting barnacles are stalked. Some, such as the goose-necked barnacle (*Lepas anatifera*) attach themselves as free-swimming larvae to flotsam such as logs and plastic fish boxes, while others, such as the buoy barnacle (*Dosima fascicularis*), secrete a spongy, white float like a misshapen table tennis ball, to which several animals may contribute. Both kinds of stalked barnacle may hitch a ride on small masses of crude oil which have weathered and hardened into tar-balls.

The association of *Lepas anatifera* with geese (Anatidae are the family of birds that includes geese) reaches back to early natural history. The twelfth-century scholar Giraldus Cambrensis encouraged,

A drifting log carried these goose-necked barnacles to a Sligo strand.
(Ciaran Maguire)

but did not invent, the idea that the migratory geese appearing so mysteriously on Ireland's winter shores were hatched from the stalked barnacles growing on drift timber: he had seen a thousand of the 'small, bird-like creatures' (this, perhaps, from their feathery feeding appendages) hanging from a single log! A more truthful association of the barnacles with birds is that they are an important food source for gulls.

The Beauty of Blaschka

Blaschka model of a radiolarian microscopic, single-celled plankton, Autosphaera elegantissima.
(Courtesy of Natural History Museum)

Elegant and exquisitely colourful as they may be in the sea, anemones, tubeworms and most other marine invertebrates quickly lose their beauty and form in jars of preserving fluid. But in 1878 the staff of the Natural History Museum in Dublin found a solution to filling the gaps in their marine collection. They heard of the glass models superbly crafted by Leopold and Rudolf Blaschka, the Dresden father and son whose remarkable art was fast becoming famous beyond Germany.

The Blaschka family could trace its origins to the glass craftsmen of fifteenth-century Venice: a tradition now brought to a portfolio of more than 700 marine animals, executed on commission for the natural history museums of the world. Incredibly perfect in every minute detail, even in the microscopic forms of radiolarians, they captured natural beauty for science and, even today, photographs of the models can be mistaken for the living animals.

Over a decade, the Dublin museum bought 530 models from the Blaschkas, of which more than 400 have survived. It is one of the largest collections in the world and in 2006 was the focus of the Dublin Blaschka Congress, drawing international workers in science, history and art. The Natural History Museum will use its present reconstruction to give the glass models an even more bewitching display. See also p.67.

CHAPTER 6

Fish and Fisheries

Pollack.
(Courtesy of NOAA Photo Library)

The tail-end of a Caribbean hurricane once left the strand below us littered from end to end with scores of washed-up fish. They were species from the rocky ground out towards the islands: muscular conger eels (*Conger conger*), tiny goldsinny wrasse (*Ctenolabrus rupestris*), and black tadpole fish (*Raniceps raninus*) that only divers see. Others we gathered for the freezer: pollack (*Pollachius pollachius*), saithe (*Pollachius virens*) and a few young ling (*Molva molva*). A marine scientist friend thought they had drowned from the shock of a sudden change in temperature as masses of water were overturned offshore. Disparate in size and colour, they all had a long, slender, round body shaped for swimming through rock crevices or between the crowded stems of kelp. Habitat and lifestyle are largely what sculpt a fish, from the jawless, snake-like lampreys and hagfish (the latter with the ghoulish role of devouring the ocean's larger corpses) to the streamlined giants of predatory pursuit.

The 1,250-odd species listed for the northeast Atlantic belong to 600 genera and 220 families, but their main taxonomic division is between those with cartilaginous skeletons (Chondrichthyes) and the bony or vertebrate fish, the teleosts (Osteichthyes). The present-day teleosts evolved around 200 million years ago, long before mammals or hominids appeared on the planet. The most obvious thing that sets fish apart from invertebrates is, of course, the jointed backbone or spine of cartilage. Along with sheltering the central nervous system and anchoring a muscular skeleton, the backbone makes possible the undulatory waves that give swimming its thrust and speed. In the typical roving hunter – such as a tuna or swordfish (*Xiphias gladius*) – the fins of a torpedo-like body are spaced for manoeuvring after prey. A tail forked like an arrowhead sheds the drag of water. Other predators count on explosive acceleration with the help of thrust from strong fins mounted at the rear.

Buoyancy within

Most bony fish depend for their buoyancy on control of an internal swim bladder, mounted amidships below the backbone and taking up about 5 per cent of their volume. They use it to maintain neutral buoyancy, saving the energy that would otherwise be spent in trying not to sink. A special gas gland regulates an exchange of oxygen between the bladder and the blood, inflating the bladder to a constant volume whatever the depth and pressure. Among the cartilaginous fish, the elasmobranchs – sharks, dogfish, skates and rays – never evolved a swim bladder. The first two gain some lift by a hydrostatic design in which the forward fins can act as elevators and a raised tail gives an upward and forward thrust. In the bottom-living skates and rays, the fins have become wings and their rippling undulations produce swimming that becomes a sort of underwater flight.

Sharks may also rely for buoyancy on a high content of hydrocarbon oil (squalene) found in their very big livers. Basking sharks (*Cetorhinus maximus*) were once killed in large numbers for this oil – initially to burn for lamplight and later for its exceptional lubrication. The lack of a swim bladder can have advantages in species that change water levels rapidly (in dashes after prey or to avoid being eaten), since too drastic an expansion of the bladder can rupture it. Without it, fish must keep swimming in order not to sink, but this perpetual motion has its own compensation since it also pushes more water – and oxygen – over the gills.

The mackerel (*Scomber scombrus*) is another fish without a bladder but with a dazzling turn of speed. It is pursued by some of the fastest creatures in the ocean, including its giant relative, the tuna. It can reach more than 32 kph, and the fish in some fast-moving schools accelerate to more than 25 body-lengths per second. For a good portion of the year, the mackerel gains some buoyancy by the oil stored throughout its body. This builds up through a summer of voracious feeding on smaller fish to reach a peak of some 30 per cent in autumn, when a trawler's catch of mackerel may actually tend to float. In his chronicle of coastal life, *The Shores of Connemara*, Séamas Mac an Iomaire describes sailing a *púcán* after mackerel and noting 'a heavy odour of oil from a smooth slick to the west' where gulls and gannets were diving. The oil becomes an energy reserve for survival through lean winters, when mackerel idle near the bottom in deep water far offshore.

Touching at a distance: the senses of fish

Nearly all fish can see, hear and smell, sometimes with great acuity. Their eyes are very similar to those of land vertebrates, alert to a broad range of wavelengths depending on the strength of light. The ability to look right and left at the same time makes up for the lack of a swivelling neck, and fish also have no general need for eyelids, since their eyes are washed by water, which also modulates the strength of sunlight. The eyes of species in the twilight zone between 200–1,000 m tend to be strikingly large and highly sensitive, and several families have long, narrow, upward-pointing tubular eyes that enhance light gathering and binocular vision. Many fish at these depths and below produce their own light for a variety of uses (see p.80), and others living on the totally dark deep seabed still have large functional eyes, probably to feed among the large variety of organisms that produce biological light, such as sea lilies, brittle stars, and sea cucumbers.

In the brighter illumination of shallow water many bony fish have excellent colour vision that comes into play in bodily mating signals. Some are sensitive to ultraviolet light, and salmon and anchovies can even detect polarised light. Like humans, fish have rods and/or cones in their eyes: rods enable them to see bright light as white, and the absence of light as black, with shades of grey in between; cones are necessary to see colour. While a good many sharks have rods and cones in their eyes, their appreciation of colour is still unproven. Many shallow-water sharks can regulate the amount of light entering their eyes by dilating or contracting their pupils just as people do. In some skates and rays, a contraction of the pupil into a horseshoe-shaped slit helps in determining distance, and others slide a flap of skin over the pupil in a squint with similar purpose. In place of functional eyelids, some sharks have a nictitating (or winking) membrane that protects the eye during feeding (others roll their eyes back in their sockets).

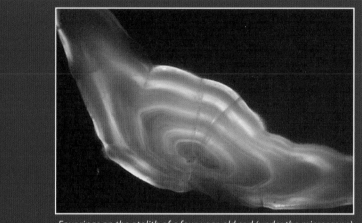
Four rings on the otolith of a four-year-old cod (under the microscope).
(Courtesy of Marine Institute)

Most bony fish have keen hearing and many use sound in communication, but they have no outer ears or eardrums to receive sound vibrations. These are carried by the body tissues to an inner ear on each side of the head and picked up by hard, free-moving ear-stones, suspended in fluid, called otoliths. These have a second function in the fish, generating signals that help to keep its upright balance in the water, but they also feature prominently in the science of fishery stock assessment: otoliths acquire winter rings that can be counted under the microscope as a reliable measure of a fish's age. In another aid to hearing, many bony fish, such as herring, have modified gas bladders and swim bladders next to the inner ear: gas bubbles increase sensitivity to sound.

As in vertebrates ashore, a fish's sense of smell is fused with that of taste, but olfaction is more sensitive and chemically specific. Taste buds are scattered around the lips and mouth, but nares, located like nostrils on top of the head, are what pick up the chemical pheromones so vital to fish communication and behaviour. The sense of smell in sharks is notoriously acute: their receptor cells can detect fish extracts in concentrations lower than one part in a billion. Once a shark picks up a scent trail it follows it by moving its head from side to side as it swims. If the scent is lost or if the slick of molecules is too wide to use for navigation, it may swim forward in an exaggerated S pattern until it can pick up the direction again. But chemical pheromones are linked to much more than potential prey or carrion. Secreted by one fish and picked up by another, they carry messages about species, sex and hierarchy and information about habitats, as in the ability of homing salmon to recognise their natal rivers.

An invaluable 'distant touch' sense in almost all fish is the system embodied in the lateral line inscribed in each side of the animal and sometimes, as in the cod (*Gadus morhua*), drawn conspicu-ously in white. It is actually a canal in which lies a series of sensory cells called neuromasts. Little hairs on the cells project into the canal, which is open to the surrounding water through tiny pores. Any disturbance of water or low frequency vibration impinges on the hairs and stimulates nerve impulses from the neuromasts to the brain. These act as close-quarter radar, helping in navigation, perhaps in clouded water, or signal the presence of nearby prey or predators (in skates and rays, a network of lateral lines on the underside can pick up movements and water-jets from bivalves and other buried animals). The signals also help in the close formation of schooling fish, keeping each in optimal position to avoid turbulence. In the deep sea too, fish, such as orange roughy, have highly developed acoustic pores on their heads and sides, and the elongated bodies of many deep species improve the precision and range of the sense.

Electricity: fields of betrayal

A variety of bony fish have developed the ability to use electricity to send out signals or aid navigation in cloudy waters. The thornback ray (*Raja clavata*), for example, can generate 4 volts (though nothing quite like the 'flashing skate' described by Séamas Mac an Iomaire: that finds its way through kelp forests by 'the light shining from its eyes'). Weak electrical currents emitted by organs and muscles can, however, betray concealed fish to their predators. Sharks can notoriously detect the electrical fields generated by other, distant animals, notably as they contract their muscles in swimming or when wounded. Dogfish, like rays, can pick up fields created by flatfish passively concealed in sand. The source of this eerie ability lies in canals in the skin along the lateral line and in highly sensitive receptors around the mouth and snout. Here they are called, rather grandly, the ampullae of Lorenzini, who first described them in 1678. The number of nerves devoted to them suggest they are at least as important to elasmobranchs as their eyes and ears. In the basking shark, this special sense may extend even to detection of muscle activity in tiny copepod zooplankton.

A final note on the varied array of sensing abilities in fish is, perhaps, offered by the deep-sea tripod fish (*Bathypterois grallator*), that prefers to rely on directness of touch. Having only tiny eyes, it spreads sensitive fin rays (up to 1 m long) like radio antennae or the legs of a tripod, to 'stand' on the ocean floor, waiting for crustacean prey to bump into them.

Different levels, different lives

In the ecological layering of the ocean, the zone from 1,000–4,000 m down, which includes almost all deep-sea life, is called the bathypelagic. From the surface to 200 m down – the realm of useful light – is the epipelagic. In between (200–1,000 m) is the twilight zone of the mesopelagic. Beyond their main differences in shape – round-bodied, deep-bodied or flat – groups of fish spend most of their lives at different levels in the ocean. Some are benthic or demersal, living on or near the sea floor; others are pelagic, hunting or feeding in the water column. Most of the seabed's invertebrate marine life is, to a large extent, a dinner table for the demersal fish – just as, indeed, most little fish are food for bigger ones, and fish eggs and larvae of all kinds are food for marine invertebrates and vertebrates alike.

Demersal fish (often referred to as 'white fish') live at or near the seabed. They can be divided into a number of groups. Flatfish include sole, plaice, megrim and lemon sole. The term 'roundfish' generally refers to fish belonging to the cod family (gadoids), such as cod, whiting and haddock, but also includes hake. Demersal fish that do not fit into either of these categories include monk/angler-fish and John Dory. Elasmobranchs (sharks, skates and rays) can be either pelagic or demersal.

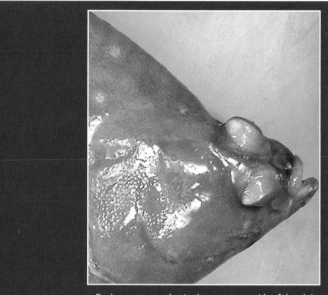

During metamorphosis, the eye on one side of the plaice migrates over the head and comes to rest close to the other. (Courtesy of Marine Institute)

Fish living on the seabed show several special adaptations. Flatfish, for example, start out round as pelagic larvae but later flatten out and settle on one side on the bottom (most North Atlantic species choose the left side). During this metamorphosis, the eye on one side migrates over the head and comes to rest close to the other. Both are now raised from the uppermost side, swivelling independently as the fish lies lightly buried in the sediment. A nineteenth-century naturalist, Frank Buckland, described a manoeuvre of concealment so rapid:

> [It] must be seen to be believed. The plaice lifts up its head and the upper third of its body and then brings it down on the sand three or four times with sharp, quick raps; a small cavity is thus made in the soft, wet sand, which at once fills with water; the fish

then works its fins on each side of its body with such a rapid motion that they seem almost to vibrate. These combined efforts enable the fish to conceal itself almost quicker than the eye can follow, and nothing can be seen but its eye, which is of a lovely emerald colour.

Such camouflage is further improved as the exposed side of most maturing flatfish takes on the colour of its seabed surroundings; the underside remains white and sensitive to prey movement through its lateral line.

Of the twenty-two flatfish species living in Irish waters, some half-dozen have familiar common names: plaice (*Pleuronectes platessa*); flounder (*Platichthys flesus*); dab (*Limanda limanda*); sole (*Solea solea*); brill (*Scophthalmus rhombus*); turbot (*Scophthalmus maximus*); halibut (*Hippoglossus hippoglossus*). The last is the giant among flatfish, at a potential 2.5 m, and feeds on smaller fish, sometimes in very deep water where it can find the low temperatures that it prefers.

Halibut on a restaurant menu is now more likely to be the much smaller, allied species, Greenland halibut (*Reinhardtius hippoglossoides*); it is dark coloured on both sides as if it has not quite decided on its lifestyle, and fished mainly in colder waters north of Ireland. As plaice and sole succumb to fishing pressures, similar but unfamiliar flatfish find their way to market. Notable among them is megrim (*Lepidorhombus whiffiagonis*), a species from the deeper slopes of the continental shelf. It lacks the fine flavour of plaice and is easily damaged in handling, but is an increasingly valuable by-catch for Irish trawlers off the west and south coasts exporting to markets in Spain and France.

In Britain, the elongated oval of the witch or pole dab (*Glyptocephalus cynoglossus*) has been presented at the fish counter as 'Torbay sole'. In the true sole family, the common, 'black' or 'Dover' sole are all *Solea solea*, living inshore around both islands and basically brown (with a black spot on one fin) but a master of camouflage whatever the shade of seabed. The 'lemon' sole (*Microstomus kitt*) is not a sole at all but more of a burly dab, sometimes blotched with pink if living over rocks encrusted with the rosy *Lithothamnion* algae.

Batoids with wings

The bottom-living elasmobranchs, such as rays, skates and angel sharks (known collectively as batoids) are more truly flat fish, being vertically compressed rather than just lying on their sides. Their pectoral fins are greatly extended into wings and completely fused to the head and body, and the lack of a swim bladder means that they sink to the bottom once they stop moving. But they are equally at home on the sands of inshore shallows and in abyssal depths, feeding on all kinds of bottom animals. There is no biological difference between the diamond-shaped rays and skates, but the latter have a long, pointed snout, rather than a bluntly-rounded one, and can grow to 2 m or more. Unlike flatfish, the mouth of the benthic elasmobranchs is on the underside, well back from the nose. Many species of batoid feed on shellfish, which they uncover by flapping their wings against the seabed, and crush with flat block-shaped teeth.

Thornbacks are the most abundant rays in Irish inshore waters, down to some 300 m, with specimen records (above 9 kg) concentrated on the east and south coasts. But seven ray species figure in commercial catches (blonde, spotted, cuckoo and painted are among the names, prompted by their back patterns). The slow-growing common skate (*Raja batis*), was overfished to near-extinction from the Irish Sea by the later decades of the twentieth century, but still appears in catches off the west and south coasts. Catch-and-release sea anglers at Valentia, County Kerry, and Clew Bay, County Mayo occasionally raise skate to match the old specimens weighing more than 54 kg.

Skate. (Courtesy of NOAA Photo Library)

As the thornback demonstrates, rays are commonly equipped at least with prickles or, indeed, stout sharp thorns curving up from the skin. Lacking scales, the skin is often coated with mucus, thought to ease the laminar flow of water in swimming and also to help prevent infection (there is research into its potential for new antibiotic compounds). Electric shocks that make fishermen cautious of handling batoids in their catch come from the Torpedinidae family, related to the true rays and skates but with rounded, disc-like bodies and a fleshy tail with a prominent fin. The electric ray (*Torpedo nobiliana*), reported at regular intervals around the Irish coast, uses shocks of up to 220 volts at 8 amps to stun its prey. In her handbook, *British Sea Fishes* (1987), Frances Dipper notes that 'Fishermen have been known to receive a shock from their line even before seeing what they have

Thornback ray. (Courtesy of Exploris Aquarium, Portaferry)

Anglerfish. (Courtesy of Marine Institute)

hooked!' and Séamas Mac an Iomaire recalls 'a sudden sting in my arm as if I had pins and needles running up my shoulder. My hand shook so much that the ray was shaken off the hook.'

Among the bottom-dwelling or demersal species of high commercial value, the name 'monkfish' has been appropriated by the fishing industry as a marketing pseudonym for the muscular, well-flavoured tail of the majestically ugly anglerfish (*Lophius piscatorius*). Its hugely wide mouth, fenced with backward-curving teeth, awaits fish intrigued by the 'lure' dangled on a filament in front of it. The angler lies half-buried in sediment, camouflaged not only by mottled colours but by a fringe of skin-tags that wave to and fro in the current like fronds of seaweed. The original monkfish – the angel shark (*Squatina squatina*) – is a flattened, bottom-feeding elasmobranch; itself quite a bizarre shape, like a cubist guitar, but nowhere near as inventive as the angler and seen by scientists as an evolutionary link between the shark and the rays. The warm shallows of Tralee Bay and Clew Bay are favoured Irish habitats.

Among the round fish of soft seabeds there are a few, such as the eel-like red band fish (*Cepola rubescens*) and snake blenny (*Lumpenus lampraetiformis*), that excavate substantial burrow systems with shafts up to 1 m deep. Other tiny gobies and blennies use the burrows of large invertebrates. But most of the gobies and blennies found around Irish shores – about twenty species of each – flit among rocks and sand with plenty of hidey-holes. Among the larger species, the hand-sized red-mouth goby (*Gobius cruentatus*), with its puffed-out vermilion lips and cheeks, has attracted special scientific attention for its colonisation of Lough Hyne (the marine nature reserve in west Cork) where it lives abundantly in the gaps between boulders. It has been known there for about seventy years. This population, and smaller ones found in Bantry and Kenmare Bays, are all in sun-warmed, sheltered water, and almost 1,000 km north of the nearest known populations in northwestern Spain.

The pipefish of coastal shallows excel in their camouflage, lying along seaweed fronds as if part of them. The most abundant around Ireland, the slender worm pipefish (*Nerophis lumbriciformis*) will even stay beneath seaweed on rocky shores between the tides. But there are larger pipefish, such as *Syngnathus acus*, whose elongated snout and stiff segmented body are more typical of the Syngnathidae. This is the ancient marine family that includes the celebrated seahorses, represented in Irish waters by two species, the short-nosed seahorse, *Hippocampus hippocampus,* and the long-nosed *Hippocampus ramulosus* (sometimes *guttulatus*).

Phantom horses

Pipefish swim horizontally with a snake-like motion, but seahorses have a classically vertical stance, poised above a curled, prehensile tail. The horny segmented plates of their bodies are part of the mechanism that allows this ventral bending, all in the cause of camouflage: a seahorse gripping the tip of a frond of seaweed with its tail becomes supremely invisible, not least to prey that the animal sucks in with a jerk of the head. In *H. ramulosus* the more frequent species around Ireland, the disguise is furthered by a crest of wispy appendages, its pattern distinct to each individual.

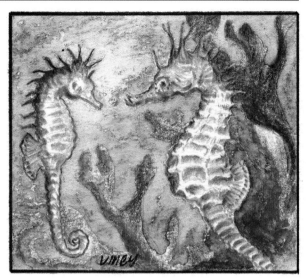

Seahorses: an elaborate courtship.

The elaborate and uncommon sexual behaviour of seahorses (see p.121) have made them a target of Chinese folk medicine and added to their attractions for home aquarium study and display. The trade in dried and living seahorses is now so huge as to threaten their species, notably in the Pacific.

In sandy shallows, the 15-cm lesser weever (*Trachinus vipera*) brings itself to human attention by injecting defensive venom from a long spine on its gill-cover into the bare feet of swimmers and paddlers, or the hands of shrimp fishermen sorting their catch. It is feared also by surfers, who gather at shelving west coast bays in the aftermath of storms. By day, the fish lies buried in the sand with eyes and black dorsal fin exposed, lunging upwards to prey on shrimps and small fish such as sand eels and gobies. It often moves in and out with the tide, which increases the risk to holidaying humans. The severely painful sting is best treated by soaking the skin in very hot water. There is also a greater weever (*Trachinus draco*), but this generally lives more deeply, down to 200 m, coming into shallower water in summer to spawn. Séamas Mac an Iomaire saw one 'striking seven or eight sand eels one after the other. It was burrowing through the sand like a pig.'

One big reward of his chronicle is to appreciate how intimately the coastal fishermen of Connemara knew their shallow-water fish. He lists, for example, six different types of gurnard, 'a nice mild, sweet, healthy, strong fish to eat' (this once shorn of spines and big, bony head) caught with handlines off the shore. The tub gurnard (*Trigla lucerna* = *an cnúdán soilseach*) and red gurnard (*Aspitrigla cuculus* = *an cnúdán dearg*) are reasonably familiar, but there were also *an cnúdán glas, an cnúdán buí, an cnúdán breac*, and *an cnúdán deilgnach*, all common at the coast by Mac an Iomaire's reckoning. He also knew three warring tribes of gobies under the wrack along the shore – 'and there's no colour in the rainbow they haven't got . . . Often on low spring tides on moonlit nights the cats go foraging, though they have no lines or hooks but only their claws. They catch a good lot of fish on the shore of every kind, blennies, gobies, scorpions and others.'

Despite their name, and the sinister reputation of the Mediterranean's Scorpaenidae family, the bottom-living sea scorpions, while equipped with sharp spiny dorsal fins, are not poisonous. Indeed, the long-spined sea scorpion (*Taurulus bubalus*) is one of the fish hunted by Ireland's coastal otters (*Lutra lutra*). The tough scales of the wrasses are no obstacle, either: Aran otters studied for their diet were as pleased to hunt the big ballan wrasse (*Labrus bergylta*) of rocky bottoms as the soft-skinned rocklings of the kelp forest, sinuous and slippery as eels.

The wrasses are colourful and territorial reef and kelp dwellers, armoured with stiff scales. Off our coasts they come in five different species: cuckoo (*Labrus bimaculatus*), corkwing (*Crenilabrus melops*), goldsinny, cook or small-mouthed (*Symphodus exoletus*) and ballan wrasse. The largest is the ballan wrasse which lives largely on shellfish.

The cod family

Rocklings are marked as members of the cod family by the barbels – sensory feelers complete with taste buds – that tuft their cheeks or chins. A single long barbel juts from the chin of the ling, a vastly longer and tapering relative – perhaps 2 m in very deep water – that haunts the shadows of reefs and wrecks. The capture of immature, inshore ling to be salted for winter was one of the earliest of Irish fisheries: 'We had for dinner fresh cod's head,' wrote Humphrey O'Sullivan in his diary of 1829, 'salt ling softened by steeping, smoke-dried salmon and fresh trout with fragrant cheese and green cabbage.' The dish figured in Joyce's Dublin and, in the west, survived as far as the mid-twentieth century.

Before the invention of fish fingers, salt cod, too, was (and in parts of Europe still is) a culinary staple. The fishery dates to the seventeenth century and, before the modern pressure on cod stocks, it could be caught almost from the shoreline to 600 m (but more usually at 150–200 m) shoaling at or near the bottom. An infant cod takes refuge in a gravelly seabed when only a couple of centimetres long. Its food then is mostly copepods, but worms, crabs, urchins and shellfish join the variety of fish in its adult diet: indeed, it will notoriously eat almost anything that will fit in its mouth, including other smaller cod. Its diet can affect its appearance: cod that feed on crustaceans acquire a brownish-golden skin while those that feed on fish take on a mottling of greenish-blue, a look nicely compared to Connemara marble in an Irish fishery pamphlet.

Among the most determined predators of cod is another (but barbel-less) member of its family. The silver-green pollack is known in today's Ireland principally as an angler's hard-fought catch from the rocks, but its northeast Atlantic territory ranges from Morocco to Iceland and Norway, and it can grow to 1 m or more. Its wealth of names in Irish attest to its value to the currach-fishing families of the Atlantic coasts (*mangach* is one of the commonest). Pollack and the closely related coalfish (or saithe, coley or *glasóg* - all *Pollachius virens)* are told apart by differences in mouth and lateral line. They swim through the pages of *The Shores of Connemara*, where a foreword by marine scientist Cilian Roden relates some of Séamas Mac an Iomaire's most memorable catches to oceanographic events among the islands: 'Indeed, the very place where he tells of catching nine pollack in a few minutes . . . was only a few yards from where, in 1986, we found the greatest population of coalfish and pollack and linked this abundance to the upwelling of cold, plankton-rich water.' As for the folk-science of cod, Mac an

Iomaire records the belief 'that when bad weather comes, the cod takes on a ballast of small stones to keep itself settled on the reef when the weather is very rough.'

The progressive development, size and separation of fins so marked in the evolution of the gadoid or cod family becomes quite striking in the haddock (*Melanogrammus aeglefinus*), perhaps the cod's closest relative and often taken in the same trawls. At the simplest extreme of fin design is the tusk (*Brosme brosme*), a large but somewhat obscure species of the northern Atlantic, not unlike the ling but with a single, continuous fin running almost right around the body. The whiting (*Merlangius merlangus*) has three dorsal fins and two anal fins. On the cod, pollack and haddock these have grown large and distinct, and the haddock, for good measure, sports a sharp point to its first dorsal fin. Below it is the large black 'thumbprint' left by St Peter when taking a coin from its mouth, an attribution shared with a similar blotch on the sides of the vertically swimming and spectacularly finned John Dory (*Zeus faber*) of the Zeidae family. The haddock stretches out a small undershot mouth to snatch bottom invertebrates, particularly brittle stars and small sea urchins and the different pattern in the prey of cod and haddock lets both fish share the same grounds without competing. A rare, jumbo haddock caught in Dublin Bay in the 1880s measured almost 1 m, but most of today's catch are half that length.

The distinctive profile of John Dory, like a vertical dinner plate with flamboyant, spiny fins. Its jaws shoot out to seize small fish.
(Nigel Motyer)

The northern hake (*Merluccius merluccius*) is a member of the wider cod group – the order Gadiformes. Tapering into a long tail and occasionally caught at somewhere near its full 1.3 m size in shoals at the edge and slope of the continental shelf, it can be found down to 1,000 m around the Porcupine Bank, but lives more commonly at less than half that depth. With strong, curved teeth (hinged inwards, like those of the angler), hake are ferocious predators, even on their own kind. They rise in shoals from the seabed at night to ambush fast-moving schools of small pelagic fish, such as mackerel or herring, blue whiting (*Micromesistius poutassou*) and squid. As if in rehearsal, very young hake feed on the bottom, by day, on schools of planktonic shrimps, and follow them at night as they rise to feed on phytoplankton at the surface.

Fish of the middle kingdom

In between (200–1,000 m) is the twilight zone of the mesopelagic: the ocean's middle kingdom. In Ireland's Atlantic waters, the mesopelagic zone begins where the seabed falls away at the edge of the continental shelf, either abruptly, as at the precipitous eastern wall of the Rockall Trough, or more gently, as at the slope of the Porcupine Seabight.

The life of the mesopelagic zone draws its energy from the sunlit surface above, notably by nightly upward migration to prey on plankton (and each other). This huge rise of organisms, outstripping every other migratory movement on the planet, was virtually unknown until it showed up on ships' radar in the wake of the Second World War. Sampled by scientists, it was found to engage a wide spectrum of ocean life, from zooplankton and crustacea to jellies and squid, but most abundantly, a range of small fish of some thirty identified families.

Most of them are small, perhaps 2–15 cm long, with a range of adaptations to a dim world and a life of varying pressure. Their nightly migrations demand strong swim-bladdered bodies and large sensitive eyes that can find prey near the surface even on dark nights. As prey themselves to predators both from above and below, their camouflage is distinctive. Dark backs and silvery sides give protection when viewed against a light background; while at greater depths an array of light-emitting organs along the lower surface of some species mimics the spectrum of the surrounding twilight, the rapid flashes from the photophores blurring the fish's outline. This has earned the Myctophidae family, in particular, the name of 'lanternfishes', and the differing patterns of photophores help to distinguish the fifteen species of the group in Irish waters.

Globally, their biomass is estimated at an enormous 600 million tonnes, and a one-hour trawl off Argentina is on record as having yielded 30 tonnes of a single myctophid species. Sampling in the North Atlantic has encouraged the prospect of trawling such widely distributed mesopelagic species as food for fish farming – 'one of the greatest marine resources that still are underutilised,' to quote a Faroese fishery scientist. Being small fish, most mesopelagic species have short lives and a low fecundity – a few hundreds or thousands of eggs – but their rate of reproduction is high, perhaps to withstand the pressures of predation. They are difficult fish to study in an aquarium, since their response to changing light conditions is highly sensitive: trying to migrate downwards, they batter themselves to death on the glass. In the ocean, their sensitivity to moonlight interrupted by clouds has produced baffling scatter-patterns rising and falling on the echo sounder screens of ships.

Mesopelagic fish sometimes load the nets of trawlers fishing for blue whiting off the edge of the continental shelf, where this small gadoid (about 30 cm long) shares with them the depths between 200–600 m (sometimes almost 3,000 m in the Rockall Trough). It gathers to spawn in early spring, notably off the Porcupine Bank, and these schools attract the main fishery. In 2004, catches of blue whiting off the west of Ireland and Scotland reached a record peak of more than 2.4 million tonnes, making this the biggest fishery in the Atlantic. Much of the catch provides oil and fishmeal for salmon farming and other forms of aquaculture.

The diminutive boarfish (*Capros aper*), no bigger than a fisherman's palm, is another source of 'feed-grade material' that has provided a new harvest for boats from Killybegs in 2006. It shades from pink to deep red depending on its depth (40-600 m or more), and its shoals are swiftly mobile. They make a light but bulky catch, and the spiny fins that frame the boarfish's oval body are apt to make them clog up the chutes and silos of trawlers and factories. Nonetheless, the target was 10,000 tonnes in the first year of trawling.

Herring the King

*With a hundred cran of the silver darlings
that we'd taken from the shoals of herring . . .*

Herring.

Ewan MacColl's enduring folk song may have been his own twentieth-century evocation, but it drew on the spirit of the many authentic ballads celebrating this staple food-fish of so much human society. Ireland's Luke Kelly and Liam Clancy helped to make the song famous: they could also have chosen among 'The Queen of Connemara', 'Bantry Bay', 'The Kinsale Herring', 'The Boys of Killybegs', 'The Herring King' and more. 'Somehow,' wrote John Molloy in his history, *The Herring Fisheries of Ireland (1900 to 2005)*, 'you don't find that same sort of excitement with any other fishery.' From sailing yawls and west coast hookers, to fleets of steam trawlers and today's pelagic tank vessels and sophisticated fish-detecting systems, the Atlantic herring (*Clupea harengus*) has survived the constant assault upon its numbers. 'Once a herring shoal has been located it has very little chance of escaping,' writes Molloy, as it is gathered into a mid-water trawl 'with a mouth opening as big as a football field.' Yet the herring's most abundant stocks can still justify Linneaeus' description, *copiosissimus piscis* – the most prolific of fish – and images of migrating herring forming massive expanses 'as far the eye can see' are by no means redundant, even in today's global plunder of ocean life.

The Norwegian spring-spawning herring, for example, shoaling in the vast, bleak waters that span the Arctic Circle, are estimated at more than 7 million tonnes (the annual trawler landings are perhaps one-tenth of that), and Norwegian and Scottish scientists have measured shoals 8 km long and containing as much as 2,000 tonnes of herring. The individual fish in such shoals must be counted in millions, since the Atlantic herring (usually no more than 30 cm long) is among the smaller species in its family, relying on countershading and bright silver sides and belly to blur its image in the shoal's swirling evasions of predators. As a feeder on swarming copepod zooplankton, snatching the animals one by one, the herring dispenses with the lateral line that alerts carnivorous fish to larger prey.

Herring swim loosely in a shoal hunting for food, but more tightly in the spawning season – also, it seems, at times when their numbers are falling. The significance of the shoal densities scribbled on wheelhouse sonar screens has been a frequent cause of argument between scientists and fishermen. It seems agreed, however, that some sort of pecking order exists within the shoal, which is usually layered to leave the smaller fish along the top. The shoal moves up and down in the water column, especially when feeding, and follows the upward migration of the zooplankton at dusk. It is a nervous, intensely alert community, reacting very quickly to noise and vessel lights; shoals break up and scatter as boats pass overhead.

They return each year to specific spawning grounds inshore, and it is this that provides the identity of different stocks, its biological details so vital to the calculations of fishery management. Ireland is flanked by three separate stocks, at the northwest, in the Celtic Sea and the Irish Sea. The northwestern stock is thought to find a stable biomass at some 110,000 tonnes. The herring of the Celtic Sea are at the southern limit of their species' distribution and the state of the stock has been uncertain: it seems only that it will need to grow much larger to withstand a projected harvest of some 20,000 tonnes a year.

Sonar perspective of the Stanton Bank, a feeding ground for Ireland's west coast stock of herring. (Geological Survey of Ireland)

The herring stocks of the far North Atlantic migrate for thousands of kilometres to feed or spawn, or to shelter over the winter in enormous shoals in the deep fiords of Iceland and Norway. The stocks in Irish waters travel no more than 500 or 600 km, but the drift of larvae from the spawning grounds creates further tantalising variables in computing the size, breeding success and recruitment of young fish in particular stocks. Larvae that hatch from spawning grounds off the southeast coast are carried into the Irish Sea. Those from west Cork and Kerry drift in currents as far as Galway Bay; those from grounds off the northwest coast of Donegal may end up off the west of Scotland.

As they cease to drift, sustained by their individual globules of oil, and begin to hunt plankton, the larvae take on the shape of little herring and start to swim in shoals. They have been swept into shallow bays, where they tend to stay for their first two years. These nursery areas, specific to the main herring stocks, are in known places around Ireland – behind St John's Point in Donegal Bay, for example, or around Lambay Island or Rockabill off the County Dublin coast. The sheltered waters between County Down and the Isle of Man offer a nursery ground both to the 'native' herring of the Irish Sea (known as the Mourne stock) and larvae swept northwards from the Celtic Sea, which return to the south coast as spawning fish. The big migrations of Ireland's Atlantic herring are those of stocks swimming inshore to spawn in late summer and autumn. The Celtic Sea herring have been feeding in the deep between the Labadie Bank (due south of Cork Harbour) and the tip of Cornwall, while the stock off the west and northwest coast range from the shelf west of Galway up to the Stanton Bank west of Scotland. Sprat (*Sprattus sprattus*) and sardine (*Sardina pilchardus*) belong to the herring family and are of increasing importance because of declining herring fishing quotas.

Mackerel on the move

'Upwards of 300 sail of French fishing vessels, some of 200 tonnes, on the coasts of Ireland, where they met with great success in the mackerel fishery, which it was thought was the cause of the great scarcity of fish experienced at that time . . .' A report from 1757 helps to register the long history of *Scomber scombrus* in the annals of North Atlantic fisheries. Mackerel is another great shoaling or schooling fish whose protein and omega-3 fatty acids have been of great benefit to humans.

Its dramatic appearances and disappearances, like those of migrating birds, have inspired endless historical conjecture. 'Initial theories on migration one hundred years ago,' as John Molloy recorded in his study, *The Irish Mackerel Fishery* (2004), 'suggested that mackerel shoals migrated down the coastline of Western Europe during summer and autumn, then crossed the Atlantic and finally migrated north-

Mackerel.

wards along the east coast of America and Canada to winter under the Polar ice cap. It was also thought that during this rest period the fish became blind and developed a thick film over their eyes and lay hidden in the mud.'

Modern tagging programmes in the northeast Atlantic, including those by Ireland, have drawn a much less tidy picture. Not only are there migrations in the winter and early spring to and from the main spawning grounds, migrations after spawning to the feeding grounds, and migrations to and from the overwintering grounds off Norway, but these have been changing over short periods. Even the spawning of mackerel is long drawn out and complicated. Unlike the herring which release all their eggs and milt 'in one great explosive event', as Molloy puts it, in a very well-defined spawning area, the mackerel spawning season starts around Spain as early as January and gradually moves northwards until it finishes in early July north of Scotland, the shoals moving continually throughout the period. They leave a trail of batches of eggs and milt all along the edge of the continental shelf from northern Spain, along the Porcupine Bank, to the west of Scotland. Most are released in the upper, sunlit reaches of water, but the earliest eggs may be spawned in the deeper waters, perhaps as far down as 600 m.

This seemingly casual egg-and-milt release must have advantages for the species: it certainly ensures that all the mackerel eggs are not released in one basket, so to speak, and spreads them through environments of varying risk. But despite the regular international egg surveys that form the basis of assessing mackerel stocks, the spawning process remains deeply mysterious. A big mackerel of, say, 37 cm can produce between 500,000 and 700,000 eggs in the season, but doles them out in batches of up to 17,000 over a spawning period of up to 90 days. Each egg contains a tiny, golden globule of oil, both for buoyancy and sustenance as the larva forms and grows.

The extraordinary span of mackerel migration and spawning and the great fertility of the species have helped to create and sustain the largest single fishery of the northeast Atlantic, currently dominated by Norway, Scotland, Ireland and Russia. In 2007, for example, the catch prescribed by ICES was some 500,000 tonnes. The Irish share was about 46,000 tonnes, most of it taken by pelagic trawlers holding catches in tanks of refrigerated sea water. Management of the stock has been subverted by misreporting of catches and discards, and illegal landings into Scottish ports. ICES finds the mackerel are being harvested unsustainably, not least in the on-board grading of bigger fish and the discard and waste of the small (but perfectly marketable) ones.

The catch of horse mackerel (*Trachurus trachurus*) is also substantial (about 180,000 tonnes from the western European stock, down from some 500,000 tonnes in the mid-1990s), but the fish's separate identity and indifferent reputation as a food-fish has belied its importance. It is the only common member of the *Carangid* family in northern European seas, with rare, vagrant appearances made by its warm-water relatives such as amberjacks (*Seriola* spp.) and pilotfish (*Naucrates ductor*), the latter sometimes accompanying leatherback turtles (*Dermochelys coriacea*) on their migrations into Irish waters. The horse mackerel is not even a close relative of the mackerel proper, but has a similar shape and shine (though with dorsal fins set closer together). Research over the last decade has shown strong links between horse mackerel migration into northern areas and the shift of water masses in the northeast Atlantic. A major fishery targets the juveniles for human consumption in Europe; the middle-aged fish go to the Japanese market, while the oldest are destined for African consumption or processing into fish-meal.

Entering the deeps

At 1,000 m, the lowest depth frequented by the hake, the last of the light has disappeared and the first flickers of bioluminescence appear in predominantly black or grey fish (the colour red, at this depth, is also darkly monochrome). We are now at the outer reaches of the continental shelf or descending the continental slope beyond; and while the deep seabed retains a great diversity of invertebrate species, the variety of fish and other swimming animals has already fallen off markedly between 100 m and 1,000 m and continues to decline as the water chills and pressure grows. Even so, a net at any depth in the Rockall Trough and Porcupine Seabight might yield forty to fifty different fish.

Nearly 1,000 species are known so far from trawling the deep-sea bottom. But unlike the general distinction in shallow waters between pelagic fish (swimming in the upper layers) and demersal species (living on or near the seabed), most of the demersal fish of the deep sea are upwardly mobile. Apart from the really benthic fish, including the anglers, skates and flatfish, the 'benthopelagic' fish that live just over the seabed do not rely on its animals for much of their food. As the ocean deepens, less and less marine snow reaches the seabed and its bigger invertebrates, in consequence, grow fewer. While scavenging fish such as hagfish and gulper eels can wait for descending corpses, most benthopelagic species swim up to find prey in the layers of water above them. Here, in the middle or mesopelagic depths of the ocean, the fish and other organisms themselves migrate upwards at night to feed on fauna close to the surface. It is the sun's energy, in the end, that finds its way down through the ocean to sustain every form of life.

While a deep-water trawl may raise an exotic mix of fish, the main commercial interest lies in a mere half-dozen of the benthopelagic species. Between 1,000–1,500 mm, the big grenadiers (or rat-tails) are both a dominant seabed family and a prime target of bottom trawling. They were originally discarded from deep-water hauls of hake because their long shape, tapering away to nothing at the tail, seemed too strange or even repellent for the market. This adaptation is common to many deep-sea species, including the notorious whip-tailed rabbit fish, whose name, *Chimaera monstrosa*, marks it as an early encounter with the curious forms of the deep.

The reason for such tapered tails is still uncertain, but a slimmed-down body may help to maintain neutral buoyancy in conditions of high pressure, serving a slow pace of life in which bursts of speed are rare. Grenadiers will eat almost anything, including carrion, and their capture of invertebrates and fish is more by stealth than swift attack. The deepest grenadier species yet recorded lives down to 6,500 m and three others, together with eels, dominate the fish of the Porcupine Abyssal Plain. But the most frequently fished of the group is the roundnose grenadier (*Coryphaenoides rupestris*), abundant on the slope of the Rockall Trough. It is another in the great order of codfish, and the 20 per cent of it that reaches the consumer in fillets has a good flavour and a long frozen shelf-life.

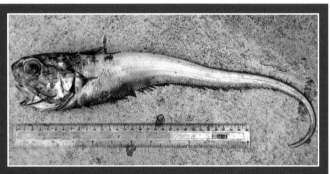

Roundnose grenadier. (Courtesy of Marine Institute)

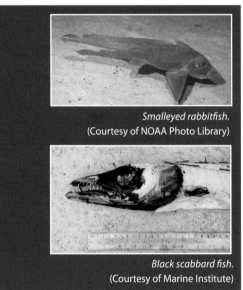

Smalleyed rabbitfish.
(Courtesy of NOAA Photo Library)

Black scabbard fish.
(Courtesy of Marine Institute)

Caught in the same trawl may well be fish that, as Redmond O'Hanlon describes in *Trawler*, stud the mesh 'with grotesque black heads, jaws agape to show ragged teeth . . . like throttled serpents.' The black scabbardfish (*Aphanopus carbo*) has the fang-like teeth of a ferocious predator, and an eel-like body that may reach 1.5 m. The head is generally chopped off by trawlermen at the first opportunity, but its fine white flesh and 'interesting halibut and chicken-like flavours' make it eminently marketable. Since the fifteenth century it has been fished in the depths around Madeira, sometimes with heavily weighted lines stretching 1,300 m down into the dark, but it is now an acceptable part of the catch in deep waters north to Iceland.

At the greatest depth of a trawl, however, half the catch may be small, unmarketable smooth-heads (*Alepocephalidae*), their pates quite bald of scales. They are the ugly rejects of a family that includes the gleaming silver-plated little argentines, once thought beautiful enough to be deep-water cousins of the salmon and subject to fishing quotas. At one early period of French deep-water trawling, the grenadiers themselves were discarded as a by-catch with the blue ling (*Molva dypterygia*), a close relative of the common ling, once fished intensively on its spawning grounds to the west of Ireland.

Down to the sharks

Two small, deep-water dogfish sharks (*Squalidae*), about 1 m long, became particular targets of deep bottom trawling. The world's deepest shark is the dark-brown Portuguese dogfish (*Centroscymnus coelolepis*), found all over the northeast Atlantic down to 2,700 m. It is targeted commercially in the Rockall Trough, together with the leafscale gulper shark (*Centrophorus squamosus*) that rarely ventures below 1,000 m (the two species are collectively known as 'siki' sharks). From growth bands on the spine of *C. squamosus*, a Marine Institute scientist, Maurice Clarke, found that it could live to at least seventy years.

This is modest enough for a deep-water species, whose slow growth, long life, late age of reproduction and slow rate of replacement can be in startling contrast to most of the familiar human food-fish. The pressure of trawling on traditional species, often with fine-meshed nets, is steadily reducing both their individual size and lifespan. However, even the biggest mackerel on record in Irish sampling programmes – 63 cm long and more than 2 kg in weight – was only about eleven years old, and a fourteen-year-old herring would now be a rarity in the Celtic Sea stock.

The orange roughy (*Hoplostethus atlanticus*) has been a celebrated example of deep-sea actuarial norms, quickly bringing home the folly of uninformed and unregulated trawling for new species. Gathered in schools above steep, rough seamounts to the west and southwest of Ireland in water of 4–7 °C the roughy takes thirty years to mature and reproduce. But it is clearly well able to nourish its stubby body (up to 50 cm of vivid vermilion: just a darkening grey shadow from 800 m down) with enough prawns, fish and squid for a life of up to 150 years. In such gradual renewal, an unconsidered human harvest can become catastrophic, as was happening to the species in the last decades of the twentieth century.

Orange roughy can live for 150 years.
(Courtesy of Marine Institute)

Reproduction: an infinite strategy

The dark mermaid's purse of a skate's egg-case at the tideline; the white spongey mass of a whelk's egg capsules caught in cast-up seaweed; the bright yellow patch of a dogwhelk's eggs firmly stuck to a rock at low tide: even such modest and familiar beachcomber's finds can hint at the myriad ways of marine reproduction.

Consider the ballan wrasse and cuckoo wrasse swimming around the reefs offshore. Most bony fish are sorted into lifelong genders, separately producing sperm and eggs; some are born hermaphrodites, producing both; and a few may even self-fertilise. But many wrasses are 'sequential hermaphrodites'. They are born female, grow into sexually mature females, and have the potential to transform into functional males later in life. The sex change correlates with social hierarchy and social behaviour.

In many wrasse species, social structure includes a large dominant male and many smaller, subordinate females. Removing the male from the group triggers the largest female to begin transforming into a male.

For almost any general reproductive behaviour, mechanism, or sexual strategy in the ocean, there is a minority doing something entirely different for its own good (or simply haphazard) adaptive reasons. Weather, temperature, amount of sunlight, moon cycles, currents and other environmental cues can influence the timing and abundance of spawning (and, indeed, of almost anything else). Apart from the mammalian couplings of whales, dolphins and seals, the reproductive life of the ocean ranges from the simple binary fission of protozoa to the sexual claspings of sharks. Some seabed organisms use both asexual and sexual strategies: among the sponges, anemones and corals, for example, the animals can multiply by budding (or even, among sponges, by fragmentation) or by the union of germ cells to produce free-swimming larvae that later settle on the seabed. In many jellyfish, the settled larvae grow into polyps that asexually bud off a series of swimming medusae – jellyfish – to continue the reproductive cycle. Most marine worms are also unisexual, unlike the general hermaphroditism of worms ashore, and their voracious larvae are among the leading consumers of inshore phytoplankton. Even among the zooplankton, the copepods that feed so many fish are sexually separate, spawning fertilised eggs free in the water.

The spawning of many bony fish can seem a profligate behaviour, as vast numbers of eggs are released to find random fertilisation in rapidly thinning clouds of sperm. Egg numbers supposedly relate to the risk of predation – the female cod, for example, produces some 4.4 million – but why the huge and largely solitary sunfish should hold so excessive a record, scattering perhaps 300 million unfertilised eggs (these found in the single ovary of a 1.4-m fish) remains a mystery: its mating has never been observed.

This sunfish travelled from Dingle to the Bay of Biscay in 2007. (Martin Lilley)

Once fertilised, most such eggs from pelagic fish are left to drift in the plankton, buoyed up by a droplet of oil and the yolk sac that nourishes the developing larva. Some spawned by demersal species sink to the bottom. Here they may mingle with the millions of eggs released and fertilised in the same fortuitous way by benthic invertebrates such as oysters, sponges or echinoderms. Oviparous reproduction, as this is called, with a general lack of care for the fate of offspring, is characteristic of most animal life in the sea.

But there are, predictably, hundreds of exceptions in which varying degrees of protection are afforded the embryonic stages and sometimes the larvae as well. Some of the larger crustaceans keep developing eggs tucked safely under their abdomens, attached by hair-like structures or in a special pouch. Some fish carry eggs along with them, held in the mouth, gill cavities or pouches on the body.

In the corkwing wrasse, found all around Ireland, the male builds a nest from seaweed, tucked into a rocky crevice, and guards it until he can attract a 'ripe' mate with an elaborate courtship display. After she has laid her eggs in the nest, he covers them with seaweed, and may even repeat the performance with another passing female. While waiting for the eggs to hatch and the larvae to drift away, he not only guards them but fans them with his tail to refresh the oxygen in the nest. Similar guardianship is found among the gobies and blennies: the female lays her eggs in old mollusc shells or under rocks, sticking them on firmly at one end, in a dense patch of eggs, and then the male guards them until they hatch. The female common octopus also attaches her eggs to a surface within her den, then stops eating to brood them constantly, keeping them clean and aerating them; soon after they hatch, she dies.

In ovoviviparous and viviparous fish, as with some elasmobranchs, one parent (usually female) keeps the fertilised eggs in her body. The developing embryo is nourished by a yolk sac formed prior to fertilisation but there is no food connection with the parent. A striking version of parental care occurs in the seahorse family (Syngnathidae), in which it is the male that incubates the fertilised eggs. They have been deposited in his body-pouch by the female, are then fertilised with his sperm, and remain there to develop, fed by individual yolk sacs. In due course, the male gives birth to tiny seahorses. This role reversal is part of the remarkable behaviour between the sexes that has made seahorses so popular as residents of home aquariums. Not only does a pair remain monogamous, at least for one breeding season, but they reinforce their bonding by three days of elaborate courtship. They meet each morning, change colours and intertwine their tails in a lengthy underwater dance before completing the mating.

The coupling of sharks and rays is more straightforward. The male's pelvic fins are modified to become copulatory organs (known as claspers) that deposit packages of sperm. But some sharks, too, are ovoviviparous; others are viviparous, in that the growing young need nourishment from their mothers' bodies before they are ready for birth. Female dogfish and rays release their fertilised eggs in tough, leathery capsules – the 'mermaids' purses' found empty at the tideline. Those from dogfish have long curling tendrils at the corners: the female swims around a rocky reef until the egg catches on seaweed or upright bryozoans or hydroids. The thornback ray's dark capsules have a long horn at each corner and perhaps twenty of them are released onto sand between March and August. The relatively small number of eggs hatched by many large sharks and rays reflects the better chances of survival that accompany the manner of their birth. But some small sharks can still be quite prolific. The common (lesser-spotted) dogfish, for example, may lay two eggs every five or six days for long periods within a ten-month breeding season. Their young may take almost as long to develop and hatch, at a length of about 10 cm.

Finding a fertilising partner in the dark is one of the challenges of the deep sea, especially when small numbers of a species are so thinly spread across an enormous area. The elaboration of bioluminescent signs and signals is the general response (see p.80), but some deep-sea species of anglerfish have evolved so unusual a strategy that, for many years, fish biologists identified the diminutive male – perhaps a mere 2 cm long – as a different fish species. Having found a mate by fast and furious swimming (and the luminous glow of her lure), the male burrows into her belly, fuses with her blood system and lives henceforth as a parasitic supplier of sperm on demand.

Looking for larvae

In the spring of 2000 a team from the Marine Institute made the first ever survey of fish larvae off the Atlantic coasts of Ireland, hauling their fine nets through fish plankton across the Celtic Sea, the Porcupine Bank and the continental shelf right up to the Stanton Bank west of Scotland. Among 100 or so species silvering their meshes (nine kinds of goby, for example, and half a dozen lanternfish, including the charmingly named chubby flashlight fish, *Electrona rissoi*), the larvae of commercial fish were to be the stars of the microscope. Abundant mackerel larvae in the western Celtic Sea and along the shelf edge off southwest Ireland confirmed the processional spawning of its migrating shoals. Blue whiting are also shelf-edge spawners, but a surprise was to find their larvae carried into the shallower waters of the eastern Celtic Sea.

Here, around Nymph's Bank and the sea west of St George's Channel, was a hotspot of larval concentration, gathering nearly all the cod larvae found in the survey, along with haddock, whiting, pollack and saithe. On the southeastern side of the channel, close to Land's End in Cornwall, they were joined by abundant larvae of sole and plaice. Along the shelf edge in the western and southern Celtic Sea, where satellite images showed oceanic waters mixing with those of the shelf, there was also a rich swirl of larvae: this time, of hake, megrim and mackerel. Satellite images confirmed the rising blooms of phytoplankton, first in the northwest Celtic Sea, where the shelf edge nears the coast, and then along the edges farther south. Such findings carry clear messages for the creation of marine protected areas around Ireland.

Fish talk and intelligence

'Fish can communicate by sound or some form of underwater sonar or fish talk. Gurnard when taken on board make distinct croaking frog sounds. Conger can cough like a human. Red bream make a thin, whining sound . . . Of course fish have throats and tongues and perhaps can sing and make merry – at least they have plenty to drink.'

These 'Observations of a Fish-Gutter' in the book *Skelligs Calling* (2003) were those of a veteran Kerry fisherman, Michael Kirby. While he may have listened in vain for a song, he was right to assume that the sounds formed part of 'fish talk'. So far, some 800 species have been listed among soniferous (sound-producing) fish, and this field of investigation is still young.

The sounds made by the cod family have been particularly well studied with new under-water listening devices, not least as a possible means of tracking their shoals. Cod of both sexes make sounds during the year, most often in situations involving territorial confrontation: in shoals recorded at spawning grounds off Norway it was the males that generated all the noise. This reached the human ear as a low rumble of grunts, each produced by drumming muscles surrounding the gas-filled air bladder. Research suggests that the sounds may be part of a male territorial ritual at spawning time, influencing sexual selection by the female; it has even evoked, for some observers, the highly competitive 'lek' behaviour (gathering for mating displays) of some terrestrial male birds. The pollack is another grunter. The male haddock, on the other hand, uses similar means to produce a series of knocks that speed up to a continuous humming as it nears the mating embrace. Ways have been found to tell which species is 'talking', and even to identify (at least in the laboratory) the sounds of individual utterers.

The sounds made by herring seem virtually confined to the night, when fish in laboratory aquariums were heard to produce bursts of high-pitched, raspberry-like pulses, lasting up to 7.6 seconds. Judged by bubbles caught on infrared video, they came from the anal duct region (prompting the mischievous acronym FRTs, or Fast Repetitive Ticks), but could also have come from the swim bladder, which has a duct beside the anus. Starving the fish produced no change in FRT-frequency, but when they were held away from access to air at the surface the sounds declined: it is the swim bladder that 'farts', using swallowed air. Clupeid fish such as herring can detect sound frequencies up to some 40 kHz – beyond the hearing of most other fish – so the swim-bladder pulses can keep herring in close contact in shoals at night without alerting listening predators.

How intelligent are fish? Intelligence is bound up with learning and thus the ability to remember; also to observe and deduce. Research seems to show that fish have a whole range of cognitive abilities, including learning from experience – and from other fish. Rather like mammals, their intelligence responds to complex surroundings: indeed, their ability to map their environment may spring from a common vertebrate inheritance of organised behaviour. In a recent experiment with Atlantic salmon, one group of parr were reared for three months in the usual, rather bleak hatchery conditions, and another in a tank furnished like a stream with plants and rocks. Half of each group were fed hatchery pellets; the other half with live bloodworms. Offered live shrimps, the best foragers were those in the enriched environment and with experience of live prey. In other experiments, 'naive' hatchery fish were seen to learn foraging behaviour from pre-trained fish they could see through a perspex wall.

Why do fish migrate?

The ocean is full of drifters; among them the billions of seasonal fish eggs and larvae. But the seas are also webbed with migratory journeys of fish, instinctual travels between environments that offer

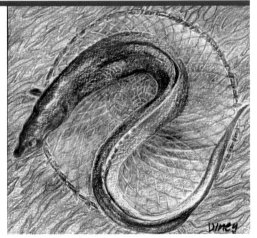

The eel's ocean migration may take longer than anyone supposed.

the best conditions for survival at various stages of their lives. Areas that are best for spawning are rarely those that offer the best feeding; neither may offer the best refuge from predators during an over-wintering retreat.

The most spectacular and mystifying migration has been that of the eel (*Anguilla anguilla*) – both from our own rivers and those of western Europe – to breed in the depths of the Sargasso Sea at the other side of the Atlantic. The wettest, darkest nights in autumn bring an exodus of silver-bellied eels from Ireland's rain-swollen streams and rivers, setting out on a journey of 6,000 km or more to spawn and then die. This extraordinary catadromous life cycle –

feeding in fresh water but breeding in a distant quarter of the ocean – is the reverse of the salmon's (anadromous) behaviour. Some scientists have wondered whether the migration began millions of years ago, in a narrower Atlantic. The European eel and its American cousin (*Anguilla rostrata*) spawn next to each other in the Sargasso: their developing larvae drifting in a parallel clockwise stream before the Americans are swept into east coast estuaries, while the Europeans drift on in the Gulf Stream and arrive in the rivers as elvers (or 'glass eels') after some two years or more.

In 2006, a project by Irish and Danish scientists attempted to track the outward migration of adult eels to their spawning grounds in the Sargasso – an area of the Atlantic measuring 2,000 km by 500 km, from which no adult eel has ever been recovered. Electronic tags fitted to twenty-two Irish eels released into Galway Bay in the autumn were designed to record depth, temperature and location on the migration route across the Atlantic, and timed to 'pop off' and surface in sequence to broadcast their data to a Danish research vessel. The final tags, it was hoped, would at last disclose the eels' spawning location, to be confirmed by catching some in a trawl. The tags, unfortunately, surfaced within the first third of the journey, suggesting the migration may take longer than anyone had supposed.

The extreme excursion of the European eel to breed, and the passive 'homeward' drift of its larvae to inshore nursery areas have dramatised dynamics that govern fish migration in general. The need for optimum feeding often provides the third move in what fishery science has called the 'migration triangle' that governs the lives of so many species. Within any such formula, however, the migratory habits of different fish, and different stocks of one species, can seem infinitely variable. Sea temperature, weather changes, and planktonic and lunar cycles can add their own complexities. Some fish seem to offer simple illustrations of migratory response to water temperature. The western stock of horse mackerel, for example, spawns in the western Celtic Sea and then moves up to feed in the southern Norwegian and North Seas, retreating southwards as the temperature falls in autumn. It overwinters along the continental slope and forms dense schools in deeper water. The southern stock of horse mackerel, on the other hand, based around the coasts of Spain and Portugal, shows a big overlap between spawning and feeding areas and in some parts scarcely migrates at all.

Bass move inshore to spawn in summer; pollack move offshore to spawn in winter. Thornback rays move inshore in summer to produce their young; ling migrate to the deep shelf edge to spawn in spring. It is often assumed that the timing of such movements occurs with little change from year to year, but climate change could bring calendar shifts in peak abundance, important to both fishery catches and their management. A British study found that flounder, for example, migrated from the estuaries to spawning grounds at sea some one to two months earlier in years that were up to 2 °C cooler; a steadily warming sea will bring its own effects.

The massive size of some migrating shoals finds a prime example from Canada, observed, ironically, on the eve of official admission of the Newfoundland cod stock collapse. In the summer of 1990, Canadian scientists using high-resolution echo sounder found the biggest school of cod ever documented in their waters, migrating inshore in a channel in the Newfoundland continental shelf: it covered an area of roughly 20 by 30 km, and contained an estimated 500,000 tonnes of cod. This was more than 80 per cent of the estimated northern cod biomass at that time.

Some new insights into cod habits have come from the European CODYSSEY research project, which released more than 3,000 tagged fish between 2002 and 2005 in the Barents Sea, North Sea, Baltic Sea, and over the Icelandic and Faroe Plateau. Along with migrations of hundreds of kilometres between spring spawning grounds and summer feeding grounds, each ecosystem showed many resident cod that remained in the same locale. The fish also tolerated a remarkably wide range of temperature, from -1.5 °C in polar fronts in deep water off the Icelandic coast to as much as 21 °C as they rested close to the seabed in the southern North Sea. All in all, the Atlantic cod showed 'a remarkable behavioural repertoire and environmental tolerance that permits individuals to occupy a wide range of marine habitats.' This still left plenty of room for mystery.

Big predators and their decline

The cover of *Nature*, the international science journal, for 15 May 2003 carried the shocking and sombre conclusion that human fisheries had removed nine-tenths of all large fish from the sea. A ten-year study by marine scientists based in Canada, sifting catch data from all over the world, computed the massive decline over fifty years of industrial fishing. From the cod, groupers and great batoids and flatfish of the continental shelves to the sharks, tuna, marlin and swordfish of the deeps, the losses must have profound and unpredictable consequences for the structure of life in the sea.

In 2007, a team of Canadian and American ecologists illustrated the changes that can cascade through ocean food webs when top predators disappear. They found that overfishing of big carnivorous sharks along the Atlantic coast of the United States had led to dramatic increases in their prey

A shoal of tuna. (Courtesy of NOAA Photo Library)

Young blue fin tuna washed ashore in Old Head, County Mayo. (Myles Heneghan)

populations. Among them, the cownose rays (*Rhinoptera* spp.) had exploded in numbers, and their consumption of scallops had ruined the livelihoods of coastal fishing communities.

While such a direct chain of consequences can be hard to demonstrate, the destruction of top predators is beyond question. One example is the pursuit of the Atlantic bluefin tuna (*Thunnus thynnus*), the mackerel's huge (2–3 m) ocean-going relative among the schooling species of the Scombridae family. Until the late twentieth century, the presence of this magnificent predator off Ireland went virtually unremarked, although fishing had begun for its smaller southern relative, the metre-long albacore (*Thunnus alalunga*). In the 1980s, bluefin of 450 kg were caught in mid-water inshore trawls for mackerel and horse mackerel off Kerry and Donegal. By the 1990s, the appearance of a Japanese tuna fleet west of Galway, setting squid-baited longlines of perhaps 100 km, brought home the astonishing value of bluefin in the *sashimi* restaurants of Tokyo. The tuna also became a prized trophy of big game angling served by west coast charter boats. These developments drew Ireland into the study of tuna migration and transatlantic moves for conservation.

The bluefin epitomises streamlining for speed, its crescent-shaped fins pressed back into grooves in the surge of acceleration to 60 kph, and its oxygen-hungry metabolism sustained by ceaseless pursuit of mackerel, herring, whiting, flying fish and squid. This driven quest for food, plus the capacity to warm itself several degrees above the surrounding water, takes the bluefin on spectacular migrations. Its home seas are the Mediterranean and the Atlantic to the west of Spain and Portugal, but many bluefin migrate northwards after spawning, up the west coast of Ireland and on to Norway, Iceland and even northern Russia. While shoals of herring thronged the North Sea, tuna would swing around the north of Scotland, sometimes in schools of twenty or more, to circle the nets of drifters as they fished off the Yorkshire coast.

There are bluefin in the western Atlantic, too, severely harassed by sport fishermen along the North American coast. The eastern and western populations were thought to be quite separate, leading the International Commission for the Conservation of Atlantic Tuna (ICCAT) to set different and greatly disparate catch quotas. Satellite tagging made possible by the 'catch-and-release' policy agreed by Ireland's charter skippers helped to show an unsuspected transatlantic mingling of the two populations at feeding time, and also the autonomy of their wanderings. Two fish tagged within minutes off the coast of County Donegal migrated to separate sides of the Atlantic and after eight months were some 5,200 km apart.

The leap in catches of big bluefin since the 1990s, together with intense capture of small specimens (chiefly by French, Spanish and Italian vessels) and unregulated fishing in the Mediterranean, has created a pressure far greater than would allow the eastern Atlantic stock to stabilise. Concealment of catches, ICCAT believes, means that while the Total Allowable Catch (TAC) for bluefin has been running at 32,000 tonnes, the actual toll is nearer 50,000 tonnes. Ireland's view is that catches

Swordfish.
(Courtesy of NOAA Photo Library)

of even 15,000 tonnes a year may not be low enough; Marine Institute scientists have urged big annual cuts in quotas until the bluefin shows signs of recovery.

That recovery programmes can work is shown by the dramatic revival of the North Atlantic swordfish, heavily overfished off America in the 1900s both commercially and by deep-sea anglers. A conservation campaign persuaded more than 500 chefs to take swordfish off their menus, and an agreed catch quota of 10,000 tonnes was followed in 2000 by protection of key nursery areas in US waters. Four years into the recovery programme, an assessment for ICCAT found the stock almost restored to a healthy level. But swordfish are a migratory species that matures at the age of five and spawns in warm waters throughout the year.

Salmon come home

The Marine Institute's Salmon Research Centre at Burrishoole, County Mayo, devoted to conservation of the northeast Atlantic salmon and improving the ocean survival of hatchery stock.
(Courtesy of Marine Institute/David Brannigan)

The Atlantic salmon (*Salmo salar*) may not be an obvious candidate for ranking among large predators, but its sea-going appetite for fish such as herring, capelin (*Malotus villosus*) and sand eels (*Amodytes* spp.) is substantial. Its stocks migrate from some 1,500 western European rivers to destinations spanning the North Atlantic from Greenland to Norway. In Irish scientific estimates, a peak of salmon productivity was reached in the mid-1970s, when 1.8 million fish returned to the island's rivers; only about one-third of that number do so today.

At the end of the last glaciation, some 13,000 years ago, the only open streams and rivers in Ireland were those draining into the Celtic Basin from the southern margins of the island. These may already have supported salmon and trout that survive as distinctive Irish races today, but as the thaw spread north they were joined by more colonising salmonids, including Arctic charr (*Salvelinus alpinus*), whitefish or pollan (*Coregonus autumnalis*), the eel, the sea and river lampreys (*Petromyzon marinus* and *Lampetra fluriatilis*), two herring-like shads (*Alosa fallax* and *A. alosa*), and at least one stickleback (*Gasterosteus aculeatus*). All the salmonids were initially cold-water fish conditioned to the habit of anadromy, feeding in the sea but migrating into freshwater to spawn.

The Atlantic has only one species of salmon, while the Pacific has half a dozen with great differences in shape and habit. Even *Salmo salar* can vary in behaviour between neighbouring islands and rivers. Salmon run into Scotland's River Tweed for eleven months of the year. Anglers on the River Liffey in Dublin may catch the first big returning fish of the year on New Year's Day, while in summer comes a second run of fish half the size, the grilse or juvenile salmon that have spent only one winter at sea. In the short hill rivers of western Ireland, with cascades and waterfalls passable only in a spate of rain, the summer run of grilse is the only passage of the year. These younger, smaller fish have returned from a brief migration, north around the coast of Scotland and on towards the Faroes and the rich feeding grounds of the Norwegian Sea. Migrations of 'spring salmon' from other, more substantial Irish rivers travel northwest across the Atlantic to eddy systems off west Greenland, where the fish may spend several winters feeding on capelin (members of the wider order of Salmonoidei) and other small shoal fish. Their round journey may reach 5,000 km, and the homing instinct that guides their return journey seems to use several senses, responding to the earth's magnetic field, the chemical smell of the natal estuary and pheromones released by other salmon in the home river.

In current estimates, made possible by long-term research based at the Marine Institute's salmon centre in Burrishoole, County Mayo, less than 10 per cent of the wild smolts (young fish) that go to sea from Irish rivers are surviving to adulthood. The prospects for hatchery fish, released in 'ranching' operations, are even poorer. The final decades of the twentieth century saw mounting international concern, initially to control commercial fishing of salmon at sea. Although many of the Atlantic salmon homing to European rivers pass through Irish waters, the Republic waited until 2006 before joining other countries in banning drift net catches of salmon, while compensating coastal fishermen.

Meanwhile Irish and European marine scientists brought new genetic tools to tracking salmon in the research programme known as SALSEA (Salmon At Sea) through marine surveys in 2008 and 2009. Sponsored by the multinational North Atlantic Salmon Conservation Organisation (NASCO) (of which Ireland's Ken Whelan of the Marine Institute is president) this is a long-term investigation of what happens to salmon in the ocean, tracking them through their DNA to know exactly where they go and what they eat, and whether climate change may be affecting their migration speeds and routes or food resources.

Toll on the sharks

The toll of commercial fishing on the sharks of the northeast Atlantic has been most drastic among the smaller dogfish species dwelling near the seabed. Some of these form part of the mixed catch of bottom trawling for deep-sea fish such as orange roughy or roundnose grenadier. Others, in shallower depths on the shelf, are familiar commercial species, still largely taken as a by-catch but also targeted with gillnets.

Most notable of these is the metre-long spurdog (*Squalus acanthias*), or common spiny dogfish, the 'rock salmon' of British fish-and-chip shops and long a valuable species for Irish fishermen. Once widely assumed to be the world's most abundant shark, but without any international agreement on its management, its stock in the northeast Atlantic has been brought close to collapse. This is a single stock, long-lived, slow-growing and late to mature, with a slow migration northwards across the shelf from the Celtic Sea. What has made the spurdog particularly vulnerable is its separation into single-sex shoals, the females avoiding the males. The targeted fishing for large females that peaked in the 1980s struck disastrously at a gestation period almost as long as an elephant's: 22–24 months until the live delivery of, at most, half a dozen infant sharks.

In the world's oceans, sharks of any sort are rare or absent from the abyssal depths below 3,000 m. While well able to handle high pressure, and conspicuous on slopes down to 2,000 m, the dwindling fish prey of greater depths is unable to meet their high energy demand or sustain the oil-rich liver they need for buoyancy. At the depth limits of today's trawling, however, the shark population is substantial, while generally of the smaller species. In the mounting catch of 'squalid' sharks (Squalidae is the dogfish family and squalene a key constituent of the liver oil), two species in particular have borne the brunt of deep-sea trawling and targeted fishing by longline and gillnet. The Portuguese dogfish and the leafscale gulper shark ('leafscale' is a distinctive skin texture) were first caught in the 1980s and along with the market for livers and fins, their fillets have been sold collectively as 'siki' to French and Spanish consumers. As with their close relative, the spurdog, the sharks' long gestation periods and small numbers of live young have led to catastrophic clearances by fishermen.

Research led by Maurice Clarke of the Marine Institute has revealed the sharks' late maturity at a large size, and their potentially long lives (up to seventy years, in the case of Portuguese dogfish. 'Of all the species caught in the deep-water fisheries in the northeast Atlantic,' Clark concludes,' deep-water sharks will have the lowest resilience to fishing pressure and the slowest replacement rates.' The EU ban on the use of gillnets in depths below 200 m, introduced in 2006, was a particular response to the scandal of 'ghost-fishing' – the death of deep-water sharks, along with anglerfish, rabbitfish and other species in the meshes of gillnets lost or abandoned in a ruthless, wasteful and largely unregulated fishery.

The deep-water sharks off Ireland are not universally small. The 7-m Greenland shark (*Somniosus microcephalus*, elsewhere called the sleeper shark because of its sluggish behaviour) is found between Ireland and Iceland, and, while generally a scavenger on fallen carrion, may rise from more than 2,000 m to attack seals and small cetaceans. Another deep-water giant that rests on the bottom by day and hunts towards the surface at night is the 5-m bluntnose six-gill shark (*Hexanchus griseus*). Its particular appetite for hake leads it regularly into fishing trawls on the slopes of the Rockall Trough, and small, immature specimens have been caught by sport anglers fishing off the southwest coast.

The oceanic, pelagic sharks found off Ireland share with tuna the cryptic uniform of bluish-grey backs and white bellies, and can often show the same leaping agility when trying to shake off a sport-angler's hook. The 4-m shortfin mako (*Isurus oxyrinchus*) is occasionally found close inshore in summer and has been caught both by tuna fishermen and sea anglers off the west coast. Its reputed 4.5 m jump when hooked joins a savage reputation as attacker of humans in a rare and ultimate frisson of angling excitement. The mako may, on the other hand, sometimes be confused with its more benign if even more robust 4-m cousin, the porbeagle (*Lamnus nasus*), which moves into Irish inshore waters in June from deep mid-waters off the west and south. Here they hunt mackerel and the females give birth to four pups, the fruit of a nine-month gestation. In 1932 a Dr O'Donnell-Brown caught a record 365 lb porbeagle shark off Achill, but the fish's role in Irish angling history is quite overshadowed by its present fight for survival in European seas.

Supplying the world's most expensive shark meat (the *veau de mer* of French cuisine), the porbeagles have become a critically endangered species, seriously exploited for over half a century on both sides of the Atlantic. The collapse of the eastern population in the mid-twentieth century led to intensive targeted fishing in the northwest, where most of the virgin biomass of porbeagles was removed in just six years. The northeast population continued to be fished without restriction until 2008 despite calls from ICES for a total cessation; then, the first ever TAC set limits close to the existing level of catch. The catches by French, Norwegian and Danish fleets have dwindled, but unknown numbers of the shark are taken by Japanese, Taiwanese and Korean longliners (and small numbers as a by-catch in several Irish fisheries). As Marine Institute fishery scientists have pointed out, most porbeagles caught on the hooks of surface longlines are taken alive and could easily be returned to the sea. Even with a minimum by-catch, however, the northeast Atlantic population could take twenty-five years to recover.

The mackerel and squid of Irish waters have attracted the virtually circumglobal thresher shark (*Alopius vulpinus*), a fast-swimming, high-leaping species with a scythe-like caudal or tail fin that can account for half of a 6-m length. It provides one of the stranger stories in Ireland's shark history with a report by an Irish ichthyologist, Harry Blake Knox, of an event in Dublin Bay in the winter of 1865. He claimed to have seen a thresher use its tail fin to swat a wounded diver – probably the great northern diver (*Gavia immer*) – which it then swallowed. The shark is better known for using its fin to lash shoals of fish into a tight formation, all the better for attack.

Like so many pelagic sharks, including the mako, the thresher is now ranked as 'Vulnerable' in the careful gradations of threat devised and monitored by the IUCN, the International Union for Conservation of Nature. For the oceanic blue shark (*Prionace glauca*) the global rating is one degree safer – 'Near Threatened'. Only its extraordinary abundance and fecundity (dozens of pups instead of the usual few) can withstand an annual mortality, mainly as by-catch, put at between 10–20 million individuals. In regional seas, however, the balance may already have tilted more severely: in the North Atlantic, there is evidence that the population has declined by 50–70 per cent.

Tagging the blues

The blue shark feeds heavily on relatively small prey, such as mackerel, and summer brings a northward movement into Irish inshore waters of juvenile females. At around 2.5 m long, they have become the prime quarry of catch-and-release sport anglers off the west and south of Ireland and no fewer than 16,719 of these graceful, slender creatures, with backs of a vivid cobalt blue, were tagged between 1970 and 2001.

The Sportfish Tagging Programme of the Central Fisheries Board was introduced in 1970 by the Inland Fisheries Trust, then responsible for developing all recreational angling. Results from sea angling competitions around the coast were showing a decline in the capture of some of the most important species, such as blue shark and tope (*Galeorhinus galeus*), angel shark ('monkfish'), skates and rays. At that time, nearly all fish caught by anglers were killed and taken ashore to be weighed and photographed. Little was known about the reproduction and migration of the trophy species, and charter boats readily volunteered co-operation in a tagging programme and a general rule of catch-and-release.

The blue is ranked as one of the weaker swimmers among pelagic sharks, and seems to use the North Atlantic gyre of currents to assist an ocean-wide, clockwise migration. Most recaptures of the Central Fisheries Board tags were by Spanish tuna and swordfish longliners working between Iberia and the Azores. Secondly, came the interception by Japanese and Korean longliners off West Africa, including the Canaries and Cape Verde. Canadian longliners working off the Grand Banks were the next biggest source of tags, followed by sport fishermen off Long Island, Montauk and Nantucket on the northeast American coast. The longest journey undertaken by a recaptured shark was 6,640 km, from Loop Head in County Clare to Venezuela; other tags have been recovered after fifteen years.

Denied the traditional satisfaction of weighing dead fish suspended on the quays, new means were needed of meeting the sport angler's sense of competition. The Shark Angling Club of Ireland was quick to promote a weight-estimation formula recommended by the International Game Fish Association. The girth of the fish is measured around its greatest width, in inches, and this number is then squared. The resulting figure is multiplied by the length of the

A catch-and-release rule for sea angling helps sustain blue shark numbers off Ireland's west coast. (Bluewater Fishing, Clifden)

shark from the tip of its nose to the notch of its tail (again in inches). The resulting figure is then divided by 800 to give the fish's weight in pounds. By such arcane calculation the game angler is satisfied to watch his hard-won trophy flash away into the depths.

The blue shark's potential for commercial inshore fishing was tested by Irish fishery scientists in experiments with longlines off Clare and Kerry in 1990. Floating 8-km longlines were baited with mackerel on 300 hooks (this based on the traditional Scandinavian longline used widely up to the 1970s off the Irish coast and elsewhere). More than 100 sharks were caught through the summer, but the commercial possibilities were not pursued.

The basking shark redeemed

'As they sleep on the Surface of the Sea, they are discovered by their Fin, which being extended above the Water, resembles the Sail of a Boat. They lye in this posture, til the Fishermen, making up to them, strike them with their Harpoon Irons . . .' Clergyman and naturalist William Henry, writing in the 1730s, was describing the start of what fishermen called a 'sunfish' hunt off Killybegs in County Donegal. The

The basking shark: oil from its great liver lit the 'lanthorns' of Dublin.

harpooning of the basking shark – the second-largest fish in the world, continued for a further two centuries. Today, its prodigious liver-oil is no longer a sought-after commodity, but such plankton-feeding sharks (another is the whale shark of the Pacific [*Rhincodon typus*], the biggest fish of all) are caught up in the wider concern about shark declines. While new research explores its migratory habits and distribution, a total EU ban on catches has been in force since 2002, and the potential trade in fins from catches on the high seas have some control through a prohibitory convention from CITES (Convention on International Trade in Endangered Species of Fauna and Flora). But the ocean's growing web of longlines creates an ongoing toll of by-catch deaths, with the corpses discarded and fishery scientists writing of a 'severely depleted' stock.

The sunfish of marine science is *Mola mola*, the scarcely less remarkable ocean wanderer sometimes seen from the summer heights of an Irish cliff as a big disc-shaped fish swimming verti-cally in the clear depths below. But the basking shark was elected the 'sunfish', *liabhán greine*, for a long period of Irish folk history (or occasionally, as in Kerry, *ainmhidhe na seolta*, 'the monster with the sails'). Under either name, it made determined hunters of the fishermen of Ireland's Atlantic coast. From the early 1700s, oil extracted from the shark's liver was used to fuel lamps, waterproof wool and timber, soothe burns and bruises and rub into aching muscles. It fuelled lighthouses around the coast, and filled the flickering 'lanthorns' in the streets of Dublin and other Irish cities; in purity and versatility, it was second only to oil from the sperm whale.

The basking shark lives in temperate seas in both hemispheres, foraging north to the edge of Arctic waters, but only in the northeast Atlantic is there any long history of exploitation. Not until 1950, after at least two centuries of shark hunting, did scientists explore in any detail its anatomy and biology. A study of sharks caught off the Scottish Hebrides was quick to address traditional exaggera-tions of its size, scaling down the reputed 12 m to a rarely exceeded 10.5 m (indeed, of more than 3,000 basking sharks spotted off the UK, only about 240 were over 8 m in length). But the shark's other vital statistics remain impressive. Swimming steadily at about two knots with its cavernous mouth agape, it can filter more than 2,000 tonnes of seawater an hour, the volume of a 50-m swimming pool. The plankton trapped by its long, bristle-like gill-rakers nourishes a liver of enormous size, often weighing a tonne, and charged with oil rich in squalene, a low-density hydrocarbon. This gives the shark buoyancy, so that in swimming forward, the tilt of the big pectoral fins is enough to lift it from the seabed or hold it at the surface.

The basking behaviour is thought to have a twofold purpose: the sharks congregate in areas – often off headlands – where currents bring plankton to the surface and concentrate it into drifts; the act of gathering may itself help them to find a mate. Occasionally a plankton front, swept inshore by winds and currents, attracts spectacular assemblies. In May 1998, they appeared in some hundreds off the Lizard Peninsula in southern Cornwall, bringing crowds of people to the cliffs to marvel, and to try to count their fins.

Cetorhinus is the only big shark to adopt the technique known as 'ram filter feeding', accumulating plant and animal plankton by swimming forward, often on a convoluted path, through the drift of floating cells (the tropical whale shark and the megamouth, *Megachasma pelagios*, are mainly suction feeders). It takes energy to forage in this way – perhaps more, at times, than the density of plankton supplies. The animal seems to live on an energetic knife-edge: when should it stop swimming and close its mouth? A shark-tracking study in the English Channel by David Simms at the Marine Biological Association in Plymouth found the animal starting to feed when there were only about 400 copepods per m^3 – a threshold far lower than biological modelling would have suggested. But *Cetorhinus*, by feeding at the base of the food chain, extracts the maximum usable energy from its nourishment. It shares with its carnivorous relatives the remarkable sensory receptors that respond to distant electrical fields generated by muscle movement and may use them to detect the very presence of the microscopic swimming copepods. It may also be guided by the scent of dimethyl sulphide, the gas produced by phytoplankton when grazed by zooplankton and thought to be used as a foraging cue by some tube-nosed seabirds, such as petrels and shearwaters.

The inshore appearance of the sharks in summer as they nose after fronts and blooms of plankton has prompted long speculation on how they spend their winter. It was widely accepted that they migrated into deep water and rested on the bottom in a state of torpor. The pattern of spring sightings suggested a single population wintering off the Moroccan coast of Africa. But recent satellite research by David Simms has shown that they remain active during winter, feeding on *Calanus* zooplankton that overwinters in deep water off the edges of the shelf. And in 2007, a female tagged off the Isle of Man by Mavis Gore and colleagues was tracked 9,589 km across the North Atlantic to a point off the Newfoundland shelf – the first evidence of a link between the European and American populations. The shark spent nine days around the Mid-Atlantic Ridge and reached a record depth of 1,264 m. A rare sighting of basking sharks mating, after four hours of courting behaviour, was reported from the north Irish Sea in June 1999. Those caught at the surface have been almost all female, and one being towed into a Norwegian harbour in 1936 gave birth to five living young.

Parasites: Ad Infinitum

Parasitism was deftly defined by the Harvard evolutionary biologist Edward O. Wilson, in *The Diversity of Life* (1992), as 'predation in which the predator eats the prey in units of less than one. Being eaten one small piece at a time and surviving, often well, a host organism is able to support an entire population of another species. It can also sustain many species simultaneously.'

In the ocean as on land, some parasites attach or embed themselves externally (ectoparasites); others live within the body's tissues, organs or circulatory vessels (endoparasites). Still more species can be harmless hitchhikers (the barnacles on whales, for example, if they do not become, quite literally, a drag) or relatively harmless lodgers, like the little pea crabs (Pinnotheridae) that take lifelong shelter within the mantle cavities of mussels and oysters.

Given a structure so perfectly shaped for burrowing through soft material, it comes as no surprise that roundworms (or nematodes) lead the ocean's roster of endoparasites, notably those of fish. But this suggests some simple form of assault and a rudimentary lifestyle, whereas the cycle of many marine endoparasites is remarkably complex. The most studied examples are those of the 'cod worm' and the 'herring worm'. Both are found in many other kinds of fish, but it is their frequent presence in commercial species that has drawn such close investigation.

The cod worm *(Phocanema deicipiens)* may grow to 4 cm long and lies curled and encased in a membrane produced by the fish tissue. The herring worm *(Anisakis simplex)*, almost colourless and half the cod worm's size, is found, tightly coiled and similarly encased, in not only herring but mackerel and whiting.

The adults of both worms live in the stomachs of marine mammals that have eaten infested fish: *Phocanema* in the grey seal and *Anisakis* mainly in dolphins, porpoises and whales. Their eggs pass out in the mammals' excreta, and when they hatch the microscopic larval worms must find a new host. Those of *Anisakis* are eaten by a small, shrimplike crustacean, a euphausid; those of *Phocanema* by a small isopod crustacean living on the seabed. When the new hosts are eaten in turn by a fish, the larval worms are released into its stomach, whereupon they bore through the stomach wall and become encased in the tissue.

Neither worm is any threat to the human consumer; even if it passes unnoticed into the frying pan or fish-finger factory, both cooking and freezing will kill it anyway.

CHAPTER 7

Managing the Catch

'The modern trawl,' wrote Sir Alister Hardy in his great mid-twentieth century survey *The Open Sea*, '[is] a gigantic netting bag with an oblong mouth some eighty feet [25 m] across . . .' Times and wonderment change. By the 1980s, the modern nets in the Irish mackerel fleet had reached some 1,600 m, and by 2005 some new herring nets had openings the size of Croke Park. They are still basically 'the same four sheets running down into one cod-end' as a Killybegs netmaker describes, but operated by computer in bigger trawlers of formidably increased horsepower and sonar of ever-finer discrimination. An experienced skipper can identify not only the species in the shoal, but whether their size is worth the time and fuel to catch them. The dilemma of the fishing industry is, indeed, that technology and catching capacity are now far out of balance with the natural replenishment of stocks.

Fishing on such a scale and with such high technology is, however, confined to the pelagic sector of the Irish fishing industry and to the bigger trawlers operating in the deeps. Of the Republic's 2,500 fishing vessels, the vast majority – more than two-thirds in 2007 – are less than 15 m long. They stay within sight of the coast (they include the traditional currachs of the west), but still give thousands of fishermen a living, or part of a living: up to 1,400 small boats spend the summer fishing

The old herring trawlers of Dunmore East. (BIM)

The Killybegs pelagic fleet. (Donie Smith)

lobster. In 2004, a scheme was launched to register all inshore boats, to help effective management and conservation of inshore stocks of fish and shellfish.

Of the 130 vessels longer than 24 m, most are multi-purpose (polyvalent) trawlers fishing for a variety of species, using several techniques, in different areas at different times of year. They may catch mixed flatfish and roundfish in the summer and move to herring in the winter and spring. They also switch areas and target species according to market or weather conditions as well as changes in quotas and restrictions. The pelagic and deep-water fleet, with about twenty-four trawlers of 40 m or more, is based mainly at ports on the northwest and southwest coasts, and ranges from the Celtic Sea to waters off the west coast of Norway. This relocation of effort by larger vessels has been matched by a recent decline in the number of Irish boats fishing in the Irish Sea.

As this book appears, more than one third of the Irish whitefish trawlers fishing the seabed for species such as monkfish, hake and megrim are being decommissioned, with compensation, as part of a general European reduction in fishing capacity. But the modernising of the remaining fleet and the expansion of aquaculture seem still to promise a profitable future. Irish bank lending for private investment in fishing vessels rose

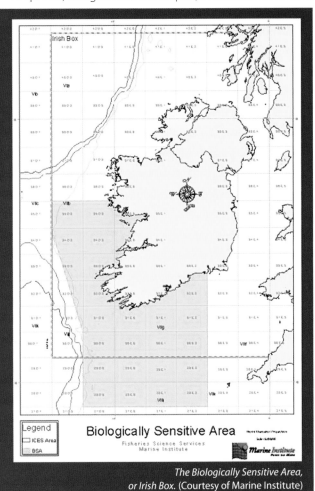

The Biologically Sensitive Area, or Irish Box. (Courtesy of Marine Institute)

to €400 million in 2005. None of this was for further factory-ship supertrawlers of the kind that have attracted such controversy and which have now passed out of the Irish fleet.

The waters around Ireland are rich in spawning and/or nursery areas for mackerel, horse mackerel, blue whiting, hake, herring, haddock and cod. Indeed, the data presented to the EU Commission by the Marine Institute persuaded it to establish, in 2003, a large Biologically Sensitive Area, called the Irish Box, where special fishery controls apply. It encloses an area of 100,000 km^2 and follows the 200-m contour line from Galway south around the coast to Waterford. In a regime enforced by the Irish Naval Service, vessels over 10 m long have to report their movements and catches to the Irish Fisheries Patrol every two hours.

The wider waters yield an annual catch of about 1.5 million tonnes, worth some €800 million, of which Irish boats haul in about one-fifth. The landings of 'small pelagics' – mainly mackerel, horse mackerel and herring – peaked in the mid-1990s, but international and Irish trawlers now hunt declining

An anglerfish in camouflage on a bed of maerl. (Nigel Motyer)

stocks, chiefly off the west of Scotland but also off the west and southwest of Ireland. Here, too, trawlers fish industrially for blue whiting to feed farmed salmon with fishmeal and oil. Landings of all the demersal species have been declining since the 1970s, with steadily fewer boxes on the quayside of the traditional gleaming roundfish: cod, whiting, haddock and saithe. Of the bottom-feeders on the Irish shelf, only hake, anglerfish (monkfish) and megrim seem to have been holding their own, to the west and south of the island; although 2007 brought a fresh abundance in several stocks of haddock and saithe across the northeast Atlantic.

The slippery squid

As stocks of traditional fish species dwindle, squid is becoming a more familiar human food even

Squid.
(Courtesy of NOAA Photo Library)

in countries like Ireland where it remained largely unmarketable up to the late twentieth century. The massive numbers of oceanic squid have yet to be targeted seriously by the large European trawlers, not least because of difficulties in catching them. An illuminating passage by Martin Wells of Cambridge University (in *Civilization and the Limpet*, 1998) explains the problem:

The lateral line of a fish detects obstructions at a distance, stops fish from careening into things. But it also allows us to fool them with nets that they could perfectly well swim through if they believed their eyes rather than their pressure sensors. Only the cod end of a trawl is fine enough to prevent escape by most of the fish that find themselves in it. Most of them have been conned by the wide-mesh wings of the trawl. Squid, unlike fish, believe the evidence of their excellent eyes, rather than their pressure detectors, and swim through the mesh while the going is good.

There are other ways of catching squid: enormous seine nets, for example, or – as in the Japanese fisheries – ships dangling lights and mechanically jigging thousands of lures. But such investment can seem doubtful in the northeast Atlantic, given the great fluctuation in squid stocks inherent in the animals' biology. As Wells writes, they 'grow like smoke, often from a few milligrams to a kilogram or more within a year: they mate, lay eggs and die.' While this annual turnover can create a huge harvest of squid, one bad spawning or feeding season can decimate the stock.

Trawling the deeps

Most deep-water fishing takes place between 800–1,200 m on the slopes of the Porcupine Bank and in the Rockall Trough. French trawlers led the way to the deeps in the 1980s, followed by Spain, the UK, Norway, the Faroes and Ireland. Many boats switch between trawling over flat ground for mixed deep-water species, such as grenadier, black scabbard and shark; or trawling over mounds for shoals of orange roughy, and traditional trawling on the continental slope and shelf (French deep-water trawlers, for example, also target black pollack in shallower waters). At the shelf edge west of Donegal, Norwegian longliners fish for ling and tusk and Spanish longliners and gillnetters fish for shark on the slopes of the Porcupine Bank. At a far greater distance, trawlers from many countries fish the Hatton Bank beyond Rockall and even the slopes of the Mid-Atlantic Ridge.

The switch to new deep-water fish was initially unregulated, and its impact on long-lived, late-maturing fish and their fragile seabed habitats was potentially disastrous. The orange roughy, with its firm sweet flesh, became emblematic of both. Schooling above the corals and rich invertebrate life of isolated seamounts, the roughy takes some thirty years to mature and spawn; it may live to the astonishing age of 150. As trawlers moved from one seamount to the next, the regulating machinery of ICES, the EU and the North East Atlantic Fisheries Commission (NEAFC) slowly caught up, imposing some sea-area closures for the species and strict catch limits elsewhere. Concern about the vulnerable ecosystems of the high seas reached the UN General Assembly in 2006, and this achieved strong international action. The NEAFC banned trawling on seamounts along the Mid-Atlantic Ridge and on areas of the Hatton and Rockall Banks, and in 2007 the European Parliament approved new controls, including a ban on fishing deeper than 1,000 m over fragile areas of the high seas.

Rockhoppers and ticklers

Like harrowing the Earth from an airplane, the impact of bottom trawling can be quite catastrophic beyond its take of target species. An area equal to the world's entire geography of continental shelves is trawled every two years, and some densely fished waters are trawled over and over: in the southern North Sea, for example, some spots are trawled 400 times a year. Many bottom trawls are fitted with heavy steel rollers and bobbins – rockhoppers as they are known, and most also have ticklers: heavy lengths of cross-connected chain that rake the seabed ahead of the net. Its cod-end, filling with fish along with rocks, mud and unwanted invertebrates, is towed for kilometres along the bottom. The mouth of a rockhopping trawl is held open by a pair of massive otter-boards, spread by the force of water as the trawl is towed, and trials with new designs off Ireland's southwest coast seek to keep the nets off the bottom, lessen the drag of debris, and economise on fuel. Beam trawling for flatfish also uses

Net remnant caught on a reef. (NOAA Photo Library)

tickler chains ahead of the net, and their replacement with electric pulses is being evaluated in trials by ICES.

Lost or abandoned nets and other fishing gear have contributed greatly to the burden of plastic debris at the sea floor. Of particular concern have been huge lengths of monofilament gillnet, originally set for monkfish and deep-water sharks off the west of Ireland. Beginning in the late twentieth century, some fifty trawlers (mainly based in Spain) were setting large numbers of bottom gillnets – totalling perhaps 250 km per boat – returning to lift them after as many as ten days and sometimes, because of bad weather, not at all. At any one time, more than 8,000 km of nets were estimated to be set by the fleet, and those never lifted continued a destructive 'ghost fish-ing', perhaps for two or three years. The practice was documented by the Deepnet Project, instigated by Norway's Directorate of Fisheries and helped by

Tuna caught in a net. (Courtesy NOAA Photo Library)

the Marine Institute, Bord Iascaigh Mhara (BIM) and Irish Naval Service patrols. The project reported 'a deep reluctance to talk about this fishery, in fact almost an unwritten law of silence.' A pilot retrieval survey hauled up some 650 nets at Rockall and around the Porcupine Bank, and 2005 saw the introduction of an EU ban on the use of gillnets to the west of Ireland and Scotland, beyond depths of 200 m. In 2008, retrieval of the nets with grappling anchors was still continuing around the Porcupine Bank, in a co-oper-ative Irish–UK project called Deepclean, funded by the EU.

Now that the supply of alternative deep-water species has proven so illusory, with stocks even of the deepest sharks on the point of collapse, fishing around Ireland is clearly seen to be 'moving down the food-web': a concept and global trend first documented in the late 1990s. Having depleted the stocks of larger, long-lived, fish-eating species, fisheries are now concentrating on short-lived plankton-eaters of lower value (such as mackerel) and invertebrates (such as *Nephrops* prawns and crabs). In scientific estimation, this leads first to increased catches, then declines.

Prawns are now the second most valuable catch (after mackerel) for Irish fishermen. In the Irish Sea, where stocks of cod, sole, whiting and spurdog have fallen to a critical condition and herring now supports a single pair of Northern Irish vessels, summer trawling for *Nephrops* is now the leading activity. The true amount of prawns caught by the fifty vessels of the otter-trawl fleet, mostly fishing out of Howth, Clogherhead and Skerries, is unknown since under-reporting or misreporting of catches is endemic in this, as in most sectors of the fishing industry. This has made it impossible, indeed, for the Marine Institute's fishery scientists to give the annual catch advice they provide for most fish species. The stock of *Nephrops* off the east coast has seemed remarkably resilient, but its abundance may reflect the loss, through overfishing, of its natural predators. Cod is the main one, and others, such as skate and angel shark, are now virtually extinct in the Irish Sea.

Ireland's part in the chequered history of Atlantic cod-fishing has been minor; but the exodus of poor Irish fishermen from the southeast coast to Newfoundland in the late eighteenth century, described in chapter 1, placed them at the heart of the great export of salt cod to western Europe. The Grand Banks fishery itself was dominated by fleets from France, Portugal and Spain for, as Mark Kurlansky noted in *Cod*, his 1998 history, Ireland 'was too impoverished to develop a distant water fleet.'

Nor, even with independence, was the Republic equipped to benefit from the huge resurgence of Atlantic cod stocks in the wake of the Second World War. By the time a significant fishing fleet was developed in the 1970s, landings of all demersal species were already declining. Irish trawlers were making increasing catches of cod in the Irish Sea, but here the cod are a virtually self-contained stock, spawning mainly in the sheltered northwest of the sea. The juveniles suffered heavily as a by-catch by trawlers fishing *Nephrops* prawns.

Under-reporting of catches of Irish Sea cod has been so general that the true state of the stock is unknown. Spring closure of the cod spawning grounds in the Irish Sea began in 2003 as part of conservation measures extending to the west of Scotland and the North Sea. Later, the fishermen of Ireland's southeast coast agreed unilaterally, with support from the fishing industries of Spain, France, Belgium and the UK, to extend the spring closure to cod spawning grounds in the Celtic Sea. Throughout the northeast Atlantic, fishing pressures have already led to cod maturing when younger and at smaller sizes, and its sensitivity to water temperature may not be helping. Cod around Ireland are living close to their temperature limits (no more than 4 °C is their ideal) and a warmer sea increases stress during reproduction.

Advice, negotiation, agreement

The management of fishing around Ireland and in the northeast Atlantic from the Arctic to Gibraltar rests on the scientific advice of ICES, or as much of it as proves politically acceptable or negotiable within the EU in the Common Fisheries Policy, or in wider international agreements. EU member states have to agree what happens to limits on catches within the Common Fisheries Zone, which comprises the Exclusive Economic Zones out to 200 nautical miles from the coast of each maritime state. For fish stocks that straddle EU and non-EU waters, negotiations are carried out under joint agreements with other states. Where highly migratory fish swim the high seas – waters beyond any national jurisdiction – management depends on such organisations as ICCAT and NEAFC.

The leap in catches of big bluefin tuna since the 1990s, together with intense capture of small fish (chiefly by French, Spanish and Italian vessels) has created a pressure enormously greater than would allow the eastern Atlantic stock to stabilise. Concealment of catches, ICCAT believes, means that the actual toll for bluefin far exceeds the TAC of 32,000 tonnes. ICCAT's recovery plan relies on a steadily falling TAC, longer closed seasons and a bigger minimum landing size. Ireland has no bluefin quota, but catches juveniles of the small longfin or albacore tuna which arrive off the southwest on migration in late summer. The EU's ban on drift nets left surface trolling and mid-water trawling as the main fishing methods, and Irish landings of albacore have fallen sharply.

Blue whiting, the small, glittering fish that ranks among the world's top ten catches, uses the northeast Atlantic with no concern for boundaries. It spawns in spring to the west and northwest of Ireland and Britain, but also in Faroese waters, Norwegian fiords and off southwest Iceland. It then moves north to feed, congregating in huge shoals between Iceland and Norway and farther north in the Barents Sea, and begins to return in autumn. Its stocks have shown huge peaks (on Icelandic estimates, close to 11 million tonnes in the spring of 2007), but so have the catches by Norway, Iceland, the Faroes and the fleets of the EU. Warned by ICES that the harvest was becoming unsustainable, the coastal states agreed in 2005 to share the stock at a total limit set by the NEAFC (which, at 1.8 million tonnes in 2007, was nearly twice what ICES advised) and to manage allocations to end 'Olympic fishing' – the race to fish between competing fleets.

Within the EU, assessments are made by various ICES working groups of stocks in different fishing areas, and these shape the scientific advice that – ideally – guides their management. This uses TACs for particular species, along with measures such as specified mesh sizes for the nets, minimum landing sizes for the fish, particular closed areas and limits on days at sea. The data used by the working groups are gathered by national fisheries scientists such as those in Ireland's Marine Institute.

The science of stock assessment and fisheries advice juggles a great many fluid facts and events, and feeds these into complex mathematic models of population dynamics. It must weigh up what seems to be happening to a particular population of fish, then model the maximum catch that will allow it to maintain or improve its numbers and reach an optimum size, both for maximum commercial value and adequate reproduction. The crucial information has to do with age – not only the age structure of the current population, but ages in the life history of the fish: age at first and subsequent spawnings; age in relation to size and mortality. Fish, like trees, have annual seasons of fast-fed growth and winters of resting, each marked with rings of varying width. In trees, the rings form in the trunk; in fish, most clearly in a bony structure called the otolith, or ear-stone. Reading the otoliths is easier in some species than others – in herring, for example, compared with monkfish, hake or mackerel. Otoliths from different stocks of fish often vary in shape and size and 'some age readers,' notes John Molloy, 'maintain that otoliths from around Ireland – particularly those from the northwest – are much more difficult to interpret than those from the North Sea.'

Sampling and the full picture

First, however, catch your fish: independently, on research cruises, but also (and vitally) by sampling those already caught commercially. Age must be related to weight and length, from sampling catches at the quayside, in chilly auction halls, and sometimes at sea. On-the-spot sampling of hauls by discard observers is essential, since young fish or unwanted species discarded at sea are part of the picture of the whole catch: indeed, they may form most of it.

Looking at the age structure of catches and landings over a number of years tells much about the dynamics of the stock. A rising number of younger fish can signal a strong recovery; a drop in the older fish in the catches can mean that too few fish are surviving to reach their growth and spawning potential. Either way, steady sampling of catches is essential to the data handed up to the ICES working groups, and their assessment of the biologically safe limits to particular fishing quotas. It also informs the fisheries advice offered in the Marine Institute's annual Stock Book, the science-based bible of the Irish fishing industry. Resistance to the activities and judgements of scientists has sometimes been precipitate: in 2005, a section of the Irish fleet withdrew its co-operation with the Institute for market sampling in several ports, so that information ceased for more than a year on the main commercial species being fished to the north and west of the island. But the Institute's insistence that 'fishers need to be an integral part of the sampling and data collection process' has begun to bear fruit in a number of voluntary self-sampling projects and even the valuable notes in skippers' diaries.

Length matters: measurement of sample fish on RV Celtic Explorer. (Marine Institute)

Catch sampling at sea. (Marine Institute)

For perhaps half a century, the organisation of most fisheries science was devoted narrowly to the state of particular species and stocks. In the later twentieth century, global concerns about human impact on the oceans distilled a far more holistic and far-reaching ecosystem approach to fisheries management: one that considers all the interactions between species and the impacts on ocean habitats and food chains. The intergovernmental Stockholm Declaration of 1972 extended the approach to include fishermen, local communities and ocean users within the ecosystem. The implications of this new relationship with nature are taking tentative effect, both through technical measures at sea and the wider involvement in decision making. Meanwhile, it stands at the heart of the Marine Strategy Directive passed by the European Parliament in December 2007.

The ecosystem approach to fisheries still needs a lot of working out, not to mention global acceptance of its precautionary principles. As emphasised by ICES, these accept that knowledge of the ocean's ecosystems is incomplete, to say the least, and that fisheries should be managed to make the least possible impact on them. Although a full implementation of agreed principles and aspirations might be difficult at this time, the status quo is not an acceptable option in the light of a growing understanding of the collateral damage caused by fisheries. Even in its routine operations, the practice of discards – the dumping at sea of unwanted, undersized or quota-barred species – has been profoundly wasteful and ecologically destructive. Nothing, it is true, is ever wasted by nature, least of all in the ocean: every dead or mangled scrap will be eaten on its way to the seabed or recycled thereafter. But the scale of discards over the past half-century has been a huge waste of a precious marine resource.

A study published by the Food and Agriculture Organisation in 2005 put the discard total in the North Atlantic at 1.3 million tonnes per year, or almost a fifth of the world discard total. To the west of Ireland and Scotland, discards ranged up to 90 per cent of catches, depending on fleets, the target species and depth. In Ireland's demersal fisheries, at least one-third of the total catch has been discarded (two-thirds in the case of beam trawls) with the casualties usually of a dozen species per haul. As the EU Fisheries Commissioner, Joe Borg, declared in 2007, discarding 'makes no ecological, economic or ethical sense.' Much of it has arisen from the EU's own system of area quotas: fishermen emptying a net of excellent but 'wrong' fish on to the deck have had no choice but to throw them away. Where several species were caught together (for example, cod, haddock and whiting) the vessel may have had quota remaining for one species but not for the others. Fishers could also choose to retain only the most valuable fish, thus dumping perfectly marketable fish of lower value. But fitting the system to end discards into an already highly complex web of regulation will not be easy. The final management system, introduced to one fishery after another, will set standards for maximum acceptable by-catches. The ultimate obligation to land all fish caught is a strong incentive for the industry to find its own technical solutions; however it could be adopted by individual countries.

Two of the countries that have already banned discards – Iceland and Norway – have stayed outside the EU. Iceland has been a role model of flexible fishery management, with a system that can be juggled to accommodate, say, a skipper's over-quota catch of haddock by swapping or borrowing between quotas. But its endgame for fish for which there is no ready market (the Icelandic fisheries research institute buys it up) is not one likely to fit the EU, with its immensely complex mix of fisheries, species and conservation controls.

Towards smarter gear

Redesigning nets to allow juvenile or unwanted species to escape has had some promising results. In 2007, the World Wildlife Federation (WWF) awarded the top prize in its International Smart Gear Competition to a new net called The Eliminator, designed by fisheries researchers at the University of Rhode Island. It takes advantage of the tendency of haddock to swim upwards when faced with a net, while cod, flounder and other species swim down: the mesh in the net's belly is 2.4 m across to let them escape. Already widely used by Rhode Island fishermen, its first trials in the North Sea produced remarkable selectivity, retaining haddock and whiting, but almost no cod. In the western Irish Sea – where otter trawling for *Nephrops* operates on the nursery grounds of whiting – the heavy by-catch and discarding of the juvenile fish has been matched by a severe decline in adults; the use of square mesh panels in the trawls, to release the juveniles, has been mandatory since 1994.

Thousands of dolphins and porpoises have died in the northeast Atlantic as a by-catch in trawls and bottom gillnets; fitting the gear with 'pingers' to discourage their approach seemed a clever and humane idea, but years have passed in solving unforeseen difficulties. A continuous pinging from static nets (a sound based on wide-band signals) is a loud and polluting undersea noise; as much to the point, the animals get used to it. BIM, concerned to dissuade common dolphins from swimming into nets alongside albacore tuna, developed an interactive pinger triggered by the dolphins' own echolocation signals. It was proofed against being set off by sounds from engines or fishing gear, and then tried on the bottlenose dolphins of the Shannon Estuary. They duly sheered away from the signals. The pings were ignored, however, by common dolphins at sea. Different cetaceans, it seems, respond to different acoustic signals, and BIM's technical team returned to the drawing board.

A recent EU regulation made it mandatory to use pingers on bottom gillnets in a number of fisheries, including areas off Ireland's south and southwest coasts, chiefly to deter harbour porpoises. While several devices are on the market, fishermen were concerned about their effectiveness and practicality. BIM tested four of them aboard Irish gillnet vessels fishing for hake. Mindful that a fisherman using 20 km of nets would need 100 pingers at a cost of some €10,000, it found the pingers effective but needing a longer, more durable life.

Marine Protected Areas

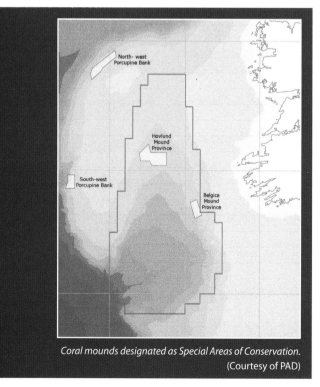

Coral mounds designated as Special Areas of Conservation.
(Courtesy of PAD)

The ecosystem approach has strengthened the arguments for Marine Protected Areas (MPAs): vulnerable spawning or nursery grounds or special seabed habitats in which fishing would be restricted or totally banned. In 2002, the World Summit on Sustainable Development in Johannesburg agreed to establish representative networks of MPAs by 2012, and to achieve sustainable fisheries by 2015. Their promotion and development in European waters has fallen largely to the OSPAR Commission, which, along with ICES, is the most prestigious international body concerned in the care of Ireland's ocean. It was originally set up to administer the Convention for the Protection of the Marine Environment of the North-East Atlantic, which Ireland, with other coastal states, signed in 1992. This succeeded two previous conventions dealing with marine pollution and dumping (the Oslo and Paris conventions – hence OSPAR, now based in the UK).

The practical value of MPAs in preserving or reviving fish stocks has been strongly controversial since the 1980s. Most commercial fish are highly mobile: indeed, the Fisheries Society of the British Isles has argued that, to be effective, individual reserves would need to cover more than 60,000 km². Others have pictured the boundaries of no-take areas being thronged with trawlers, 'fishing the line' intensively for the spillover from freshly abundant stocks (a scenario that has been presented both in favourable and unfavourable lights). Benefits from networks of quite modest closed areas have satisfied many marine scientists from studies of existing reserves worldwide. Grossly over-trawled areas may take decades to recover first their seabed invertebrate life and later their bottom-dwelling fish, but closing relatively undamaged habitats can bring a marked revival within a few years. There have also been dramatic improvements of shellfish catches from the drift of larvae beyond closed boundaries.

Most migratory fish should also benefit from protection of sensitive habitats used at key stages of their lives. The network of MPAs assembled by OSPAR is aimed at an 'ecological coherence', protecting areas that best represent the range of species, habitats and ecological processes. This, of course, includes the whole spectrum of life in the ocean, not merely commercial fish species, and adds to the network of Special Areas of Conservation (SACs), both terrestrial and marine, created under the EU's Habitats and Birds Directives. Ireland has about ninety marine SACs, of which some twenty have been nominated as OSPAR MPAs. The dozens of bays, estuaries and offshore islands among the marine SACs earned their protection initially for birdlife or conservation of shoreline habitats, but marine research by the National Parks and Wildlife Service has since begun to document their underwater ecology. Around Kerry's Blasket Islands, for example, the porpoise population has come under special study (see p.162) and the Shannon Estuary is already closely managed for the welfare of its bottlenose dolphins.

The four clusters of deep-sea coral mounds given statutory protection by SACs cover a total area of 2,500 km² and comprise the Belgica mounds, the Hovland mounds, and those at the southwest and northwest of the Porcupine Bank. In these areas bottom trawling and fishing with gillnets and longlines is prohibited. The mounds will lead Ireland's list of MPAs, but some important inshore fish spawning and nursery zones may not be far behind. The Marine Institute has stressed the great challenge to fisheries science posed by the MPA concept, which demands new kinds of data in assessing the conflict between human activity and conservation objectives. It is obviously difficult to protect mobile or widely spread species without closing extensive areas of sea, and its effectiveness can be hard to demonstrate. In Irish waters, the variety of national flags on the trawlers adds to problems of monitoring and enforcement. The Institute has argued strongly that involving stakeholders throughout the process of defining an MPA and in decisions on its management would bring 'a higher chance of compliance'.

Saving the shellfish

Along with the major *Nephrops* fishery, Ireland's shellfish are – or should be – a leading resource for coastal communities as small farming continues to decline. The fortunes of the brown crab, so long a prime quarry of inshore fisheries, have become quite uncertain. After fourteen years of a steady increase in landings, mostly from the northern stock off Donegal, a recent substantial fall in catches seemed ominous. More and more of the landings have been made by offshore 'super-crabber' vessels, operating in rough weather and able to use as many as 3,000 pots each, rather than by the small boats of traditional inshore fishing communities; the crabs are increasingly intercepted during their landwards migration in spring. Many lobsters, too, are taken as a by-catch in the brown crab fishery, but local co-operatives are now keen to enforce size limits, and the notching and release-of-females scheme to enhance natural egg production has handled some 100,000 hens since 1990. Lobsters live at least twenty years and possibly up to fifty, so the hens' potential fertility is prodigious.

The gross overfishing that destroyed virtually all of Ireland's native oyster beds in the nineteenth century has been echoed on a lesser scale by assaults on the island's limited resources of native cockles, razor clams, surf clams and carpet clams or palourdes. In *Alive, Alive-O* (2004), his vivid history of Irish shellfisheries, Noel Wilkins described the 'clam boom' of the mid-1970s, when the French market for palourdes reached such values (up to €6 a kilo) that hundreds of gatherers descended on the natural beds in Galway Bay and wiped some of them out in months. The species is still valuable, but their patches are now very small and isolated and some populations have been killed off by coastal developments.

A greater, mechanical plunder began in the 1990s, when boats using hydraulic fluidised dredging engaged in a free-for-all harvest of a newly discovered razor clam bed off Gormanstown in County Meath. By the time further fishing became uneconomic, some 20 km^2 of fine seabed sand had changed in structure and the long-lived commercial razor clam has been virtually ousted by other seabed invertebrates. Later, suction dredging arrived at the rich cockle beds of Dundalk Bay, an SAC and Special Protection Area for Birds covering more than 4,000 hectares of sand and mudflats. Displacing traditional small-scale harvesting with rakes in shallow water, and operating close inshore at the top of the highest spring tides, the dredgers took exceptional tonnages for export and damaged great quantities of cockles by repeatedly gathering and discarding the same small juveniles.

The Marine Institute's fishery scientists repeatedly called on Government for proper management of the harvest and enforcement of a closed season, not least because of the importance of the cockle beds to the bay's great winter flocks of oystercatchers and other migrant waders, some 50,000 strong (an example, indeed, of the ecosystem approach). By 2007, with the Dundalk stock reduced and dredging now scooping the smaller cockles of Waterford Harbour, the fishery was at last being controlled by closures, management and conservation regulations. An almost parallel sequence of overfishing, closures and eventual regulation of catches was seen at cockle strands in Scotland and on the UK coast of the Irish Sea.

Another fishery of native molluscs – that of whelks – is concentrated off the southeast Irish coast, targeting mainly the animal's spawning and nursery ground. As the numbers of whelks diminished close to shore, Arklow fishermen took their pots as far out as 25 km. Demand from Asian customers more than doubled the value of the catch between 1997 and 2003, when some 9,000 tonnes earned approximately €5 million at the quayside (this with an inshore fleet that an unkind EU study described as 'relict', being largely composed of boats built in the 1950s). Landings have since fallen to the lowest on record.

King scallops are landed into more than forty ports around the coast, but notably into Kilmore Quay and Dunmore East, harbours closest to the widely spread deep-water stocks of the Celtic Sea, the southern Irish Sea and the western approaches to England and Wales. What was once a fishery of sandy bays and inshore waters has progressively extended to new grounds farther and farther offshore, so that the return has increasingly to be measured against rising fuel costs and the condition of the landed catch. Unlike the small inshore scallop fisheries of the west coast, the offshore stocks of the south and east are fished by large boats, up to 36 m, each towing as many as 34 spring-loaded dredges. At the peak of recent activity, in 2002, well over 500 sharp-tined dredges were ploughing the patches of rough sand and gravel that scallops prefer. The Irish Box covers part of the main scallop ground south of Waterford, and in 2007 new EU limits on scallop-fishing effort brought a protest by the Wexford fleet, which blockaded the Rosslare ferry port. A quarter of its whitefish trawlers are now being decommissioned, and developments in research and organisation are directed to a more sustainable offshore scallop fishery.

King scallops seem an obvious candidate for aquaculture. Wilkins described an extraordinary turn in their fortunes in 1979 that led to a fever of economic speculation. In that year, conditions in Mulroy Bay, County Donegal, produced the biggest scallop spatfall ever recorded in European waters from an adult stock of some half a million individuals. As Wilkins put it, the event prompted 'thoughts of Mulroy Bay spat supplying the whole world' and an Irish scallop industry to match the vast aquaculture enterprise of Japan. Rearing the Mulroy spat in captivity, however, was to prove extremely difficult, and in the 1980s the adult stock in the bay was greatly reduced by pollution from tributyltin (TBT), a deadly substance widely used as an anti-fouling coat on boat hulls and since completely banned.

Seeding the mussel grounds

In sheltered bays, mussels grow on ropes below barrel-buoyed longlines. (Marine Institute)

As yet, the cultivation of scallops remains at the margins of Ireland's shellfish aquaculture industry. More than half its annual value comes from mussels processed and frozen for export: some 37,500 tonnes in 2006. They are harvested mainly from managed cultivation on the sea bottom but are also grown in many sheltered bays on ropes suspended from barrels or rafts, above the reach of predators. Both methods mean moving spat or small seed mussels from good spatting grounds to good growing grounds, a pattern developed as beds of native wild mussels were depleted.

Bottom farming of mussels creates the highest volume and value of all shellfish operations, but it is highly dependent on great banks of seed mussels created in the Irish Sea by larvae drifting from spawning beds on the coast and in estuaries. They are dredged up under licence, with allocated tonnages, for replanting at commercial farms in Wexford and Waterford harbours and in northern sea loughs, notably in large beds at Lough Foyle. The severe demands on the seed mussel beds and their shifting locations and patterns of growth have brought urgent research to support a science-based management.

Mussel bed. (Courtesy of Marine Institute)

Moving on from such mature shellfish industries as mussels and oysters, the future of Irish aquaculture is being energetically promoted by BIM and the Marine Institute. They have encouraged the farming of new species such as abalone (*Haliotis tuberculata* and *Haliotis discus hanai*), Manila clam (*Tapes semidecussata*), and have supported hatcheries raising millions of juvenile purple sea urchins for growing in intertidal rock pools and juvenile lobster for introduction to the sea. Their 'Farming the Deep Blue' international conference, held in Galway in 2004, signalled an ambition to lead Europe, if not the world, in taking finfish farming out to sea.

Moving fish farms offshore

Salmon farms were early to claim Ireland's sheltered inshore waters, but their performance has been beset by problems of fish disease, by ecological controversies and by competition from Chile and Norway. In 2007 their sector was seen to be operating at less than half its productive capacity. Ireland's salmon farmers were among the earliest, however, to test fish cages designed for exposed situations, and much of their production comes from sites with 'moderate' exposure to the west coast's winter seas. An organic farm in the lee of Clare Island, County Mayo, has been a notable pioneering success.

The advantages of moving farmed salmon out to sea have long been acknowledged: more vigorous waves in deeper and oxygen-rich water rear muscular, healthy salmon that look and taste better. Stronger tides flush through the cages and disperse their waste. In the wake of the 'Farming the Deep Blue' conference, the first five offshore locations on the west coast have been chosen for intensive exploration. All have some shelter and deep water of 25–40 m. Three are in the lee of large islands: Gola off Donegal, Inishturk off County Mayo and Inisheer in Galway Bay. The fourth, at the Skerd Rocks off Connemara, is sheltered by a necklace of rocks and breakers; the fifth, reckoned the most adventurous in exposure, but with the deepest water, is in Dunmanus Bay, County Cork.

Moored in the lee of Clare Island, County Mayo, this organic salmon farm is washed by swells from deep water.
(Marine Institute/Alan Drumm)

In 1980 farmed fish supplied just 9 per cent of those eaten by people; the figure is now nearer to half that. Since the capture of wild fish will at best remain static, while the global appetite for fish continues to soar, the output of aquaculture would need to double to around 90 million tonnes by 2030, to meet the demand. Perhaps 10 million tonnes of that will need to come from marine finfish farming, much of it offshore. Given present technology, Ireland's present emphasis on salmon seems likely to continue, at a far larger scale, rather than turning to other commercial species for offshore farming.

The onshore farming of turbot is already widely established in France, Spain, Portugal and Chile: indeed, their farmed tonnage now exceeds their wild catch. Ireland's one commercial farm, in Connemara, reported a harvest of 60 tonnes in 2003. Juvenile turbot are readily available on the open European market and they can be reared in systems that recycle, and in warm sea water to keep them growing in winter. The costs of rearing cod, however, have discouraged its farming in Ireland, while Norway and Scotland have made substantial investments in the technology.

Sinking the cages

For the offshore fish farmer, the hazards posed by harmful algal blooms and invasive masses of stinging jellyfish are quite as severe as the potential damage from storms. Early warning systems at some distance out to sea (perhaps, indeed, from satellite scrutiny) and submersible cages to sink the fish below the surface concentrations of algae or jellyfish, are likely to become part of offshore production. Indeed, making Ireland a centre of new technology informs the ambition of BIM and the Marine Institute in setting up an Irish-based International Council for Offshore Aquaculture Development, an initiative significantly welcomed by the EU's Fisheries Commissioner, Dr Borg.

A living . . . or part of a living

The scale of the projected offshore salmon farms, like that of today's pelagic trawls for mackerel and herring, is at an opposite extreme from the hundreds of ageing small trawlers that, along with half-decked lobster boats and currachs, account for some 1,800 of Ireland's fishing vessels. Their inshore ocean is bounded by coast and near horizon, and the periodic intrusion of pelagic freezer trawlers, nudging into shallows in pursuit of shoaling sprat, is a reminder of their distance from the industry of high technology and capital debt.

Traditional drift-netting for salmon using currachs in Killary Harbour, County Galway.
(Marine Institute/David Brannigan)

Some 3,000 fishermen are supported by the inshore fleet, concentrated mainly on the west and south coasts. They include the former salmon drift netters, now withheld from their quarry. Traditionally, the inshore fisherman engaged in a succession of fisheries, with different gears, as each species came into season. Today, as Edward Fahy has described, 'an individual fisher is privileged to have a single local stock' that supplies a living, or part of a living, for part of the year. Thus, while the gear still ranges over shellfish dredges, pots, nets, hook-and-line and small otter-board trawls, the use of even two of these on any one boat is rare. Fishing effort is also intermittent, with less than half of working days actually spent at sea. Yet of the dozen or so kinds of shellfish, including several crab species, and two fish (conger eels and bass) in the list of 'mainstay' inshore species, only the green shore crab could be considered under-exploited.

The catch or harvest of wild inshore species was worth more than €32 million in 2005. This chapter has already described some of the periodic free-for-all assaults on resources, such as razor

Angling for bass – but only two fish per day. (Courtesy of Fáilte Ireland/Central Fisheries Board)

fish, cockles, palourdes and brown crab. Intensive exploitation of shrimp (actually the common prawn, *Palaemon serratus*) is beginning to arouse similar concern. This is a surprisingly recent commercial fishery, using baited 'Chinese hat' traps and targeting berried females, which began in southwest Ireland in the mid-1970s and spread to the east and north. Conger eel – a standard bait for the lobster pots it so often invades – has become the target of directed longline fishery. Irish trawl fishers joined in at a point when conger was thought to be already fully exploited, and there are now arguments for restricting the catch to recreational anglers.

Bass (*Dicentrus labrax*) should not really appear in the list at all, since commercial fishing for it was banned in 1990. It is now an angler's prize, with a minimum length of 40 cm, a closed season, and a limit of two fish in twenty-four hours – the only marine fish to enjoy such protection. This followed the near-total depletion of Ireland's share of the stock that began in the 1960s and 1970s. Bass are a warm-water fish with spawning concentrations at the mouth of the English Channel: indeed, some of those reaching Ireland could result from a drift of eggs and larvae to our waters. Once here, they return each summer to the feeding grounds of the southeast coast. Climate change is encouraging the fish to range north (they are taken more and more often by Northern Ireland fishermen) but the restriction to anglers is likely to remain: the Republic's stock of bass is still nowhere near recovery and an illegal trade in the fish is thought to be substantial.

In Cornwall and Devon, fishermen in small boats sprouting bamboo rods troll commercially for bass (otherwise and increasingly a farmed fish), but they observe a minimum landing size, lift the fish with landing-nets, and rush them ashore without a scale out of place to upmarket restaurants that boast of their 'ecological' sourcing. Such a profitable application of traditional handlining has been copied by mackerel fishermen at Dunmore East, fishing with feathered jigs as their grandfathers did, and packing the biggest fish in ice for swift delivery ashore at premium prices.

After a thorough survey of inshore fishing in 1999, BIM crafted an ambitious framework for management, completed in 2005. A network of advisory committees and species groups, structured from local to national level, now has a substantial involvement of fishermen in agreeing science-based management plans for crabs, lobster, crawfish, shrimp and molluscs. These will, it is hoped, change the scene summed up in the Marine Institute's 2007 Stock Book: 'Demand for marine product has increased and the resources display every sign of being over-exploited. Meanwhile, effort increases in a relentless race to survive which can end only in greater hardship for a growing number of inshore fishers.'

Failures of management

In the wider waters too, Europe gropes towards better management. In December 2007, a few days before the fishery ministers of Europe gathered in Brussels for their annual, all-night ritual of negotiations on national fishing quotas, the European Court of Auditors delivered its latest report on fishing in EU waters. It was a formidable indictment of the workings of the Common Fisheries Policy. Management failure, the Court concluded, was made evident in continuing overfishing and falling catches. Monitoring of stocks depended on unreliable facts and figures and ineffective inspections; infringements went undetected or attracted no proper sanctions. The Community's fleet still had too much catching capacity – 'an incitement to non-compliance with catch limitations.'

Earlier in the year, the European Commission published a scarcely less critical review of progress towards conservation. Despite reforms, and some success in long-term recovery plans, some 80 per cent of fish stocks were still being fished outside safe biological limits. The main (and unchanging) reason was that the TACs agreed at the December gatherings are much higher than those recommended by fishery scientists, by an average in recent years of between 42–57 per cent. Even at that, many TACs are (in practice) consistently overshot. Only three of the thirty-three stocks of known status are fished compatibly with management for maximum sustainable yield – the pledge of the World Summit on Sustainable Development in Johannesburg in 2002.

Fin whales off the coast of west Cork. (© Padraig Whooley/IWDG)

CHAPTER 8

Marine Menagerie

Cetacea, Seals, Turtles, Birds

Sperm whales, photographed by the Air Corps to the west of Mayo. (Irish Maritime Squadron)

'No doubt there are those who will begin here with a sense of incredulity ... Some, indeed, may have difficulty in believing that any serious whaling has been undertaken in the vicinity of Ireland: nothing could be further from the truth.' In *Irish Whales and Whaling* (Blackstaff, 1981), the Belfast zoologist James Fairley was addressing a broad audience. Few people at that time had any sense of the cetacean life around the island, still less of the regular presence of some of the largest whales in the world.

A quarter of a century later, whales and dolphins enjoy something near their proper place in the roster of Irish wildlife. This is almost entirely due to a relatively small, partly amateur, network of researchers and observers established in 1991. The Irish Whale and Dolphin Group (IWDG) have opened a new chapter in Irish natural history – one that acknowledges that nearly half of our native mammals live in the sea. Mighty animals such as fin whales (*Balaenoptera physalis*) and humpback whales (*Megaptera novaeanglia*) can sometimes be seen (if distantly, through telescopes) from Irish headlands, and even seasonally promised, with some confidence, by the skippers of west Cork's whale-watching charter boats. Even deep-ocean sperm whales (*Physeter macrocephalus*) are being gathered into the national ken: prompted to keep a lookout by the IWDG, the Irish Air Corps in the spring of 2007 photographed nine of them passing in a group along the edge of the continental shelf at about 160 km west of the Mullet Peninsula, County Mayo.

Their sighting calls up the Norwegian whaling operations based on that stretch of the County Mayo coast (on the Inishkea Islands and the Blacksod Bay side of the Mullet Peninsula) between 1908 and 1922. At least 800 great whales were killed in that time from small and powerfully fast steamers with crow's-nest lookouts and harpoon guns mounted in the bows. The first season saw the capture of six 'nordcapers', the 18-m northern right whale (*Balaena glacialis*) that became the 'right' target of whaling because it swam slowly in coastal waters and obligingly stayed afloat when killed. Today, as everywhere in the eastern Atlantic, sightings of its V-shaped blow off Ireland are extremely rare.

After the first successful sweeps, the Mayo whalers needed to go much farther from the coast to find their quarry – ultimately to the Rockall Bank, some 400 km distant. The record season was in 1920, when the Blacksod company produced 3,995 barrels of oil from 101 fin whales, 12 sperm whales, 9 blues (*Balaenoptera musculus*) and 3 sei (*Balaenoptera borealis*). But both Mayo whaling stations ended in commercial failure. Later in the century, perhaps well into the 1970s, Norwegian whalers searched around Ireland for the small, 10-m northern bottlenose whale (*Hyperoodon ampullatus*) and the similar-sized minke whale (*Balaeoptera acutorostrata*), both of which could be processed on board. In 1976, a new Wildlife Act protected all cetaceans from 'wilful interference' within the state's fishery limits, and in 1991 the sustained lobbying of the IWDG helped to bring the government declaration of a sanctuary for whales and dolphins within Irish waters.

In the early subsistence living of coastal communities there had, of course, been local opportunistic slaughters of inshore dolphins, porpoises (*Phocoena phocoena*) and pilot whales (*Globicephala melaena*). Indeed, 'the driving ashore of pilot whales on the south coast,' writes Fairley 'seems to have been of fairly frequent occurrence in the nineteenth century at least.' In the early eighteenth century there was also an intermittent whaling industry in Donegal Bay, where local fishermen, already skilled in harpooning basking sharks, were employed, without much success, to hunt fin whales close inshore.

A fin whale lunge-feeding off west Cork.
(Courtesy of Padraig Whooley/IWDG)

An Ulster entrepreneur, Thomas Nesbitt, invented what may have been the first workable harpoon gun and succeeded in killing two or three whales a year in the bay, but he was finally defeated by problems in exporting fast-decomposing blubber to England. His enterprise may well have inspired the clergyman-poet James Sterling (1701-1763):

Who first discovered whales upon our coast
Such quantities as Britain cannot boast;
Ev'n Donegal produces equal store
To what is found on Greenland's foreign shore.

Away from such ventures, and pending the great leap in popular and scientific interest towards the end of the last century, Irish knowledge of the natural history of whales depended largely on the regular strandings of dead or dying animals. These have ranged from massive hulks of whales more than 20 m long, baleen hanging slack in their jaws, to whales not much bigger than dolphins but with jaws lined, or at least dotted, with teeth. Such a cardinal difference has marked out the Mysticeti (baleen whales) from the Odontoceti (toothed whales and dolphins); but size is not everything since the huge, square-headed sperm whale has no baleen sieves but a massive lower jaw with twenty-six pairs of teeth, the size of goose eggs, with which to seize deep-sea squid. Among its smaller relatives, dentition ranges from the sinister array of the killer whale (*Orcinus orca*) to the few, erratic molars of small beaked whales (True's, Cuvier's, Gervais' and others) whose deep-sea lives are still largely mysterious.

Anatomy of diving

Humpback whales visit Ireland's south coast on migration from northwest Africa. An IWDG expedition photographed their breaching behaviour off Cape Verde. (© Simon Berrow)

Much of the early modern research into whales was focused on their ability to dive to great depths and stay submerged for ages (sperm whales for more than an hour) while having smaller lungs, bulk for bulk, than humans. A big part of the answer is the enormous oxygen-storing capacity of myoglobin (muscle haemoglobin), a pigment that turns the meat of the sperm whale almost black. A radically slowed heartbeat and long glides without active swimming also help to economise on oxygen use. The lungs collapse as pressure increases, reducing the risk of nitrogen dissolving in the blood. Whether this does, in fact, protect whales from the 'bends' that can afflict human divers has been questioned in the wake of autopsies on beaked whales that beached themselves in the Canary Islands after exposure to military underwater sonar.

It was US naval use of coastal hydrophones in the Second World War to warn of approaching submarines that began to reveal the cetacean world of communication by sounds, many of which reverberate through the oceans. Whales and dolphins generate an infinite range of clicks, creaks, grunts, whistles, ringing 'boings', hammerings, trumpetings and the long, patterned sequences of more gentle tones now described as 'song'. How they are all produced is still far from clear. In the toothed whales, which use sounds to locate (and, perhaps, disorientate) their prey as well as for communication, clicks and whistles are produced by forcing air past 'phonic lips' in their nasal structures and focusing it for echolocation through tissues in the bulbous 'melon' of the head. Baleen whales have no phonic lips, but are thought to use the larynx, even though it has no human-style vocal chords and the animals do not have to exhale to make the sounds. These are sometimes extremely loud – as in the 188-decibel moan of the blue whale, which can travel hundreds of kilometres underwater (the sound of a jet aircraft at take-off measures 110–140 decibels) or be elaborately phrased and protracted, as in the long – perhaps thirty-minute – courtship songs of species such as the humpback whale.

The potential impact of human interference with cetacean underwater hearing is now considered very seriously. Canada, for example, has banned the use of seismic air-guns in its western waters. As Ireland opens its deeper frontier waters to new rounds of oil/gas exploration, starting with the Slyne, Erris and Donegal basins off the west coast and the Porcupine Seabight to the southwest, the effects of undersea noise on whales and dolphins have been considered in Irish Offshore Strategic Environmental Assessments (IOSEAs) made for the government's Petroleum Affairs Division. Theoretical modelling suggests that baleen whales, in particular, may shy away at 20 km from an air-gun's seismic bang of 248 decibels, while field research suggests an even more distant sensitivity, and one likely to be shared to some extent by seals.

On the other hand, baleen whales regularly migrate into waters off northwest Australia and California with consistently high seismic activity, and along coasts which have known decades of seismic surveys. The Irish assessments have, however, stressed the 'great uncertainties as to how sound travels and decays in strength' and how little is known of the long-term effects of man-made sound on marine animals. Meanwhile, it proposes that 'slow, soft starts of the air guns' would give them time to move away, and that simultaneous seismic surveys should work at least 100 km apart.

In the UK, the Ministry of Defence has funded research to help the Royal Navy avoid using sonar on NATO exercises in areas of high cetacean density. This has been made possible by the successive EU-funded SCANS aerial and shipboard surveys of small cetaceans around Europe's Atlantic and North Sea coasts. The most recent of these surveys, in 2005, found minke whales and common dolphins (*Delphinus delphis*) particularly abundant off Ireland's Atlantic coast.

As whales diminish in size, the taxonomic overlap with dolphins can grow confusing (the killer whale, for example is the largest of dolphins, and belongs to the family Delphinidae, as does the pilot whale which is next in size). Dolphins, says James Fairley, are 'simply small toothed cetaceans with beaks' – but neither killers nor pilots are exactly small or have noticeable beaks. Even modest exploration of Ireland's whales and dolphins tempts one to settle for their order – the Cetacea – and take each animal as it comes. There are twenty-four species in Irish waters, all but a handful of which have been stranded ashore. Their detailed descriptions and behaviour at sea are presented comprehensively in the IWDG *Guide to the Identification of the Whales and Dolphins of Ireland*, by Jim Wilson and Simon Berrow (2006) and will not be repeated here.

The most spectacular encounters to date have occurred off the southwest of the island. One of early significance was described by Peter Evans, an Oxford University research scientist, in his *Natural History of Whales and Dolphins* (1987). In the autumn of 1968, sailing southwards past the Old Head of Kinsale in County Cork on a seabird expedition, 'we saw a distant shape above the horizon. I concluded that it was a ship many kilometres away . . . Imagine my surprise when the ship came into view again and revealed itself to be a fin whale, twice as large as our own [10-m] boat. It broke the surface allowing us to see the entire back and small curved dorsal fin before sending a plume of steam into the air and descending once more in a shallow dive. That was my first introduction to whales – and one I shall never forget.' It led to him helping to set up a Cetacean Group in the UK Mammal Society. 'Up to that time,' he writes, 'our knowledge had come either from earlier whaling activities off the Scottish and Irish coasts, or as a result of animals being washed up on our shores. No information had been derived from live sightings.'

Eight in a pod

This was the move that also inspired Simon Berrow, with colleague Emer Rogan in NUI Cork, to set up the IWDG. It brought another founder member, Padraig Whooley, to live in Cork and take his telescope to regular three-hour watches from the Old Head of Kinsale. From the late 1990s, his sightings of fin and sei whales – as many as eight in a pod – were seminal excitements in the group's exploration of the rich cetacean life offshore. Later, as watching effort moved out to sea, the first humpbacks were photographed at close quarters, lifting their tails high before diving in a characteristic salute.

Humpbacks can be identified by unique patterns on the underside of the flukes. (Captain Budd Christman, NOAA Corps)

A lot remains to be learned about the seasonal movements of whales around Ireland. Migrations of the big baleen whales between wintering and breeding grounds in warm, temperate waters (such as those off northwest Africa) and summers in krill-rich feeding grounds at the Arctic Circle have long been accepted, though the ocean's slow warming and cooling may put their movements somewhat out of phase with human perception of the seasons.

A year-long acoustic study in the mid-1990s, funded by oil/gas companies, used bottom-mounted hydrophone arrays to monitor the songs of the whales from the Faroe–Shetland area down to the Bay of Biscay. The pulsing moans of the fin whale rang through the sea at every latitude, with the highest counts of individuals between October and January. Off western Ireland, the vocal peak of the

The minke, smallest of the rorquals, is the most common whale around the Irish coast.
(© Padraig Whooley/IWDG)

blue whale came in November and December. Fewer than 500 blue whales may now visit the North Atlantic, and while thirty to fifty of these massive creatures are thought to pass through Ireland's ocean each year, actual sightings have been rare. Its slim, vertical blow, or spout, can be up to 9 m high and visible from kilometres around.

Song recordings have suggested an annual north–south migratory passage of 300–500 fin whales off Ireland. But the number of sightings off the south coast between June and November encourages the IWDG to think there may be a separate, sedentary population that takes shorter journeys offshore. As many as twenty have been seen together in summer, hunting herring and sprats off the coast of County Cork, sometimes sharing a few kilometres of sea with as many minke whales lunge-feeding at the surface. It is off the south coast, too, that humpback whales have been identified individually by the unique black and white pattern on the underside of the tail. They are found to come back each year, staying inshore for months after late summer, with one of them showing special loyalty to an area off Galley Head in west Cork. Acoustic studies point to a more usual use of deep waters along the edge of the continental shelf as a migration corridor between waters off northwest Africa and those off sub-Arctic Norway. This also seems to be the route of the sei whale, recorded in summer off Ireland's southwest and northwest coasts but difficult to distinguish from the fin whale without a close view.

A century ago, the fin was the commonest baleen whale in Irish waters. Today the most frequent is the small, slim, 10-m minke (named for a Norwegian lookout called Meincke who, in a story passed on to whalers the world over, mistook a distant school of little piked whales, as they were once called, for blue whales). It has the pleated, expandable mouth typical of the rorqual but also – at least in the northern hemisphere – an uncharacteristically wide appetite. While Antarctic minke stick to sieving krill from each big gulp of water, those of the Atlantic continental shelf hunt many small fish and even squid. Usually hunting alone or in small groups of four or five, they often herd or chase fish into a group, or drive them from the deep to the surface, before dashing through them with mouth agape: a tactic that can even capture larger fish such as cod and haddock. Such furious activity is sometimes on view in the mouth of the Shannon Estuary, where minkes feed on summer sprat beneath a circling halo of kittiwakes and shearwaters.

Matrilineal killers

Even when doing nothing, a pod of half a dozen killer whales can carry a powerful aura of drama, especially when met unexpectedly close inshore, say, in a sound between the Blaskets or the narrows of Strangford Lough. The small parties seen around Ireland do not generally deserve the collective term 'pod', since they are mostly matrilineal family groups. But the very tall dorsal fin of the male signals the streamlined bulk of this most awesome of Delphinidae, a ruthless pack-predator in the wild, however biddable and intelligent as an aquarium performer.

The most abundant middle-sized cetaceans in Irish waters and those most likely to be stranded ashore, dead or alive, are the bulbous-headed, long-finned pilot whales. Large numbers have been recorded along the edge of the continental shelf, and the waters off southwest Ireland are thought to be an important breeding ground. The whales live in tight family groups but often gather in schools of up to fifty or more, and one recent sighting, off Cape Clear, was of about a hundred. In deep ocean their herds may be many times larger, feeding mainly at night on squid and fish rising towards the surface. But they also frequent the bays of the North Atlantic, including those of the Shetland and Orkney Islands and, notably, the Faroes, where pilot whaling has been carried on for centuries. Historically, some 1,500 animals have been killed in a season, presenting scenes of mass slaughter in the shallows.

The 'active and boisterous' common dolphin.
(© Padraig Whooley/IWDG)

There was comparable hunting on the coasts of Newfoundland, where reports of herds being led by a single male are probably what gave the pilot whale its common name.

Certainly there is leadership among pilot whales but it is hard to pin down its role in the live beachings for which the species has a tragic reputation. In Ireland the most recent event was in March 2002, when more than thirty went aground at Castlegregory in Tralee Bay, County Kerry. Many were helped back to sea (including a calf born on the sands) with the aid of rescue pontoons supplied by the IWDG, but eighteen of the whales were lost. An even sadder outcome attended a mass stranding at Cloghane, a few miles away, in 1965, when sixty-six pilot whales were beached and, in the words of the IWDG, 'After locals satisfied themselves that the meat was not for the Kerry palate, the whales were fed to the mink in a local mink farm.'

The gradually shelving contours of Tralee Bay, next to the Dingle Peninsula, have close similarity to places on New Zealand's coastline that are the sites of repeated strandings of long-finned pilot whales and beaked whales, sometimes in several hundreds. To some scientists, this suggests a flaw of echolocation, but other scenarios abound. Many rest on proposing an instinctive – or altruistic – group bonding in following sick animals ashore. The persistent restranding behaviour so often shown by individual whales or dolphins is deeply dismaying to human would-be helpers. This has prompted the conclusion, offered on one Irish dolphin website, that 'we should not be afraid to admit that we don't know [why cetaceans strand]. It is at least a possibility worth considering that it represents a deliberate choice by conscious and intelligent animals acting under impulses of which we have little or no conception.'

Among smaller cetaceans around Ireland, the largest schools are formed among the abundant common dolphins, especially in winter. In February 2001, for example, they quartered Cork Harbour for days, perhaps for shoals of sprat, in groups ranging from 300–1,000. Farther out on the shelf, their herds may be numbered in several thousand, sometimes mixed with other species. The IWDG describes them as 'active and boisterous', often bow-riding with yachts and ships and even large whales, and a school in a leaping feeding frenzy, sharing their prey with plunging gannets, is among the most spectacular sights of Ireland's ocean. Such large numbers invite many casualties, particularly from by-catch in fishing nets, with the consequent arrival of dead dolphins at the tideline.

Mixed deep-sea herds may include schools of striped dolphin (*Stenella coeruleoalba*), a warm-water species seen increasingly farther north as climate changes. The Atlantic white-sided dolphin (*Lagenorhynchus acutus*) also associates with other species, especially pilot whales, and regularly strand alive, singly or in groups, on western coasts. The much larger Risso's dolphin (*Grampus griseus*), distinctively scarred with white body scratches, is usually seen alone or in small family groups. It is a largely oceanic animal, but it has been shown to calve in Irish waters in late spring and early summer, and is sometimes seen hunting, perhaps for cuttlefish, close to shore.

Bottlenoses: biggest dolphins

The best-known dolphins, however, remain the big bottlenoses (*Tursiops truncatus*), especially since the advent of 'friendly' individuals, such as Dingle's Fungie, and the development of dolphin-watching and well-publicised scientific study in the Shannon Estuary.

There are bottlenose dolphins in temperate and tropical seas around the world, mainly in coastal waters and varying geographically in size and appearance. The Atlantic dolphins are the biggest, the males reaching some 3.8 m. While they have been seen as far north as Svalbard (an archipelago in the Arctic Ocean roughly midway between Norway and the North Pole), their general range seems to extend not much beyond the north of Scotland. Moray Firth, in the northeast of Scotland, has one of Europe's few surviving resident bottlenose populations, and the Shannon Estuary has another. Such local dolphin groups were once common in Irish estuaries and sea lochs where today they are rarely seen at all. While bottlenoses are often encountered in Irish coastal waters, especially in the west and southwest, the great majority live farther offshore, with many sightings in the Celtic Sea. Around Europe, the highest density of bottlenoses has been found on the Biscay continental shelf.

They typically establish groups of some 130 individuals, comprising several sub-pods (a social structure common to many cetacean families). Conservation has concentrated on protecting important coastal sites (both the Shannon Estuary and the inner Moray Firth are SACs for the species) but the photo-identification of individual dolphins has shown them travelling far beyond their boundaries. At Moray Firth, in particular, a real expansion of range to the outer coasts by a more or less stable population, together with fatal attacks on the inlet's porpoises (which compete with the dolphins for food), suggest a growing shortage of fish. On the other hand, a group of bottlenoses off Cornwall and Devon has been found to have a large range of several hundred kilometres of coastline.

The Shannon Estuary is the home range and nursery ground for a large group of bottlenoses, their

number reaching a peak in May, June and July. They are drawn by the seasonal abundance of salmon, hunted in strong tidal races, and by sheltered eddies in which to calve. Since 1993, when photo-identification began, the Shannon Dolphin and Wildlife Foundation has catalogued some 200 individual animals, from nicks in their fins and other more subtle markings. A survey in 2000 found a summer population of 113 dolphins living in a seemingly 'fluid and gregarious social structure.' Some of their identities have since been matched to underwater acoustic recordings of individual and distinctive whistles. The growing confidence of identification, together with a lot more photographs of west coast dolphins by IWDG members and others, will help in exploring the wider range of the Shannon bottlenoses. The dolphin-

Bottlenose dolphins in the Shannon Estuary.
(© Simon Berrow)

watching tourism of the estuary has developed in an ideal co-operation with the scientists – Simon Berrow, Brian Holmes and Emer Rogan, all zoology graduates of NUI Cork – who have led the study of the animals. In some 200 trips a year, the two boat operators rarely meet on the estuary, yet can offer almost total certainty of encounters with the bottlenoses at a respectful but photogenic distance.

The human acquaintance

Since Fungie, the 'friendly' dolphin, first made his overtures to swimmers at Dingle Harbour in 1983, three others have regularly interacted with humans: at Dunquin on the same peninsula; at Fanore, County Clare, and Inis Oírr in the Aran Islands. Fungie, however, has sustained a local tourist industry with his reliable eagerness to engage acrobatically with boats, divers and swimmers. Similar behaviour is a worldwide phenomenon, still rare but apparently increasing, and perhaps reflecting local fragmentation of bottlenose populations. The species is widely known for its high intelligence and social nature, and 'solitary-sociable' individuals may have been excluded or displaced from their group, finding a substitute in playful human company with the occasional bonus of free fish. In 2006, there were at least four friendly dolphins around the UK, with one well-studied 3-m male known variously as 'Georges', 'Randy' and 'Dony', travelling widely, touring marinas and harbours in France, southern England, Belgium and Holland.

Ireland's smallest (up to 1.5 m) and most plentiful cetacean, the harbour porpoise, is more adventurous than its common name suggests. While there are discrete inshore populations, notably in the Irish Sea, porpoises roam out abundantly across the shelf of the Celtic Sea and have even been sighted in deeper waters above the Rockall and Faroes Banks. The name in Irish, *muc mhara* or sea-pig, can be read two ways: 'herring-hog' was a common name in English, reflecting its reputation among fishermen, but porpoises were also driven ashore for food on the Blasket Islands where, according to Tomás Ó Croimhthain in *The Islandman*, 'you could hardly get anybody to exchange a porpoise for a pig.'

Modern threats to the porpoise in European waters have been chiefly their unwanted capture, totalling many thousands, in trawls and static tangle-nets. One consequence has been the development of loud acoustic 'pingers' activated by the sonar clicks of the porpoises themselves (see p.145). There have also been moves to protect some of their inshore haunts, as in the designation of the Blasket Islands and of Roaringwater Bay in Cork as SACs. In 2007, counts began around the Blaskets, using visual patrols and underwater microphones, to establish a baseline for the density of their numbers.

Seals: 'people of the sea'

Grey seals hauled out. (Nigel Motyer)

For all the ingenious fictions of folklore attaching to the seals of Ireland and Scotland (the *People of the Sea* in David Thomson's memorable collection of 1954), the past history of human dealings with the animals was routinely bloody and utilitarian. Tomás Ó Croimhthain's chronicle of life on the Blaskets, at the end of the nineteenth century, offers his witness, as a boy, of the slaughter of seals by islandmen in a dripping, candle-lit sea cave. 'It's odd the way the world changes,' he reflected in the 1920s. 'Nobody would put a bit of seal meat in his mouth today. They melt it down for light, for it is cram-full of oil. Moreover, if you made a present of the skin to a gentleman, he'd hardly deign to accept it from you.'

For the following half-century, official bounties were paid on both grey (*Halichoerus grypus*) and harbour seals (*Phoca vitulina*) as a fishery protection measure but the Wildlife Act of 1976 gave

Harbour seal at Rathlin Island.
(Nigel Motyer)

the animals protection. Today, as the number of grey seals continues to rise steadily around Ireland and Britain, the popular objection to culling continues to frustrate commercial fishermen convinced of their intolerable competition. The northeast Atlantic grey seal ranges through a vast area, stretching from the Kola Peninsula in northern Russia to Brittany, but the bulk of the population is found around Britain and Ireland and was estimated at some 113,000 in 2003.

The grey seal on the American side of the Atlantic may be a bigger animal, but the full-grown male of Ireland's coast is still, at around 2.3 m, a burly pinniped (Pinnipedia is the order of the seals), and towers over the harbour seal which is no more than 1.6 m. The two can often be seen resting together at haul-outs on the same rocks, where the difference not only of size but colour, head-shape and nostrils (meeting in a V in the common seal, vertical slits in the grey) can be compared. But they breed and moult at different times, in different places, and the terrestrial colonies of the harbour seal are closest inshore, even on estuary sandbanks at low tide; while greys keep their distance on offshore islands and reefs, in sea caves, or remote and undisturbed corners of the mainland.

Both species spend most of their lives in or under the water and can be energetic travellers. But while the harbour seal ventures up to 50 km on fishing expeditions along the coast, diving to perhaps 50 m for flatfish and sand eels and spending no more than five minutes underwater, the greys roam far more widely: Scottish seals have been found 450 km off our southwest coast. Greys also dive more deeply, often to around 120 m, aided by the same physiological means as whales and dolphins: spare

Harbour seal mother and pup. (Michelle Cronin)

oxygen stored in blood and muscle, and a drastic slowing of the heartbeat. The blubber under their skin, about one-third of their bodyweight, gives a similar insulation.

There are harbour seals in colder coastal waters right around the globe, and those around Ireland share in a stock that extends to Murmansk in the north and the Baltic to the east. It suffered the bulk of the losses in outbreaks of phocine distemper virus (PDV) in 1988 and 2002, which caused the deaths of some 44,000 seals. Most of these were in the North and Baltic Seas, but there were also substantial losses around Ireland. At Strangford Lough in County Down, for example, the prime harbour seal habitat of the western Irish Sea, the 1998 outbreak cost some 200 lives, about one third of the colony.

Uncertainty about the general fate of harbour seals around Ireland brought home how little was known of their total number and distribution. Unlike grey seals, whose pups stay ashore for several weeks, harbour seal pups can swim with their mothers from birth, making a breeding-season census difficult. Instead (in a survey carried out by the National Parks and Wildlife Service [NPWS] in association with NUI Cork and St Andrew's University, Scotland), a helicopter equipped with a thermal-imaging camera sought out the harbour seals as they moulted at their haul-outs in July and August. Even at a respectful distance of 500 m, the infrared images could find seals tucked among rocks and seaweed and offer distinguishable profiles where harbour seals were mixed with greys. Sample 'ground-truthing' counts checked on the aerial accuracy. Near-identical surveys in Northern Ireland and the Republic produced a minimum all-Ireland total of 4,153 harbour seals, with an unexpectedly high concentration in the bays and inlets of the southwest.

A similar combination of aerial photography and ground checks was brought to a survey of grey seals in the Republic during their autumn pupping season in 2005. The project, also for the NPWS and led by Oliver Ó Cadhla, produced the first really confident estimates to serve as a baseline: an estimated 1,574 pups were born, bringing the population to a 'robust' minimum estimate of 7,083 (a further 100 pups, at most, would be added from Northern Ireland).

There are seven key breeding colonies: in southwest Donegal; the Inishkea group of islands off Mayo; islands off northwest Galway; the Blaskets off Kerry; the Saltees off Wexford; Lambay Island and Ireland's Eye off County Dublin. Other clusters of white-furred pups identified smaller sites along the Atlantic coastline from west Cork to Donegal. There were increases in pups at most of the colonies studied consistently since 1994, highest in the biggest breeding colony at the Inishkea islands. At the Blaskets, however, where some sixty seals and pups were slaughtered in an illegal cull in 2004, there was a small fall in pup production.

The appetite of seals

With the doubling of the grey seal population around Britain since 1985 and the decline in stocks of commercial fish, the pressure for culls has been unremitting. In Ireland, it was the grey seals' appetite for salmon caught in drift nets that prompted massacres on the Blaskets and, in the 1970s, the Inishkeas. In Scotland, the forays of seals into salmon rivers accelerated research using DNA to identify which fish the seals were eating from residues in their scats, collected at haul-out sites. Much had already been learned from remains in scats such as fish otoliths and squid beaks, but lengthy feeding experiments by the Sea Mammal Research Unit at the University of St Andrews refined the ability to measure not only exactly what populations of grey seals consume, but in what lengths and amounts. The results from a major survey in 2002, analysing scats from western Scotland and the Shetlands, confirmed a lot of what had been found from studies off the west of Ireland and in the Irish Sea: that grey seals will eat what they can get, that this varies from place to place and season to season, and that most of it is less than 30 cm long.

The basic prey of the 40,000–50,000 grey seals in the Hebrides remains sand eels and gadoids (especially cod and haddock), with some switch to herring in recent decades and new bottom-living fish in the diet such as lemon sole, rockling, sea scorpion, and dragonet (*Callionymus* spp.). With each grey seal eating about 5 kg of fish a day, the 77,000 tonnes consumed in 2002 in the Hebrides area were broadly in line with the rise in local seal numbers since 1985. A threefold rise in per-pinniped consumption of haddock and herring (this especially in the Outer Hebrides) was dourly noted by a fishing industry now apparently resigned to the failure of its calls for culling. Whether the seals will make it impossible for cod stocks in the region to recover, or whether declining stocks will limit the seal populations, were questions the Scottish scientists felt unable to answer without more research.

The management of seals in the interest of fisheries is an issue now to be set within the new ecosystem approach adopted by ocean scientists. It will also, no doubt, continue to be influenced by the humane concerns of the wider public. The Irish Seal Sanctuary has steadily gained in recognition and support, rehabilitating and releasing sick or injured animals found in difficulties around the island; plans for a marine conservation centre at Balbriggan are under way. Similar work is carried out in the purpose-built Seal Rescue Centre at the Exploris Aquarium at Portaferry, beside the narrows of Strangford Lough: it has released well over 200 harbour and grey seals since 1989.

Turtles: leatherbacks and others

One day in December 2006, a big leatherback turtle swimming in mid-Atlantic towards South America, took a deep dive through the blue, its powerful front flippers arcing through the clear tropical water. It was hunting jellyfish to eat, that much seems certain, but the search that took it down – and down – into fading light and falling temperature must have been compelling indeed. It reached the extraordinary depth of 1,280 m, by far the greatest dive for a leatherback ever recorded. Logged by the depth recorder strapped to its back and duly relayed by satellite to a computer in NUI Cork, this was the most dramatic event of the turtle's long journey to its nesting ground from its capture off the Dingle Peninsula on the last day of June.

The long journey was also of another kind. Irish schoolchildren were following it on a website set up by scientists, learning in the process about the leatherbacks' biology and diet and their regular summer migrations to Irish waters. In their grandparents' time, the turtles were exotic specimens – rare 'sea monsters', almost – towed in from their entanglement in fishermen's ropes for pathetic exhibition on the quaysides. Now, as an endangered species, they have earned a more enlightened study: protection under the Wildlife Act, and ready release, where feasible, by fishermen retrieving their pots and buoys.

A leatherback turtle nesting at a French Guiana beach. (Tom Doyle)

The air-breathing leatherback is the world's biggest turtle and heaviest reptile, its form shaped in the Jurassic period 200 million years ago, with a normal lifespan of up to a century. Indeed, 2007 set a further record for the biggest animal found in Irish waters: 2.5 m from flipper tip to flipper tip, with the ridged black carapace 1.68 m long and the weight of its barrel of a body judged to be at least half a tonne. It was found floating, dead, off County Cork, with a large piece of plastic lodged in its gut: an increasingly frequent fate globally, as the turtles mistake submerged plastic bags and balloons for the jellyfish that are their food (see also p.172).

The turtles' long migrations, some clearly transatlantic, may last two or three years between returning to beaches to breed; from their main 'rookeries' in French Guiana and Surinam, on the northern coast of South America, and Gabon in West Africa, the turtles regularly swim north as far as Newfoundland and Norway. This passage into cold waters is made possible by their ability, unique in reptiles, to retain the heat generated by muscular activity and conserve it beneath blubber and the thick, cartilaginous shell. The core temperature, perhaps 8 °C higher than that of the surrounding water, is also a function of the turtle's great size (a model known as 'gigantothermy') and may assist the leatherback's deeper dives.

Jellyfish are the main diet of the leatherback turtle.

Development of satellite telemetry has added hugely to knowledge of the leatherbacks' behaviour. Many of its gelatinous prey – salps, jellyfish and siphonophores – migrate vertically in the water column, rising nearer the surface at night and sinking deep by day. Thus the turtles dive more busily (and shallowly) at night and much less often during the day (but more deeply and for longer until the jellyfish start moving upwards at dusk). Even so, dives deeper than 500 m seem rare, and about an hour below water seems to be the leatherback's limit.

Scientists are still wondering how a diet 'composed almost entirely of water', as one study puts it, can meet the energy needs of such a large animal and make such long migrations worthwhile. But a striking finding of the INTERREG Irish Sea Leatherback Turtle Project, carried out by NUI Cork and the University of Wales, Swansea, has been the annual rendezvous of the leatherbacks with massive concentrations of the big, substantial *Rhizostoma* jellyfish in certain bays of the Irish Sea. While the Bay of Biscay is a known 'high-use' area for the turtles, the INTERREG study calculates that perhaps 400 may feed in Ireland's area of continental shelf and that, on an average summer's day, some 25 may be swimming close around the coast.

Ridleys and loggerheads

Ocean currents and storms bring two more species of turtle to Ireland, but these are usually juveniles, rarely much bigger than a leatherback's head. The origin of one species is fairly certain, since the last few thousand of the little Kemp's ridley turtle (*Lepidochelys kempii*) nests on a single beach north of Tampico in the Gulf of Mexico. There have been under a dozen records of strandings of the ridley in Ireland, usually freshly dead in winter, but many more of the common loggerhead (*Caretta caretta*). Neither turtle has the leatherback's ability to generate warmth and tolerate cold water. A run of winter storms can sometimes leave a scattering of dead or dying loggerheads on shores in the southwest, and in 1992 a pair of living, but weak, survivors were cared for in the Bray aquarium and returned to Madeira.

The loggerheads have hatched on beaches from Carolina to Florida, and have a migratory pattern, guided by Earth's magnetic field, that normally keeps them within the warm water of the Gulf Stream and North Atlantic gyre. They travel eastward across the Atlantic, turn south off the northern coast of Spain and follow the course of the gyre to reach the coast of Florida again. The powerful jaws of the loggerhead (hence the name) are designed for crushing shellfish and crustacea as a carnivore feeding on bottom invertebrates, and it rarely dives deeper than 40 m. While its food includes jellyfish, its ocean-going diet is not fully known. Floating plastic and balloons, both easily mistaken for jellyfish, are thought to cause many deaths.

Puffin portrait. (Nigel Motyer)

Birds of the ocean

Summer colonies of breeding seabirds on Ireland's wilder coasts offer some of the most spectacular sights and sounds of European wildlife: towering cliffs stacked with nesting guillemots (*Uira aalge*), razorbills (*Alca torda*) and fulmars (*Fulmarus glacialis*); island summits snow-capped with gannets (*Sula bassana*) or whirring with puffins (*Fratercula artica*). In spring and autumn, poor weather brings the mass migrations of seabirds within binocular range of the Atlantic headlands. Watching long and purposeful processions pressing north or south above the waves and picking out unfamiliar skuas, petrels and shearwaters, one senses most sharply the otherness, the special life, of oceanic birds. The rich waters of the northeast Atlantic shelf, along with every safe niche or hideaway a breeding seabird could desire, have made Ireland and Britain a strategic stronghold for the avian populations of the temperate ocean. The islands host the breeding of about 8 million of them, from 25 different species.

The very forms of seabirds are shaped by survival far from shore. Some, like terns and kittiwakes (*Rissa tridactyla*), are essentially aerial species with slender frames and short, light legs, ranging over vast distances in winter and plucking food from the surface or from brief dips into the waves. Others, notably the auks (guillemots, razorbills, puffins), have powerful legs set well back, and short narrow wings for propulsion in deep dives. The gannet, Ireland's largest seabird, has a strengthened skull and shock-absorbing air sacs to take the impact of plummeting aerial dives from as high as 40 m. Its subsequent take-off, on the other hand, is not so easily achieved, and best launched from the top of a wave into the lift of a helpful breeze.

Flight above the ocean is very different from that above land. The sea offers few rising columns of heated air on which a bird may soar. The obstacle of a moving ship, on the other hand, creates an upward air current in which a gull may glide indefinitely, and long breakers on the shore give a similar zone of lift. Wind is what supplies the energy for ocean flight, rising in speed as it lifts above the

A gannet with catch.
(Nigel Motyer)

frictional drag of waves. The soaring of an albatross uses this to gain altitude, tacking as it travels in a series of rises and falls: it even nests on the windward side of islands, needing only to stretch its wings to be lifted. Hardy ocean wanderers such as shearwaters and fulmars also have long, stiff wings on which to glide with minimal effort, but depend more on up-currents deflected from the waves.

Webbed feet for thrust against water are almost universal, as are glands to expel salt after sips from the sea, and others for preening feathers with waterproof waxes and fats. The order Procellariform of 'tube-nosed' birds (fulmars, petrels, shearwaters and albatrosses) also have a specially-developed sense of smell that helps them in their ocean foraging. The nostrils in their horny sheaths can detect the scent of distant dimethyl sulphide (DMS), a gas given off by phytoplankton, especially when zooplankton are grazing on it. This is a precious directional cue to the presence of fish and krill at particular points in an 'odour landscape', such as shelf breaks, upwelling fronts and seamounts. Experiments have shown that petrel fledglings have a nose for DMS even before they leave their nesting burrows (learning it, perhaps, as parents bring them food). Irish birding enthusiasts, on open sea boating expeditions to watch and take close-up photographs of oceanic species at sea, now go equipped with a phial of this concentrated, pungent and evil-smelling chemical, to spill into the waves. Such an expedition, setting out past Tory Island, County Donegal, in September 2007, rapidly summoned out of nowhere a rare array of tube-nosed birds: Leach's and Wilson's storm petrels (*Oceanodroma leucorhoa* and *Oceanites oceanicus*), sooty and great shearwaters (*Puffinus griseus* and *Puffinus gravis*), and fulmars.

Seabirds' lives can be unexpectedly long, compared with those of most landbirds. A Manx shearwater (*Puffinus puffinus*) trapped at the Copeland Islands bird observatory off County Down in 2003 had been ringed fifty years before – a northern hemisphere record, but a figure not unusual in the lifespan of the larger ocean species. In the smaller birds, such as puffins and kittiwakes, twenty to thirty years is not unusual. With such long lives, however, comes late maturity and few eggs in a clutch: petrels, gannets, guillemots, puffins and razorbills all lay a single egg.

Surviving to adulthood, full-grown seabirds have the air to themselves and few predators except at the nest. Their choice of breeding places stresses safety as well as food supply. Most big colonies are confined to offshore islands, or cliffs with ledges accessible only by air, a precaution pointed up by the periodic destruction of mainland tern and gull colonies by marauding foxes, mink, cats and rats. Manx shearwaters and European storm petrels (*Hydrobates pelagicus*) not only rear their chicks at the end of long burrows or under rocks but return from fishing to feed them after dark, when predatory great black-backed gulls (*Larus marinus*) and peregrine falcons (*Falco peregrinus*) are at rest. Ireland has some thirty summer colonies of storm petrels, mostly using burrows, or holes in scree or old dry-stone walls on the slopes of bare, uninhabited islands well offshore. The birds that nest on the Stags of Broadhaven, County Mayo, for example, feed at the distant edge of the Rockall Trough, which holds the main concentration of feeding birds off western Ireland.

The great shearwater, gliding with least effort off Tory Island. (Anthony McGeehan)

Among them are gannets that may have travelled huge distances to find food for their young. Birds from the Great Saltee Island off County Wexford, for example, have been satellite-tracked on foraging flights up to 240 km from the nest. A gannet diving vertically with folded wings suggests a spearing of fish with the powerful, pointed bill, but in fact it grabs its prey: sometimes in a brief plunge and quick re-surfacing to swallow; sometimes in a half-minute pursuit of a school as much as 20 m down. Like the fulmar and other seabirds, it will also follow trawlers, to scavenge from their catch and offal.

The spread of the fulmar in the North Atlantic has been one of the most spectacular phenomena of recorded bird history, its population increasing steadily since the mid-eighteenth century from a few original colonies in Iceland and St Kilda. It arrived to nest on the cliffs of Mayo in 1911 and still continues to increase: some 39,000 pairs now breed around Ireland. The biggest regional concentrations are still on islands at the north and west of Scotland (St Kilda alone has more than 68,000 pairs) but there the rise in numbers has markedly slowed or stopped. Early explanations for the bird's great expansion focused on the obvious boost in food supply from whaling and fishing: fulmars are still the main species in the clouds of birds feeding around trawlers. But recent closer study has found other factors at work in some population changes: many fulmars feed their chicks, for example, from the nightly rise of planktonic copepods, especially *Calanus finmarchicus*, a species in regional decline in recent decades. At one sober estimate, up to 100,000 fulmars drown each year in the northern Atlantic through snatching at baited hooks as they are launched from longlining fishing vessels.

The potential threat to seabirds from oil spills prompted the Irish Government's Petroleum Infrastructure Programme to commission an extensive survey, Cetaceans & Seabirds of Ireland's Atlantic Margin, from the Centre for Marine Research at NUI Cork (CMRC). Carried out over more than two years from 1999, and spanning all seasons, it studied seabird populations in the entire area to the west of Ireland, from the Rockall Trough and Hatton Bank to the Porcupine Seabight. They totalled some forty species, from the 'kleptoparasitic' great skuas (*Stercocarius skua*) that bully other birds into dropping their catch, to the starling-sized storm petrels that fly out to the shelf margin from their breeding colonies on Irish islands to gather food for their chicks.

While large flocks of coastal gulls intensify the numbers of seabirds in areas such as Galway Bay and the Shannon Estuary, those above the offshore deeps are boosted by gannets and fulmars following the fishing fleets. But there are deep offshore hot spots for richness of species, including the east and northeast slopes of the Porcupine Seabight, the lee of the Porcupine Bank, and the northeastern margins of both the Rockall and Hatton Banks. Here, the main items of prey include the schools of small, pelagic fish, such as sand eels, herring and sprat, along with squid and the larger zooplankton.

The vulnerability of seabirds to oil spills is clearly greatest in those that spend much of their time on the surface of the water, diving after prey. In inshore waters, the auks, such as razorbills and guillemots, are at special risk. Manx shearwaters, too, are seen as highly vulnerable. They number about 40,000 breeding pairs on the Kerry islands alone, foraging far out near the Porcupine Bank. They swim frequently and congregate in large 'rafts' near their breeding colonies at evening. Breeding gannets, while they are commonly pictured in flight or plummeting after prey, spend much of their time on the water preening, washing and sleeping, and very large resting rafts have been seen in company with trawlers.

In winter, many seabirds simply move offshore to fish in deeper water, but others undertake distinct migrations or roam the ocean for thousands of kilometres. The CMRC survey found that the Rockall Trough and its neighbouring banks and basins offer feeding grounds for many long-distance migratory species, such as skuas and shearwaters, and wanderers such as Irish-bred puffins. These, for example, may turn up anywhere from Newfoundland and Greenland to the Canary Islands, dipping their heads in the water to peer for planktonic crustaceans. The tube-nosed fulmars and petrels also wander widely, guided to good feeding grounds by the scent detection described above. Other birds follow migration paths to distant areas of upwelling. Young Irish gannets, for example, head for the waters off West Africa, while older birds with good fat reserves remain offshore to the west of Ireland, fishing in all but the worst winds.

Terns (*Sterna* spp) may press on to South Africa, and the incredible Arctic tern (*Sterna paradisaea*) even to the edge of Antarctic pack-ice. Terns actually welcome a moderately wind-ruffled sea: it helps them to hover and conceals them from fish just below the surface. Manx shearwaters skim the waves to fish in cool currents off Argentina. They choose calm, anticyclonic conditions in which to begin their migration but are often driven off course by strong winds and pressed into bays on the way. Bad gales that last for days can displace seabirds by hundreds of kilometres. The smaller, lighter species that count on snatching food from the surface, such as the petrels, can be weakened and exhausted and end up washed ashore dead or blown inland, occasionally in great numbers.

Such hazards are natural for seabirds and irrelevant to their numbers. But foraging patterns and even the spread of some seabird populations have been changed by the ready supply of offal and fish discarded from trawlers. The massive human harvesting of large predatory fish, and a steady, long-term decline in the average size of many stocks, have increased the numbers of small fish available to seabirds and so helped the growth of some of their populations. Tighter fishing controls and an end to the wasteful discarding of fish could have an opposite effect. But a shortage of normal prey due to oceanographic effects of climate change could prove of greater consequence than changes in fishing activity. Years of dramatic reproductive failure for surface-feeding kittiwakes and Arctic terns at the northeast of Britain led to a ban on commercial sand eel fisheries in the North Sea, but the scarcity of the birds' staple prey was also blamed on changing currents that failed in their usual delivery of sand eel larvae. As with so many other predators in the food chain, seabirds may have to adapt, and their numbers find swift adjustment to an ocean environment altered by climate change.

Meanwhile, seabirds account for many of the 260-odd species known to have suffered from the great proliferation of plastic debris in the world's oceans. Of the global production of some 100 million tonnes of plastic a year, about one tenth ends up in the sea, where its durability tends to be even greater than on land. The particular peril of plastic bags to jellyfish-eating turtles was mentioned above. Their resemblance to squid is also killing whales: in 2002, a dead minke whale washed up on the Normandy coast had in its stomach no less than 800 kg of plastic bags and packaging.

An insidious danger to birds and marine species arises from the plastics industry itself. It manufactures each year more than a billion kilos of tiny polymer resin pellets, called 'nurdles', which are the raw material of plastic manufacture. Inevitable spills in transport around the world send millions of these pellets sifting into sewers and then the sea, where they float as (usually) white, translucent discs resembling fish eggs or other zooplankton. A stomach full of nurdles can be the path to rapid starvation.

The Perils of Plastic

Of the 100 million tonnes of plastic produced in the world each year, about 10 per cent ends up as ocean debris. At every scale – from the largest piece of monofilament net left tangled on the seabed or the supermarket bag writhing in the sunlit water column, to tiny industrial pellets floating at the surface – plastic has become the most widespread form of human pollution of the sea, found from the Equator to the Poles. It is also one of the most lethal to marine life, above or below the surface. At least 267 species, ranging through seabirds, whales, turtles, seals and fish, are known to have suffered through entanglement or ingestion. Some kinds of plastic will endure for centuries before degrading, especially at the seabed. As others finally fragment into micro-particles, their toxic components are already entering the diet of benthic animals.

Concentrations of plastic debris vary across the oceans. The doldrums at the heart of the North Pacific Gyre, an area twice the size of France, are notorious as the Great Pacific Garbage Patch, clotted with consumer waste. In the northeast Atlantic levels of floating debris are far lower, increasing as wind-driven currents enter narrower waters, such as the Irish Sea and English Channel. But research trawls found debris averaging well over 500 items per square kilometre on the bed of the Celtic Sea. Lethal 'ghost fishing' by huge stretches of lost or discarded bottom gillnets set off the south and west of Ireland eventually brought EU curbs on their use in deep water.

As this book was written, a great leatherback turtle was found floating dead off Cork, its gut blocked with plastic bags it had swallowed in mistake for jellyfish. A basking shark drifted dead into Brandon Bay in Kerry, its jaws tangled in plastic net. Gannets strangled with six-pack webbing and dead fulmars with shredded plastic in their stomachs are regularly tossed up at the tideline. Sprinkled there too are tiny pellets of polymer resin known as 'nurdles'. As the raw material of plastic manufacture, more than a billion kilos are shipped around the world every year, with inevitable spills in transit. Usually white, translucent and the size of fish eggs or other zooplankton, their resemblance to edible prey is seen as endangering survival among seabirds and other marine species.

CHAPTER 9

Ocean Resources

The New Industry

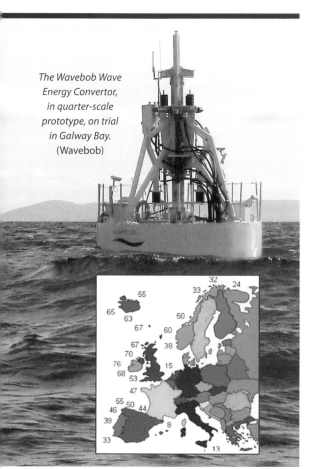

The Wavebob Wave Energy Convertor, in quarter-scale prototype, on trial in Galway Bay. (Wavebob)

The European Wave Energy Atlas shows that the west of Ireland receives the most powerful waves in Europe. (SEI)

Who knows where the wave began – what particular Atlantic wind spent some of its energy heaping the water and spinning it into a wheel, a swell rolling on like a great hoop in the sea, kept rolling by every fresh touch of wind at its crest, every new shiver of energy? It became a wave somewhere out in the bay, steepening as the swells crowded in towards Galway and the seabed shallowed to Spiddal's granite shore. It lurched at the steel wall of the buoy and rose abruptly within its hollow chamber, squeezing the air tightly above it, like compressing a spring. In that moment, one kind of energy became another, and then another as the turbine spun, and another as electricity was born . . .

Harnessing power from the waves has to be a very old human vision: think of the water mills of ancient Greece and Rome. A French hydraulics engineer Pierre-Simon Girard, patented the first water turbine in 1799. But perfecting a machine to produce electricity reliably, with low maintenance, at sufficient scale, in waves of sufficient power and yet to be storm-proof and durable year after year, has taken the best technological minds and international engineering skills many decades, many failures, and much money.

Even today, the machines on trial off Connemara began as models tested in a wave tank at NUI Cork. They were built to quarter-scale for their winters in Galway Bay and have still, in 2008, to confront the worst storms at full scale for long enough to prove their worth. But at least the special possibilities of Ireland's waves and wind, urged half a century ago in the nation-building exhortations of Seán MacBride, have now been taken up by native entrepreneurs, with government support from the Marine Institute and Sustainable Energy Ireland (SEI) under the Ocean Energy Strategy launched in 2006. They also joined forces to commission a Wave Atlas, plotting the contours of accessible wave-power around the coast at different times of year. Its theoretical contribution to the grid worked out at 75 per cent of the electricity Ireland used in 2006.

The potential energy of tidal flow is another stirring prospect. A classic example has been the French use of the La Rance estuary, on the Brittany coast, where turbines mounted in a tidal barrage built in the 1960s generate 240 MW of electricity. This has encouraged the British plan to build a 16-km barrage across the Bristol Channel. But the great cost and environmental impact of such dams has prompted alternatives, such as monopole-mounted propellers, like those of wind turbines, spinning slowly underwater in offshore tidal currents. Several such projects are already on trial off English and Scottish coasts, and another is being tested in the fierce tidal flow at the narrows of Strangford Lough in Northern Ireland. A study of such currents around the Republic, commissioned by the SEI, found that, at the present early stage of technology, a flow of at least 2 m per second is imperative. The strong tides of the east coast offer the best prospects; in the west, the Shannon Estuary is seen as the only real resource.

Wind farms and sandbanks

The first turbines of the Arklow Bank wind farm, seen from the shore. (Courtesy of Airtricity)

The untrammelled power of ocean wind, comparatively free choice of sites and a minimum of environ-mental objections have made offshore turbines the favoured habitat of wind generation. Easy access to the national grid and concentrated populations were further incentives to sites on the east coast, where stable sandbanks offer shallow sites well offshore and waves are not severe. The first seven giant turbines of the Arklow Bank wind farm at 124 m, taller than the Dublin Spire from blade-tip to wave, are predicted to grow to 200 at this site alone, some 10 km out from the shore. In late 2007, the five largest offshore wind companies in Ireland, launching an industrial association, claimed an advanced readiness to provide some 40 per cent of the island's electricity. One of them, based in the Galway Gaeltacht, proposed a 100 MW wind farm at the Skerd Rocks off south Connemara; the rest were planned for the Irish Sea, including projects for the Kish and Bray sandbanks and 220 turbines spaced out across 55 km² of the great Codling sandbank off north Wicklow, the closest at 13 km from the shore.

These Irish Sea sandbanks are founded on moraines formed in the melting of the last Ice Age and form part of a tide-driven transport of sand from deeper banks in the Celtic Sea to the east coast of Ireland. Their richness of marine life, explored in several benthic surveys, varies with the texture of the sediment. At the Arklow Bank, for example, the abundance and diversity of species is highest at the northern end, where fine sand grades into cobbles, shells and pebbles. Nearby, off Wicklow Head, is a notable reef built by the honeycomb worm, *Sabellaria*, and rich in attendant species. This is in a Special Protection Area and considered at a safe distance from the planned layout of wind turbines.

The trend towards mounting each tower on a single pile driven into the seabed means that the physical 'footprint' of wind farms is likely to be small. A Marine Institute study of underwater impacts raised the benefits of a habitat protected from trawling, but called for further ecological research – into, among other things, the possible effects on marine life of electromagnetic radiation from a network of cables in the seabed. A separate assessment commissioned for the Codling Bank project extended to just that sort of detail, but concluded that migrating salmon, for example, which use geomagnetic fields to find their way home to their spawning river, were unlikely to be confused by the cables' low radiation. Collision risks for seabirds were also seen as small, since even at the highest tide the minimum distance to each rotor's arc would be 30 m. Manx shearwaters, guillemots, shags and razorbills all fly below 7 m, and even high-fliers such as kittiwakes and gannets were judged as 'unlikely to be at significant risk.'

Kinsale Head Rig. (Courtesy of PAD)

Drilling at the frontier

'Some urgency', in an official understatement, attends Ireland's quest for new sources of offshore gas. About 80 per cent of the national supply is imported, mainly from Britain, which itself has begun to import from eastern Europe. The gas fields off Ireland's south coast, in production since 1978, are moving towards depletion, to be

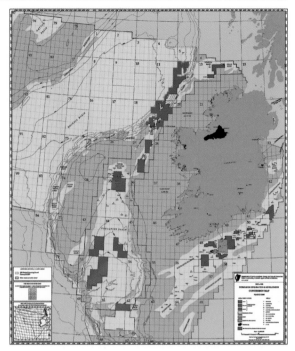

Petroleum Exploration and Development concession map for licensing of Irish blocks 2008. (Courtesy of PAD) Deep blue: exploration licences; Yellow: licensing options; Red: lease/reserved area.

replaced in part by gas from the Corrib Field west of Erris Head in County Mayo. Urged towards greater energy self-sufficiency by the EU, the new rounds of exploration licences, begun in 2007, are taking seismic surveys and drill-rigs to the 'frontier acres' of Ireland's continental shelf, in deep Atlantic waters harrowed by some of the harshest weather in the world.

The first of the licences are for new blocks in the Slyne, Erris and Donegal basins – great steep-walled hollows in the outer shelf to the west and northwest of Ireland – and for the Porcupine Seabight in even deeper water. That basin has seen only six exploration wells drilled in the past decade, but between existing activity under previous licences, and that arising from the new ones, up to ninety-five wells of various kinds may be drilled in the four Atlantic basins over the next few years. The scale of the new exploration, spanning areas totalling some 88,000 km², attracted the EU directive that regional plans should be underpinned by environmental assessments. Two Irish Offshore Strategic Environmental Assessments (IOSEAs), commissioned by the state's Petroleum Affairs Division, have shown particular concern for the impacts of noise from the seismic surveys on whales, dolphins and seals (see p.156) and on spawning fish, so that known spawning areas will be avoided at critical times.

Unless there are major discoveries, Ireland is forecast as only a small producer of gas for the immediate future. There is, however, increasing interest in the possibilities of extracting methane (of which the Corrib Field gas has a high content) from hydrate deposits in deep marine sediments. In the Marine Institute's assessment, 'Ireland is believed to have a major, but unquantified, offshore methane hydrate resource that, given the appropriate extraction and utilisation technology, may be of future significance.'

Methane hydrate is a crystalline solid in which each gas molecule is surrounded by a cage of water molecules and is 'frozen' into something looking like ice by a combination of great pressure and low temperature. It can be stable in seabed sediments at water depths greater than 300 m and can cement loose sediments in a surface layer several hundred metres thick. Globally, there are vast amounts of carbon bound up in this way – perhaps 10,000 gigatonnes – but the commercial energy potential lies in intensely concentrated hydrate formations, perhaps with free gas trapped beneath them; 1 cm³ of hydrate yields 158 cm³ of natural gas.

The hydrates can make sediments unstable in certain conditions, such as rises in sea temperature.

Theoretical research into their presence around Ireland has been largely concerned with hydrates formed in glacial times that may later have produced great submarine slides at the edges of the Rockall Trough and elsewhere (they may, indeed, still present problems in the safe location of ordinary gas production wells). Given the seabed temperatures of the western Irish shelf, it is theorised that the hydrates would be found as stable, buried deposits at water depths below 1,100 m. No evidence of their presence has been gained in the extensive seismic surveying for ordinary natural gas – this would need more specialised seismic techniques. But, given the present costs and problems in extracting the gas, any deposits off Ireland seem most unlikely to compete with more accessible hydrates, at high methane concentration, already discovered elsewhere in the world. Methane's role in climate change as a potent greenhouse gas adds to the caution needed in its liberation from the seabed.

Biodiscovery: a different world

Biotechnology, the prime partner of science in the twenty-first century, explores a virtually undiscovered planet in the ocean. The sea's physical environment and chemistry, its buoyancies and pressures, light and dark, are so alien to terrestrial experience that special 'spacecraft', with their own life-support systems, are needed for humans to explore it. The life forms watched through a bathysphere's thick windows, or by robot seabed cameras, or even those hauled up in fishing nets, are adapted to a wholly different world; their genes and circuitry, enzymes and toxins are all correspondingly strange. Eighty per cent of living organisms live in aquatic ecosystems, yet new species are discovered constantly and the biochemistry of very few is known to science.

The exciting potential of biodiscovery is set out in *Sea Change*, the Marine Knowledge, Research and Innovation Strategy for Ireland launched by the Marine Institute in early 2007. The prefix 'bio' is indeed hard-worked in its pages: bioactive substances, biocomplexity, biopharma, bioremediation, biomaterials, biofilms, bioinformatics, and bioscreening. All evoke the dazzling new products and processes the ocean's biodiversity could make possible.

The US, UK and Japan are well established in the field, and the sort of commercial bioprospecting once aimed at a dwindling rainforest has already produced new drugs from marine organisms. In the year 2000 alone, medical literature listed 78 marine chemicals with a therapeutic potential. A Spanish company, PharmaMar, has become a world leader in finding anti-cancer agents in such animals as sea squirts, sponges and soft corals. Many produce toxins designed to repel predators that are sometimes also potent for the destruction of human tumour cells. The Elan Corporation, a neuroscience company founded in Ireland, has produced a painkiller from the venom of a predatory marine snail. These are some of the invertebrates now being screened by the thousand in automated laboratories on the chance of finding a new bioactive molecule with a possible pharmaceutical use. Only one in 10,000 is likely to survive the long pipeline of assessment and clinical trials that ends in a safe and marketable product – this, perhaps, after ten years and a cost of many millions of euro.

Marine sponges from Ireland's inshore waters have been the first focus of a research programme that marries the Marine Institute with existing scientific expertise and infrastructure. Quite apart from the sponges' own biochemistry, the bacteria they filter from the surrounding water may come to constitute as much as 40 per cent of their substance, and it is now thought that the bacteria are equally likely to produce the 'interesting' new molecules. Scientists in the Environmental Research Institute at NUI Cork have been extracting all the DNA from the sponges and screening it for genetic signs of bioactive compounds. They hope, eventually, to sample bacteria directly from seawater.

The harvesting of marine life for such new purposes could obviously present problems of over-exploitation, and there have already been examples, notably around Florida and in the Caribbean, of reckless collection by 'drug prospectors'. This has prompted researchers to consider ways of farming the organisms or, more durably, of synthesising the new compounds, much as medicine needed to synthesise the active ingredients of terrestrial herbs.

Ireland's seabed, as we have seen, has several unusual, if not unique, sources of organisms, notably on the carbonate mounds and coral reefs of deep, cold water. Such extreme conditions make their biochemistry even more exotic and novel, their high degree of unrelatedness to other organisms the particular lure for bioprospecting. And while radical new human therapies may be the most dramatic (and perhaps profitable) reward, new compounds from marine plants, animals and bacteria have a vastly wide range of other applications, from paints, cosmetics, adhesives and other functional materials to foodstuffs, 'nutraceuticals' (diet supplements) and veterinary products for aquaculture. Other connections can be less obvious: the sea mouse *Aphrodita* may hold the clue to new communication technologies, and the bacterium *Rhodoferax ferrireducens* may provide new developments in battery technology. In all this, the enrichment of Ireland's scientific research and technological skills and processes, could prove immense.

Seaweeds: the changing harvest

At low tide, lush growth of golden Ascophyllum *wrack fringes a sheltered inlet of south Connemara.* (© M. D. Guiry /Algaebase)

Ireland has been far from indifferent to the exceptionally lush and varied growth of the seaweeds that fringe the island: coastal dwellers have drawn on them over centuries for fertiliser, animal fodder, seasonal cash crops, occasional health foods and remedies, and chewable snacks. The plants a modern Ireland has largely relegated to a peasant past are now, however, one of the most intensely studied and promoted of marine resources. Kelps, wracks, red seaweeds and coralline algae appear to hold limitless promise in enriching diet and health, along with ever-proliferating uses for their colloids and fine biochemicals in medicine and industry.

The 'edible wings' of Alaria esculenta *kelp, grown on longlines in a bay on the Cork coast.* (Irish Seaweed Centre)

Farmed Asparagopsis: *a natural treatment for acne.* (Irish Seaweed Centre)

By 2020, in the *Sea Change* projections of the Marine Institute, the 'current hybrid of a declining wild harvest and fledgling aquaculture production' of seaweeds will have grown into a science-based sector worth €30 million a year. Along with sustainable cropping of wild species, farmed seaweeds will be the raw material of new medicines, therapies and health foods, and of continuing biotechnological research. Coastal communities will share in adding value to this rich natural resource so long associated with poverty, hunger and hard labour.

Ireland has been harvesting kelp since the seventeenth century, mostly as the thick stems of *Laminaria hyperborea* cast up in storms. The dried sea rods were burned (or rather melted) in stone ovens built at the shore, first for the soda and potash used in pottery glazing and the manufacture of glass and soap, and later for extraction of the iodine that disinfected wounds right up to the Second World War. Plumes of dark, pungent smoke rising from the kilns and drifting inland are within the memory of many west coast communities. Rising before winter dawns, whole families competed to be first at the shore, wading into the surf to seize the slippery *Laminaria*.

The value of kelp for iodine collapsed when a cheaper source was found in Chilean nitrate deposits. But the proliferating uses of seaweed's alginic acid, a stable gel and emulsifier in a host of products and processes, continued to support the dwindling collection and drying of sea rods. For more than fifty years it has also sustained the more organised harvest of knotted wrack, *Ascophyllum nodosum*, in the sheltered bays of Connemara and Donegal, for export as milled seaweed to an alginate plant in Scotland.

With the creation of the Martin Ryan Institute in NUI Galway in 1992 as the home of the university's marine science, the potential of Irish seaweeds was given an entirely new impetus. Under its Director, Michael Guiry, it has created a world-class database of marine algae (www.seaweed.ie) and the Institute holds both the Irish Seaweed Centre for research and the Irish Seaweed Industry Organisation. A project in conjunction with the Marine Institute surveyed the great biomass of industrial seaweeds growing along the entire west coast. It concluded that the annual harvest of *Ascophyllum* could be doubled quite sustainably along 1,200 km of coastline. There are also some 10 million tonnes of *Laminaria* spp., but the value of the offshore kelp forest to ocean ecosystems and the stability of vulnerable shores compel a measured approach to its harvesting. This takes on a special importance in considering kelp as a raw material for bioethanol production (the keynote address to an international seaweed conference at NUI Galway in 2008 was 'Algae and biofuels: *Quo vadis*?'). Kelp's high levels of carbohydrate make it a tempting alternative to giving up land to biofuel crops that should really be

Large-scale seaweed farming takes up many bays in Japan. (Irish
Seaweed Centre)

growing food. But the better route may lie in farming micro-algae that produce high levels of oil for
bio-diesel.

Beds of coralline maerl (see p.46) are another precious ecosystem in which sustainable dredging
must balance its value to seabed life with value to commerce, horticulture and medicine (in bone
therapy, as one current example). That said, there are more than 8 million tonnes of live and dead
maerl, mainly in the inner and outer reaches of Galway Bay.

For the future, the greater emphasis is on farming seaweeds of high value, either as sea vege-
tables or for further processing and extraction, and also on discovering fresh treasures among the
less-considered of Ireland's 500-odd species. No more than a dozen of the larger ones have been
put to commercial use. Japan, by contrast, makes culinary use alone of some 50 seaweeds, its people
consuming almost 7 kg per head each year, from seaweed cultivation and processing that employs
some 80,000 people. Dried sheets of seaweed, called 'nori', commonly used as a wrap for sushi or
for savoury parcels, are the single most valuable marine product grown by aquaculture: worldwide
production is worth some €1.8 billion. The nori seaweed is *Porphyra* – the 'sloke' of the west of Ireland
and the 'laver' of Wales.

Europe's discovery of Japanese cuisine has revived or revealed the culinary potential of other red seaweeds already well known in Ireland, such as the chewable, salty dulse, or dilisk (*Palmaria palmata*), and gelatinous carrigeen (*Chondrus crispus*). The first is under trial cultivation in tanks in Connemara, and as plants growing on 'seeded' longlines in the open sea. The filmy kelp *Alaria esculenta* (meaning 'edible wings') has also been grown in this way, as potentially an equivalent to Japan's *wakame*. Its remarkably fast growth, up to 10 cm a day, has been enhanced by breeding *Alaria* hybrids, crossing Irish plants with strains from the Pacific and North Atlantic.

One of many alternative uses for *Alaria* is in bodycare products, in which the potential of seaweeds ranges between the cosmetic and the 'parapharmaceutical'. The little-known red seaweed *Asparagopsis armata*, for example, which anchors itself to other seaweeds by barbs on its fronds, is being cultivated in Connemara for use in anti-dandruff and anti-acne products. The hot seaweed baths whose benefits have endured in several west coast resorts since Edwardian times are now part of the 'thalassotherapy' offered in a new generation of spas (*thalasso* is the Greek word for sea).

Not least among seaweed's new promises is its potential for 'bioremediation' – clearing up marine pollution. Seeded into discharge waters from sewage treatment plants and onshore aquaculture, it can help keep bays and estuaries free of eutrophication while nourishing its own growth in the process.

Mining the seabed

Ireland's glacial past and continuing coastal erosion have left the island with vast deposits of sub-tidal and offshore sediments: millions of cubic metres of gravel and perhaps a hundred times that in sand.

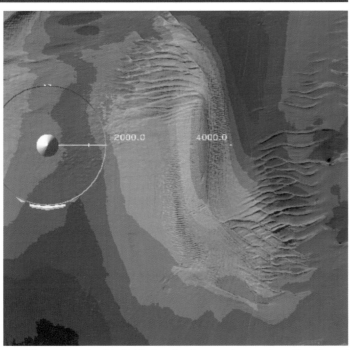

The undersea bank in Dublin Bay rises from sand-waves shaped by tides and currents. (Courtesy of Geological Survey of Ireland)

The greatest volume lies in the central and southern Irish Sea and off the southeastern and northwestern coasts, with smaller deposits in a few western bays. The drifts vary greatly in thickness, from a few centimetres over rock to 70 m or more in sandbanks off the east coast. Some have filled palaeochannels carved by ice age flows.

Given the huge demand for aggregates in the building boom that began in the late twentieth century, it might be expected that dredging would have made inroads in at least some of these reserves. But the state has hesitated to license extraction in the Irish Sea, where the chain of offshore banks gives protection to the coast. There are also practical limits to recovery of material in the frequent periods of substantial waves, swells that stir the sediment and tidal currents that corrugate its contours. By 2007 there had been no commercial extraction of aggregates from the seabed, but continuing extension of land-based quarries, and mining of sand and gravel from glacial landforms such as drumlins, eskers and moraines.

The location of sand and gravel resources was one objective of INFOMAR, the programme of inshore mapping that followed the INSS. How best to manage a sustainable exploitation of the huge drifts of the Irish Sea has, however, been given special study by the Irish Sea Marine Aggregates Initiative (IMAGIN), led by an Irish/Welsh scientific consortium and funded by the EU's regional development programme. Nature conservation, fishing, navigation and coastal protection had all to be considered, together with the costs and benefits, in devising a 'strategic framework and scientific rationale' to guide policy.

Sandy deposits containing heavy minerals – even gold and platinum – are found on continental shelves worldwide, from the beach to the outer edge. In the 1980s, reconnaissance surveys by the GSI identified a long list of industrially-valuable minerals with largely unfamiliar names (rutile, magnetite, zircon, sphene, epidote, chlorite, staurolite, etc). There were several potentially commercial deposits, notably off northwest Donegal, Mayo and south of Wicklow Head on the east coast. But while there has been research to trace the minerals' origins on land, any further development will depend on world market prices.

Mining the metalliferous minerals of the deep sea is unlikely for the foreseeable future in the extreme conditions of the northeast Atlantic: there are easier and more immediately promising places to go. The minerals are of two main kinds. Metallic oxides include the manganese nodules lying around on the seabed at 5,000 m or more and thin cobalt crusts on the rocky slopes of seamounts. Current developments concentrate, rather, on the riches in massive sulphide deposits at extinct hydrothermal vents containing copper, zinc, gold and silver. Two major exploration companies, mobilising many millions of dollars, have sought leases in national waters in the Pacific Ocean, and mining on the sea floor off Papua New Guinea is due to begin in 2009. Environmental concerns must attend all major disturbance of seabed life, of which dredging is among the most severe. It is good that Ireland's demand for offshore aggregates has arisen late, and with greater ecological awareness.

CHAPTER 10

The Great Change

Climate and Ocean

The oceans cover two-thirds of Earth's surface and their contact with the atmosphere has a profound influence on moderating climate. They transfer heat around the planet in their currents. They exchange it with the atmosphere, storing vast amounts in their upper layers, giving it up slowly to the winds and releasing it again in rain. Yet of all the oceans' swirling parameters, warming is the most inconstant: shifting by latitude, depth and season, the flow and mix of currents and the cyclic atmospheric oscillations. The North Atlantic is warming, like the rest of Earth, and climate change is already affecting patterns of marine life. But separating its effects from the inherent variability of the sea, and regional and local differences, demands long-term observation and the widest spread of data that science can provide.

The annual report cards of the UK's MCCIP express the best consensus of research institutes and universities in these islands. The report for 2007–08 confirmed the general rise in sea surface temperatures of up to about 0.6 °C per decade since the 1980s. But it stressed the strong regional variation between, say, the English Channel and the continental shelf off Scotland, and predicted perhaps no more than 0.2 °C per decade at Rockall. Along with fewer but fiercer storms and greater wave heights, it had troubling expectations, offered with 'medium confidence', about acidification of the ocean. Not only will increasing saturation of the sea with CO_2 leave more accumulating in the atmosphere, but its acid effect on marine shells and skeletons will begin to be seen within this century (see p.27)

As temperature zones of climate change, a northward shift of 1,000 km in warm-water plankton species has been matched by a retreat of colder-water plankton. Particularly significant has been the northward shift of the dominant plankton copepod *Calanus finmarchicus*, to whose reproduction cycle the cod and other fish species are adapted, and the increase of the southern *C. helgolandicus*, whose larvae are abundant at a different time of year. The seasonal timing of plankton production has altered, with some species appearing six weeks earlier than they did twenty years ago.

The changes documented by the MCCIP go some way to explaining the movements of fish stocks, and to suggest the kind of mismatch of reproduction and food supply that rapid climate change may lead to. But most fish, in any case, tend to prefer a specific temperature range: in the loss

The swordfish is moving north.
(Free Encyclopedia)

Flying gurnard are netted off the west coast.
(Wiki Media Commons)

Trigger fish.

of cod from the Celtic Sea and its replacement by smaller, pelagic fish, the changes in temperature, plankton species and fishing pressures may all play a part.

In sorting out the northerly movement of fish species, sightings of solitary swordfish as far north as Norway, or the flash of barracuda (*Sphyraena sphyraena*) or blue marlin (*Makaira nigricans*) at the entrance to the English Channel, have offered dramatic summer headlines. More significant may be lesser fish actively seeking out cooler temperatures in summer, as in recent summer migrations of anchovies (*Engraulis encrasicholus*) and sardines, from the Bay of Biscay as far north as Donegal and Scotland. They are typical of the greater sensitivity of pelagic fish to climate change. In the western English Channel, for example, the relative abundance of herring and pilchard (large sardines) has swung back and forth in response to climate over the past 400 years, the pilchard taking over in warmer periods.

In Ireland, visitations of exotic warm-water fish have been rare. In the autumn of 2003, two individual flying gurnards (*Dactylopterus volitans*) were netted off Achill and the Aran Islands, and their fan-like pectoral fins were much admired. The trigger fish (*Balistes carolinensis*), with its sturdy vertical diamond shape, has become an increasingly familiar 'strange fish' trapped in lobster pots along the west of Ireland in summer, its migrations often ending in death in a chilly autumn. The long-fin tuna, whose migrations follow the 17 °C isotherm, could well roam beyond its present summer limits at the west of Ireland, along with the strongly migratory Atlantic bonito (*Sarda sarda*). Other species whose larvae or young are now found only off Ireland's south coast, but which may increase in range, include red mullet (*Mullus surmuletus*), red gurnard, bass (*Dicentrarchus labrax*) and John Dory.

Exploding pipefish

A remarkable phenomenon, widely attributed to climate change but possibly with other causes, has been a population explosion in the northeast Atlantic of the gold-coloured snake pipefish (*Entelurus aequoreus*). As the largest and most oceanic of the family (the female reaches 60 cm) it is relatively rare around Ireland, generally hiding among kelp. From 2002, however, the Continuous Plankton Recorder in ships crossing the Atlantic began trapping unprecedented numbers of the pipefish's juveniles, as far

Snake pipefish: a population explosion.
(NOAA Photo Library)

west as the Mid-Atlantic Ridge. Numbers appearing in trawl catches began to multiply hugely, and many fish washed up dead on British coasts. Since 2004, they have been increasingly recorded in the food brought to chicks by seabirds nesting in colonies around Ireland and Britain, and as far north as Iceland and the Faroes. But the horny structure of the pipefish (a close relative of the seahorse) makes it difficult to swallow and young puffins and kittiwakes have starved amid a litter of uneaten fish. Where sand eel stocks have declined, perhaps displaced by climate change, the pipefish is clearly not much of a substitute.

Away from the kaleidoscope of fish movements, the slower climatic successions of species and communities on rocky shores provide more ready access to the pace of change. The fact that Ireland and Britain straddle a biogeographic boundary between cold temperate northern waters and warmer, Lusitanian southern waters – and many intertidal species reach their northern or southern cut-off points at these islands – make them an ideal location for study. The west coast of Ireland, however, warmed by the North Atlantic Drift, already holds a good many southern species, while the much cooler Irish Sea is more exclusively boreal in its fauna and flora.

A four-year project, Marine Biodiversity and Climate Change (MarClim), led by the UK's Marine Biological Association, used records from the 1950s onwards and resurveyed almost 500 sites to assess and predict the trends. Its Irish partners (NUI Cork and the Galway–Mayo Institute of Technology) drew on existing surveys of Lough Hyne, Bantry Bay, Kinsale Harbour, Sherkin Island, Carnsore Point, Clare Island, Dublin Bay, and on the coastal explorations of the EU-funded BioMar project. That may read as a substantial roster of data sets, but the patchiness of research and general paucity of long-term studies has been a readily admitted handicap. In 2005, a 'Marine Foresight' study for the Marine Institute pressed for more surveys of tidal and shallow-water communities and the urgent creation of a National Inventory of Marine Fauna and Flora.

A striking finding of the MarClim project was that southern intertidal species are spreading northwards (and eastwards, in the English Channel, towards the colder North Sea) far faster than the northward advance of southern terrestrial organisms. Warm-water animals are extending northwards at up to 50 km per decade, compared to the global average among species in land systems of 6 km per decade. Earlier reproduction and juvenile survival in mild winters are hastening their settlement. Examples are the typically southern Chthamalid barnacles, at the northernmost edge of their range in Ireland and Britain. Irish researchers also made a particular survey of the spread of

*The toothed topshell
(Osilinus lineata).
(Courtesy of Marine Institute)*

the invasive Australasian barnacle, *Elminius modestus* (see 'Underwater aliens' p.82).

A historical study of special value was conducted around Irish shores in the 1950s by Alan Southward and Dennis Crisp. Southward, who died in October 2007, was the most influential British marine biologist of his generation and his work with Crisp was among the first to show climate-driven changes in marine ecosystems. In 2003, an Irish research team was able to revisit seventy-two of the shores and, using the same methods, found apparent decline among some northern species. In MarClim's overall report, the toothed topshell (*Osilinus lineatus*) and the flat topshell (*Gibbula umbilicalis*) were among southern 'indicator' species showing northward advances (sometimes to the very top of Scotland) or becoming significantly more plentiful.

Change in the rock pools

Climate change will show up in rock pools, as milder winters encourage fish such as blennies and gobies to stay for much more of the year, rather than moving to deeper water. Other species, such as the vivid snakelocks anemone, may be able to live higher up in the intertidal zone. On the other

*Purple sea urchins growing in intertidal rock pools.
(Cilian Roden)*

hand, much hotter summers may take their toll on species exposed at low tide. *Climate Change and the Irish Marine Environment*, a document prepared by an NUI Maynooth science team in 2003, discussed the impact of greater desiccation on colonies of barnacles and mussels, and on heat-sensitive kelps such as *Alaria esculenta*. Long heatwaves may be fatal to some starfish in rock pools, but helpful to the spawning and recruitment of other shallow-water species, such as the purple sea urchin (*Paracentrotus lividus*). But this and other shellfish could be threatened by new

fish predators from warmer waters, such as the eagle ray (*Myliobatis aquila*) and gilt-head sea bream (*Sparus aurata*) – the latter, already reported from the south coast, would however, be welcomed by Irish sea anglers.

The team also predicted a 'coastal squeeze' at estuaries, as urbanisation spreads its concrete to the shore and sea level rises covering long-established mudflats, salt marshes and sand flats. These are habitats with value not only to the sub-tidal marine ecosystem but as vital winter feeding and roosting grounds for migratory birds. Indeed, sea level rise and severe storm surges could deprive many birds of their breeding grounds and winter refuges as sand dunes, shingle ridges and lagoons are overrun.

Sea level rise: how soon, how far?

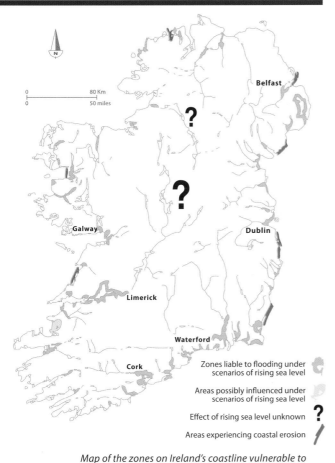

Map of the zones on Ireland's coastline vulnerable to sea level rise. (Based on a map by Robert Devoy)

Zones liable to flooding under scenarios of rising sea level

Areas possibly influenced under scenarios of rising sea level

Effect of rising sea level unknown

Areas experiencing coastal erosion

It is a long time since the world's ocean was at its present level: by some geological estimates, about 250 million years. Only 'yesterday' on that scale – say 18,000 years, towards the end of the last Ice Age – so much water was locked up in glaciers and ice caps that the sea level was about 100 m lower than it is today and quite out of sight from any point on the present shores of Ireland. The melting and retreat of the ice produced dramatic changes in relative levels of both sea and land – the sea rising from the thaw of ice into water and the land rebounding, over time, as the colossally heavy burden of ice disappeared. Fossil beaches on northern Irish coasts, raised well above present tidelines in the profile of the shore, are a reminder of this fluid past (and of the island's continuing slow tilt to the south).

Until the very recent past, sea level continued to creep upwards at a minuscule rate, estimated from geological data to average between 0.5–1 mm annually over thousands of years. Through the twentieth century, monitoring rested mainly on data from tidal gauges, but satellite measurements have added a precision independent of any vertical movement of land masses. In 2005, NASA estimated that sea level had risen by 1.8 mm a year in the last fifty years, but 3 mm a year over the last dozen. Roughly half that has come from thermal expansion of water as the planet warms and the rest from melting glaciers and polar ice sheets on land (melting sea ice makes little difference: it is already floating and displacing most of its volume).

The consolidated report of the IPCC, issued in 2007, made future projections based solely on continuing thermal expansion of the seas. Even though the Panel expects the Greenland ice cap to disappear, the destructive flow and rate of melting of Arctic ice in particular have seemed too unpredictable to model. Even without it, sea level is expected to rise by a minimum of 40 cm by 2015 and by a 50–100 cm by 2090, depending on the rate of climate change.

The impact on land masses depends greatly, of course, on their topography and statements such as 'for every centimetre the sea rises, around one metre of coastal land is lost to the sea' will obviously carry more meaning on the low, muddy delta coasts of Bangladesh than in Ireland where close to half the coastline is rocky and cliffed. The other half of our 7,500 km of coast, however, holds extensive

Erosion of sandhill coastal barriers.
(Michael Viney)

vulnerable stretches of sandy bays, estuarial mudflats and low cliffs of glacial till, as well as beaches, sand and gravel barriers protecting low land behind.

The western cliffs take the full thrust of storm-driven waves, often of 15–20 m as they roll in from the deeps. The waves' size and direct impact lessen substantially as they travel the Celtic Sea coasts, but sandy shores and glacial cliffs along the south and east are already eroding at up to 1–2 m a year. The most critical human and economic threat is from storm surges entering narrowing bays and river estuaries such as those at Galway, Shannon, Cork and Dublin, particularly at times of peak tides and heavy rain. The extreme event of February 2002, when Liffeyside housing was flooded in Dublin, saw a storm surge of 2.95 m. Allowing a further 0.5 m for sea-level rise, and a nominal safety margin has produced guidelines of 4 m above present sea level for any new basements on the east coast, and withdrawal of new building to 100 m from vulnerable shorelines.

Nature will adapt to climate change, as always, replacing one kind of community with another and selecting survivors to inhabit altered ecosystems. The northward movement of warm-water species is unlikely to be wholesale, nor will all northern species retreat on all fronts, for each has its own ecological profile and even, quite often, a long life left to live. Extremely rapid change or extreme climate events could, indeed, have massive incidental casualties (intense and protracted blooms of toxic phytoplankton or jellyfish suggest themselves as causes) and continued overfishing of key species may help to tip some ocean ecosystems to near-irreversible decline. But the chances are that rocky shores and their pools will evolve to an equal but different biodiversity, and that with any luck, there will still be eager children to enjoy them.

CHAPTER 11

Frontiers of Research

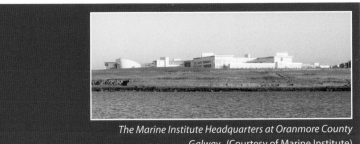

The Marine Institute Headquarters at Oranmore County Galway. (Courtesy of Marine Institute)

There was no shortage of respect for scientific research in Ireland's most famous political family, the de Valeras. Máirín de Valera, as a botanist in University College Galway, clambered around the shores of Connemara to produce the first, four-shilling topographical guide to the seaweeds of Galway Bay. Her mathematician brother, Éamon, as Taoiseach, created Dublin's Institute for Advanced Studies. But the new state's economic investment in science went little further than agricultural research for most of the twentieth century. The Marine Institute, set up in 1991, has helped to create a whole new vision of the sea as a national resource of wealth and knowledge. Its existence – along with that of its two purpose-built research vessels – has also reinvigorated marine research within the universities, helped by funding from the Higher Education Authority.

How marine research has grown: moored together in Galway docks are the RV Celtic Voyager, for decades the Marine Institute's only ocean-going research vessel, and (right) her purpose-built successor, RV Celtic Explorer. (Marine Institute)

The Martin Ryan Science Institute, NUI Galway. (Michael Guiry)

In 1991 also, Tony Ryan, founder of Ryanair, made a private donation of £3 million for the construction of a marine science institute at NUI Galway. The Martin Ryan Institute (named for his father) is now the focal point of the university's marine research, and is sited across the bay from the new headquarters of the Marine Institute in Oranmore. The MRI is now well funded by the state and has become particularly identified with the industrial and research potential of the seaweeds of the west coast; it is home to the remarkable global database of algae (www.algaebase.org) built up by the MRI's Director, Michael Guiry. But it also continues the mapping and characterisation of the west coast's seabed species and habitats, and monitors current impacts of climate change. Its laboratories at Carna in Connemara, established more than thirty years ago, have been an important centre for aquaculture research, and it supports marine studies in the Galway–Mayo Institute of Technology.

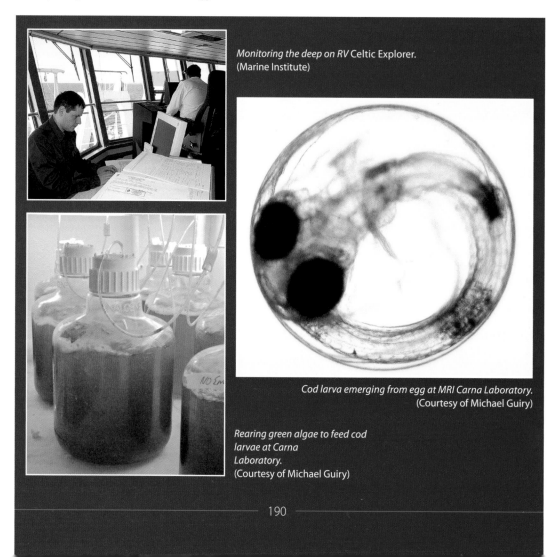

Monitoring the deep on RV Celtic Explorer. (Marine Institute)

Cod larva emerging from egg at MRI Carna Laboratory. (Courtesy of Michael Guiry)

Rearing green algae to feed cod larvae at Carna Laboratory. (Courtesy of Michael Guiry)

The Marine Institute, directed by Peter Heffernan, has its own fifty-four laboratories. Their everyday analysis and research serves fisheries and aquaculture, and includes the monitoring of shellfish quality and harmful algal blooms. Some are now also geared to the Institute's new biodiscovery programme, isolating and identifying new bioactive substances in marine organisms. Studies to further this programme are being funded by the government in NUI Galway, Queen's University Belfast and NUI Cork as part of the Beaufort Marine Research Awards. These new grants, initially totalling €20 million, were set up to further the research priorities of the Marine Institute's *Sea Change* strategy, published in 2006. The Institute has separately funded 'biodiscovery' PhD scholarships in NUI Dublin and Dublin City University. Their subjects give the flavour of the new priorities: isolation and synthesis of bioactive natural products from marine sources; exploiting marine biodiversity to develop 'drugs for normalising neural communications in disease'; characterisation of the anti-inflammatory potential of marine extracts.

The screening of bioactive compounds is also an expertise at NUI Cork, where the Coastal and Marine Research Centre groups biologists, computer scientists, hydrographers, geographers and engineers in multidisciplinary projects. These include coastal erosion and climate change impacts, sand and gravel resources, and population studies of marine mammals and seabirds. The Centre's biological work on sponges is now specifically important to the biodiscovery programme. The CMRC is entirely funded by research grant income, and complemented by three other marine research groups within the college: the Hydraulics and Maritime Research Centre, the Aquaculture and Fisheries Development Centre, and the Aquatic Services Unit. This mass of expertise, brought together under the umbrella of the college's Environmental Research Institute, was extended further in 2008, as the Cork Institute of Technology, the Naval Service and the National Maritime College in Ringaskiddy were brought together as a 'maritime campus' with €10 million to spend on ocean energy research.

The wave tank in the Hydraulics and Maritime Research Centre at NUI Cork tests model prototypes of wave energy turbines, while the Wave Energy Research Team at the University of Limerick has one of the most advanced turbine test facilities in Ireland, built with financial support from the Marine Institute. Limerick's Mobile and Marine Robotics group is also collaborating with NUI Galway in developing robotic systems for the remotely operated and autonomous underwater vehicles (ROVs and AUVs) so essential to ocean exploration.

Research Initiatives

Habitat mapping is another sector drawing expertise from several Irish universities. The MESH project, for example – Mapping European Seabed Habitats – is the EU's project to create complete and consistently informative maps from a mass of varying or incomplete national data. Marine scientists in Trinity College Dublin and the Ulster Museum in Belfast carried out Ireland's part in the early BioMar project, funded by the European Commission, that developed ways to characterise coastal underwater biotopes – a system now invaluable to MESH. Trinity scientists continue involvement in seabed mapping (in such projects as INFOMAR and IMAGIN), and the underwater photography for BioMar by the Ulster Museum's Bernard Picton provided core images for the superb Encyclopaedia of

Marine Life of Britain and Ireland at the museum's natural history website, www.habitas.org.uk.

Marine research at Queen's University Belfast (QUB), has been largely concerned with the culture of shellfish and seaweeds: the C-mar specialist unit, based at Queen's Marine Laboratory, develops new techniques in aquaculture and supports training initiatives in mariculture throughout Ireland. QUB researchers also have particular expertise to offer the Marine Institute's biodiscovery programme in identifying cryptic and new species of invertebrates and algae, in genetic structures of biodiversity, and in investigating the applications of marine materials in medicine. At the University of Ulster in Coleraine, the Centre for Coastal and Marine Research concentrates on coastal environments, from the physical processes to human impacts on the coastline.

Marine research in the Republic's regional institutes of technology gains from an exchange of ideas with the Marine Institute's Third Level Liaison Group and selective support from the Institute's 'commercialisation fund'. In the Marine Research Group of the Dublin Institute of Technology, four of the five schools in the Faculty of Science are actively involved in marine research, notably in fish contamination and human health issues. At the Waterford Institute of Technology, a multidisciplinary Estuarine Research Group monitors human ecosystem impacts and sustainable use of resources. At the Galway–Mayo Institute, the Marine Institute has funded studies on brown crabs and turbot, and also the monitoring of the west coast's whales and dolphins. At the Sligo Institute of Technology, marine studies have been enriched by the development of Mullaghmore as a diving centre.

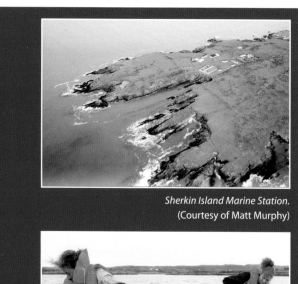

Sherkin Island Marine Station.
(Courtesy of Matt Murphy)

Plankton sampling at Sherkin.
(Courtesy of Matt Murphy)

Sherkin Island Marine Station in Roaringwater Bay, County Cork, is an independent, family-run, research enterprise. Staffed seasonally by volunteer scientists, it has monitored the species of the rocky shores of the island, and of those at similar sites between Cork Harbour and Bantry Bay, since the station's foundation in 1975. This is one of the longest and most extensive surveys of its kind and has supported an educational programme and many popular publications.

As the agency responsible for the sustainable development of the Irish seafood industry at sea and onshore, BIM undertakes technical and applied research – in, for example, conservation refinements of fishing gear – and funds professional, peer-reviewed research for its Fisheries Resource Series of publications (as in recent studies of lobster, brown crab and scallop stocks).

Foreign research cruises

In any year, up to perhaps fifty foreign marine research cruises take place in Irish waters, the scientists involved having informed the Government of the aim and nature of their work. Under the UN Convention on Law of the Sea, the Marine Institute has the right to place an Irish observer aboard, partly to authenticate what is done but also to take an active part in the research, learn as much as possible about scientific work and develop overseas contacts. The observer scheme is open to anyone with a background and active involvement in marine research (and some seagoing experience) and the Institute enthusiastically supports participation, together with financial help. Foreign research cruises for 2008 by British, Russian and Dutch vessels were mainly biological surveys related to fish spawning, behaviour and survival; but studies of North Atlantic Deep Water flows and ocean mixing were serving a broader oceanography.

In a single generation, human knowledge of the Atlantic Ocean has deepened profoundly, together with the keen realisation of how much still remains to be known.

In Ireland, even a decade has brought a quite new sense of the sea and the relevance of marine research to the island's fortunes. Unlike the exploitation of natural resources on land, each new step in marine development depends heavily on the initiative and expertise of scientists. To a degree unique in history, they help control the balance between exploitation and conservation and mediate human intrusion on the sea. We hope this book will help win some wider appreciation of their task.

Ready to descend: the French ROV that served international science teams in exploring Ireland's deep cold-water coral reefs.
(Courtesy of Geological Survey of Ireland)

The Ocean Online

The modern array of instruments for ocean research is already impressive: underwater vehicles, robot or manned; television cameras; plankton recorders; buoys that pop up to talk to satellites. All are adding, day by day, to what we know about the sea. But most of the data is gained in glimpses and samples, scattered through space and limited in time. Stand-alone instruments moored to the seabed or submerged in the water column run out of information storage and battery power; they also miss an awful lot of what goes on.

In what has been termed a 'quantum leap' in ocean research, great swathes of sea floor are to be lined with sensors, linked by fibre-optic cable, accessible by broadband, and fully interactive with computers ashore. They will serve observation stations monitoring not only the seabed but the water column above. The system will give round-the-clock access to the ocean's physical processes, a running record of their changes and transient events, and an unparalleled camera 'window' on the traffic of ocean life, from the burgeoning of plankton to the passage of migrant whales.

The new technology grew out of pioneering work at the University of Washington, on America's Pacific coast, by oceanographer John Delaney and his colleagues. His first sensor network will cover a large sector of the Juan de Fuca tectonic plate, where the Pacific Ocean is being pushed under the North American landmass. But Ireland and Europe are quick to follow. With advice from Delaney, who visited Ireland in 2008 to address the Royal Irish Academy, the Marine Institute is embarking on two sensor networks.

The first, Smartbay, will reach across Galway Bay as far as the Aran Islands: a relatively shallow loop with environmental monitoring stations linked to the Institute's headquarters. Later a much more ambitious project, Celtnet, developed with European partners, will come. The powered fibre-optic cable will extend from Waterville in County Kerry, out over the continental shelf, down into the Porcupine Seabight, out onto the Porcupine Abyssal Plain at around 3,000 m depth, and back again. There will be seven underwater observation stations spaced along the loop, presenting ocean vistas only dreamed of since Jules Verne.